Poppies

A Guide to the Poppy Family
in the Wild and in Cultivation

Poppies

A Guide to the Poppy Family
in the Wild and in Cultivation

Christopher Grey-Wilson

Timber Press · Portland, Oregon

First published 1993

© Christopher Grey-Wilson 1993
All colour photographs and line drawings by the author
unless otherwise stated

All rights reserved. No part of this publication may be
reproduced, in any form or by any means, without
permission from the Publisher

Typeset by J&L Composition Ltd, Filey,
North Yorkshire

and printed in Hong Kong

First published in North America in 1993 by
Timber Press, Inc.,
9999 S.W. Wilshire, Suite 124,
Portland, Oregon 97225, USA

ISBN 0–88192–232–3

Contents

3. Subfamily Papaveroideae

4. Subfamily Platystemonoideae

Allied Genera (formerly Subfamily Hypecooideae)

Illustrations

COLOUR PHOTOGRAPHS
(between pages 96 and 97)
(by the author unless otherwise stated)

1. *Chelidonium majus*, photographed in Suffolk
2. *Chelidonium majus* 'Flore Pleno'
3. *Chelidonium majus* var. *laciniatum*
4. *Dicranostigma lactucoides* in the Marsyandyi Valley, Nepal
5. *Eomecon chionanthum*
6. *Glaucium corniculatum* in cultivation
7. *Glaucium flavum* in the Greek Peloponnese
8. *Glaucium flavum* var. *fulvum*, Greek Peloponnese, Mani Peninsula
9. *Glaucium grandiflorum* in cultivation (photo: Jack Elliott)
10. *Hylomecon japonicum* in cultivation (photo: Brian Mathew)
11. *Macleaya microcarpa* (photo: Graham Rice)
12. *Sanguinaria canadensis* 'Plena'
13. *Stylophorum diphyllum*
14. *Stylophorum lasiocarpum*
15. *Dendromecon harfordii* (photo: Sean Hogan)
16. *Dendromecon harfordii* (photo: Sean Hogan)
17. *Dendromecon rigida* in the wild, California (photo: Mache-Parker Sanderson)
18. *Eschscholzia californica* in Snell Valley, Napa County, California (photo: Mache-Parker Sanderson)
19. *Eschscholzia californica* in cultivation
20. *Eschscholzia californica*, Riverside County, California (photo: Sean Hogan)
21. *Eschscholzia californica*, cultivar trials, Sahin, Zaden, Netherlands
22. *Eschscholzia californica* 'Milky White' and 'Purple Robe'
23. *Eschscholzia caespitosa*, Tolumne County, California (photo: Sean Hogan)
24. *Eschscholzia glyptosperma*, Kingston Range, California (photo: Mache-Parker Sanderson)
25. *Eschscholzia lemmonii* (photo: Sean Hogan)
26. *Eschscholzia lobbii*, Butte County, California (photo: Sean Hogan)
27. *Eschscholzia parishii*, Kingston Range, California (photo: Mache-Parker Sanderson)

LINE ILLUSTRATIONS IN THE TEXT

Acknowledgements

I am extremely grateful to the following for information and advice in the preparation of the text and, in most instances, also, for the loan of photographs: James Cobb, Jack Elliott, Sean Hogan, Alan Leslie, Brian Mathew, Ron McBeath, Harold McBride, Graham Rice, Mache-Parker Sanderson and Joe Sharman. To my wife, Christine, I am endlessly indebted for her fortitude in reading and re-reading the original manuscript.

Various poppy fruits: 1. *Papaver rhoeas*, 2. *Papaver hybridum*, 3. *Papaver spicatum*, 4. *Papaver argemone*, 5. *Argemone sanguinea*, 6. *Meconopsis cambrica*, 7. *Meconopsis horridula*, 8. *Meconopsis napaulensis*, 10. *Cathcartia villosa*, 11. *Stylomecon heterophyllum*, 12. *Romneya coulteri*, 13. *Hypecoum imberbe*, 14. *Hypecoum pendulum*, 15. *Bocconia frutescens*, 16. *Stylophorum diphyllum*, 17. *Stylophorum lasiocarpum*, 18. *Roemeria hybrida*, 19. *Chelidonium majus*, 20. *Sanguinaria canadensis*, 21. *Papaver somniferum*, 22. *Platystigma linearis*, 23. *Platystemon californicus*, 24. *Eschscholzia californica*, 25. *Glaucium flavum*

Introduction

Poppies are amongst the most-loved and cherished plants in our gardens. Their bold, yet seemingly delicate, flowers in a great range of bright colours make them a striking feature in the flower border. A bed of Himalayan blue poppies, a drift of red corn poppies, the huge and majestic blooms of the oriental poppies, the brazen colours of the Iceland poppy, to the more delicate little pastel blooms of the alpine poppies, are endearing characteristics of this group of plants. Most in fact have rather short-lived flowers, but a succession of buds open over a period and thus continue the show for many weeks.

It is somewhat surprising therefore that a book on poppies has not been produced until now, especially as there are so many different species and forms in cultivation. By poppies I mean not only the true poppies, *Papaver*, but all the members of the poppy family. These include the famous blue poppies, *Meconopsis*; the Mexican or prickly poppies, *Argemone*; the Californian poppies, *Eschscholzia*; the plumed poppies, *Macleaya*, the horned poppies, *Glaucium*; the oriental, alpine, Iceland and annual poppies, *Papaver*; the Tree Poppies, *Romneya*; and many more besides. With so many different poppies to consider it has not been possible to include every species in this book. In fact there are many annual species, especially of *Papaver* itself, that are rare or little known. I have concentrated on the species and forms in cultivation, together with those striking or particularly interesting species, both from a botanical as well as a horticultural point of view, that are not at present in cultivation, but really deserve to be introduced.

Each genus is dealt with separately, although the genera are grouped into their respective subfamilies (p. 23). Apart from general cultivation notes more specialised cultural requirements are considered under the appropriate genus or species. The species in each genus are dealt with in strict alphabetical order for convenience. I have included important synonyms to avoid confusion or ambiguity and these are also all listed in the index at the end of the book. In addition, botanical authorities are given for all recognised species and synonyms. The authority or author's name (often abbreviated) refers to the botanist who first described the species and gave it its name. For instance *Papaver rhoeas* L., the common Corn Poppy, was first described by the Swedish botanist Linnaeus (Carl Linné) in 1753. Such matters need not concern the gardener to any great extent save to recognise the fact that it is important to be able to put an accurate name on a particular plant. How often do we unwittingly purchase a plant from a nursery or garden centre or sow a packet of seeds under one name only to find that it is already in the garden under quite another name? Just as it is important to know the names of ones friends and associates so it is equally important to have standardised names for plants and the fact that species names are in Latin should not in any way inhibit their use. The standardisation of plant names throughout the world comes from an agreed set of rules, *The International Code of Botanical Nomenclature*. This technical and demanding book need in no way concern us here; suffice to say that it sets out various rules by which the correct name for a particular species can be ascribed and determined. Of course for many plants, in fact the majority in our gardens, the names are well established and cause little concern. Name changes, the scourge of horticulturist and gardener alike, are rarely undertaken lightly and without due thought and detailed research. Nor should they be, as repeated 'fiddling' and changing of plant names can only cause concern and ridicule.

It was, in fact, Linnaeus who established the modern system of naming plants with the publication of his *Species Plantarum* of 1753. Each plant consists of two names, the generic one, such as *Papaver*, and a specific one, such as *rhoeas*. The two brought together give the plant its unique and individual name by which it can be distinguished from all its brethren.

In many ways cultivar names present far more of a problem. They have much easier names to understand at first glance – 'Goliath', 'Ladybird', 'Midnight' and 'Orange Glow' for instance. Cultivar names are always presented in single parentheses and with a capital letter commencing each word. Modern cultivars are generally easy to trace and readily recognised. This is certainly not true of some of the older names where the correct identity of the plant in question is uncertain, especially where the plant may have become very rare or indeed may have apparently disappeared from cultivation. In some cases one cannot always be certain what a particular plant found lingering in an old garden is and, indeed, if it complies fully with a particular cultivar name. In this respect the National Council for the Conservation of Plants and Gardens (the NCCPG) has done stirling work in locating old and rare cultivars. More important is the establishment of national collections of a great range of garden plants along with active efforts to propagate some of the rarities and make them more available to the gardener. For instance, in Britain there are national collections of both *Meconopsis* and *Papaver* (oriental types).

The availability of plants has been made simple through the annual publication of *The Plant Finder*, which lists in alphabetical order the names of species and cultivars of herbaceous plants, trees and shrubs, ferns, orchids and so, and which nurseries supply them in Britain and Ireland. *The Plant Finder* does not include annuals and for these (there are many annual poppies of varying genera) one must browse through seed catalogues and lists. Specialist societies such as the Hardy Plant Society, The Royal Horticultural Society, The Alpine Garden Society, the Scottish Rock Garden Club and similar organisations produce their own seed lists; these are extremely useful and frequently include rarities not found elsewhere.

The Poppy Family
Papaveraceae

The Poppy family is a relatively small one with some 23 genera and about 250 species in total, distributed primarily in the northern temperate hemisphere, but with representatives in southern Africa as well as South America.

In the main, the family is a fairly homogeneous one and its members are readily recognised. Despite this, however, it is worth reviewing the various features of the genera that, combined, give the family its distinctive character.

THE PLANT

Most of the species are herbs, annual, biennial or perennial, although *Bocconia*, *Dendromecon* and *Romneya* (all American genera) are woody shrubs or subshrubs. When cut, the stems or leaves generally ooze a white, yellow, orange, or sometimes colourless latex; most parts of the plant possess a well-developed system of channels that secrete latex and this is very noticeable in plants such as the Opium Poppy, *Papaver somniferum*. Perennial species may be clump-forming or spread by means of underground stolons. Some species of both *Meconopsis* and *Papaver* are monocarpic perennials, taking a number of years to reach maturity but, having flowered, they seed and die.

THE STEM

Most species have a well-developed leafy stem, although plants may have all the leaves basal and the flowers borne on leafless scapes, as for instance in *Papaver nudicaule*, the Iceland Poppy, or *Meconopsis quintuplinervia*, the Harebell Poppy. The stem may be simple (unbranched) or branched, usually rounded in section, but sometimes ridged, smooth or variously adorned with hairs or bristles, or indeed a combination of these various features.

THE LEAVES

The leaves are alternate and without stipules, entire to variously lobed to deeply dissected. They are often aggregated into basal rosettes, which may be persistent or die away during the winter to leave a resting bud. The leaf-surface may be smooth or variously clothed with hairs, bristles or spines, or even pimply.

THE INFLORESCENCE

Flowers may be solitary on basal scapes, borne on branched stems or organised into more formal inflorescences. The typical inflorescence is a raceme or panicle, or it may be a cyme, but rarely a spike. In many of the monocarpic species of *Meconopsis* and *Papaver* the inflorescence may be paniculate in the lower part, but racemose above (i.e. the lower flowers are borne on lateral branches, the upper directly from the main axis of the inflorescence). In *Bocconia* and *Macleaya* the numerous small flowers are borne in diffuse panicles. The inflorescence is terminate, with a flower, often the first to open, terminating the main axis, i.e. at the top. The flowers may be bractless or subtended by a bract, which is often leaf-like.

THE FLOWER

Flowers in the Poppy Family are generally large and showy, often brightly coloured, with a relatively simple structure. There are two or three sepals in a single whorl; these closely envelop the flower in bud, but soon fall once the flowers begin to open, so that they are absent from the mature flower in most instances. In *Eschscholzia* the sepals are united into a single hood-like structure that falls away in one piece. The sepals may be smooth, hairy or bristly. The petals are borne in two whorls (rows) and are most frequently four in total, although six is common in *Argemone* and up to sixteen in the Bloodroot, *Sanguinaria*. The petals are frequently crumpled in bud and have a silky texture, often being very thin and, in some cases, semi-transparent. In many cultivated forms of *Papaver* there are double or semi-double flowered forms in which multiple petals occur and these generally wholly or partially replace the stamens. The genera *Bocconia* and *Macleaya* are unique in the family in being petalless and in having small, relatively inconspicuous flowers. There are usually numerous stamens, which form a conspicuous boss in the centre of the cup- or bowl-shaped flowers. In *Hypecoum* and *Pteridophyllum*, sometimes placed in a separate family (p. 23), there are only four stamens. The ovary consists of two or more fused carpels, but usually with a single compartment with intruding placenta that carry the ovules (unfertilised seeds) – the number of these placenta is equal to the number of carpels. The stigmas are equal in number to the number of carpels comprising each ovary; these are sessile or borne on a distinct style or styles.

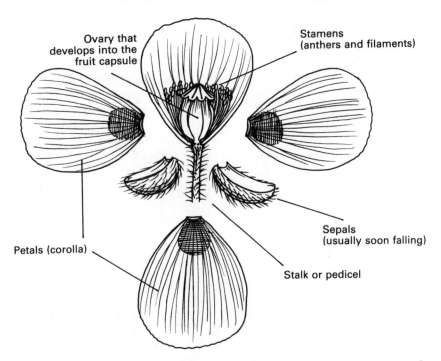

Ovary that develops into the fruit capsule

Stamens (anthers and filaments)

Sepals (usually soon falling)

Petals (corolla)

Stalk or pedicel

Diagram of a typical poppy flower

THE FRUIT

Superficially, the fruit is more variable than any other feature and the characters of the fruit are often very useful diagnostic features for separating the different genera. Most have a capsular fruit that opens by slits or apical pores, but the capsule shape varies from long and linear to elliptical, pear-shaped or globose. Linear capsules may split from the base, as in *Eschscholzia*, or from the top, as in *Glaucium*. Such capsules may dehisce explosively to expel the seed violently, flinging them well away from the parent plant. In the capsule type that dehisce by apical pores (*Papaver* and *Meconopsis*) the dispersal of the seed is passive, the seeds being knocked out by the wind, like pepper from a pepperpot. In some genera there is a distinct style, in others there is no style at all. In *Papaver* the capsule is crowned by a stigmatic disk with radiating stigmatic rays. In *Platystemon* the carpels are more or less free and follicle-like, being united only towards the base. The fruits contain numerous seeds, which often possess an oily endosperm.

In summary, the features that distinguish Papaveraceae are the presence of latex, the two-to-three parted flowers, with sepals and petals in whorls of two or three, the quickly deciduous sepals, the crumpled or wrinkled petals, the large number of stamens and the usually unilocular ovary and capsular fruits.

Cultivation

Although more detailed and specific cultural requirements are included under the different genera some comments are useful at this point. In general terms it has to be said that the majority of poppies in cultivation are not difficult to grow, with the exception of some species of *Meconopsis*, which demand more specialised conditions if they are to succeed. However, this particular genus has a certain air of exclusiveness that it certainly does not warrant and all who love poppies should certainly be able to grow one or two species, particularly the beautiful Himalayan Blue Poppy, *M. betonicifolia*. Unfortunately many people in the past have purchased a packet of seeds of this charming and eagerly sought species only to find that nothing germinated or that the resultant seedlings quickly rotted away. However, with care, it can be raised and flowered successfully, even in drier areas, and plants are often available at good garden centres.

Most poppies will thrive in any average, well-drained garden soil. Nearly all (again with the exception of one or two species of *Meconopsis*) will grow equally happily in an alkaline, neutral or slightly acid soil, although few will tolerate very acid conditions. With the exception of the Welsh Poppy, *Meconopsis cambrica*, most species of *Meconopsis*, *Cathcartia* and the various forest poppies of the genera *Chelidonium*, *Eomecon*, *Hylomecon*, *Sanguinaria* and *Stylophorum* thrive best in a moist, humus rich soil – one which has had plenty of organic matter added to it. No poppies like waterlogged soils or heavy clays that retain a lot of moisture during the winter months. Most species in these genera prefer sheltered semi-shaded places in the garden, being particularly effective in the dappled shade of the woodland garden, where deep leafy, moist soils are greatly to their liking.

Many of the more robust perennial species, as well as the hardy annual types, make fine border plants. The smaller alpine poppies (*Meconopsis* and *Papaver*) are ideal for pockets on the rock garden or scree, or in a large trough or container.

There is some evidence to suggest that the glorious blues of the finest *Meconopsis*, *M. betonicifolia*, *M. grandis* and *M. horridula* for instance, are developed best on acid rather than alkaline soils. Although they will thrive perfectly happily on alkaline soils the pure blues may well become muddied with pink or purple. To overcome this, special acid beds can be prepared in much the same way as for other acid-loving plants.

Most of the annual poppies, especially species of *Argemone*, *Eschscholzia*, *Hypecoum*, *Papaver* and *Roemeria*, prefer open sunnier positions in the garden and in deep shade become drawn, weedy and produce fewer flowers. They are also tolerant of far drier soils and drifts in the flower border can be very effective. Rigorous thinning of the seedlings is essential to allow plants sufficient space in which to develop. Supports, wires or branched-sticks placed around and amongst the young plants of the taller-growing types will provide them with support at maturity and help prevent them being blown over or weighed down by heavy rainfall. Many of the larger annual types such as the Shirley, Iceland and Californian Poppies, *Papaver commutatum* and *Dicranostigma franchetiana* are good fillers for gaps in shrub and herbaceous borders.

Perennial poppies in genera such as *Glaucium*, *Macleaya* and *Papaver* will succeed best in the average flower border. Most will thrive in a sunny position under similar conditions to the annual species and cultivars.

The smaller alpine poppies are low and tufted with solitary flowers borne on leafless stalks. These rather delicate looking plants prefer very well-drained conditions in full sun and, despite their appearance, they are mostly very hardy and wind resistant. However, in the wild they are plants of rocky places, screes and moraines, and require very well-drained conditions in our gardens. The rock garden, scree, raised bed or trough is much to their liking, where the gritty coarse compost mimicks their native homes in high mountain regions or Arctic tundra.

The shrubby genera, *Dendromecon* and *Romneya*, are natives of sunny California where they grow in hot dry habitats. In our gardens they require all the shelter and sun that is possible. In fact romneyas are surprisingly hardy and although cut to the ground during severe winter weather they can normally be expected to sprout again from below ground during the following spring. Even in my East Anglian garden, where cold winters and biting east winds are the norm during the winter, this exciting shrubby poppy has survived and flowered for a number of years. Although often grown in open borders it is perhaps at its best against a sunny sheltered wall, where it will grow far taller than in more open positions. Beware, however, of its suckering and somewhat invasive tendencies. *Dendromecon*, on the other hand, is much less often seen in gardens because it is a far more tender shrub and needs careful protection during the winter if it is to survive outdoors. If cut back by severe weather it will not sprout again from below ground level.

PROPAGATION

Most poppies can be grown from seed. In fact with the annual species, the monocarpic ones and those that tend to be short-lived perennials, seed is the only sure means of maintaining and increasing these plants in cultivation. For these types a regular regime of collecting and storing seed is essential, otherwise the plants will soon be lost.

Seed should be collected the moment it is ripe and quickly dried in a cool place. It can be stored in dry packets or containers in a cool place or refrigerator until required. Seed should be thoroughly cleaned of chaff as this might harbour harmful pests or diseases. Some poppy seeds have a long viability but others, unfortunately, soon decline or go into a dormancy which appears to be difficult to break without very specialised cultural techniques such as the use of growth hormones. In any event the longer seed is stored the poorer will be the resultant germination. For this reason it is often recommended that seed of the rarer types, and especially some of the *Meconopsis*, is sown the moment it is harvested. If this is done early enough in the summer then the resultant seedlings can be quickly pricked out and good young plants established before the onset of winter.

Seed of many poppies, particularly *Meconopsis* and some *Papaver* species, require light to germinate and should be only very lightly covered when sown. A very thin layer of silver sand or vermiculite will allow enough light to reach the seeds whilst, at the same time, keeping the vicinity of the seeds sufficiently damp.

Seeds of the hardy annual poppies present few difficulties. It can be direct sown where the plants are to flower; seedlings generally dislike being pricked out or moved. Seed can be sown in the autumn or early spring. I always prefer the latter as the problems of overwintering young seedlings outdoors during very cold or very wet winters are too great. The advantage is that, if the young plants come through the winter satisfactorily, then they will come into bloom long before their spring-sown cousins. Always sow thinly to avoid wasting seed and to limit the rather irksome task of thining out the seedlings. In some gardens the annual and some of the perennial species seed around freely and there is often no need to sow fresh batches each year, although be prepared for seedlings coming up in the most unlikely places. There are even fortunate individuals (mainly in cooler moister gardens) who boast of self-sown Blue Poppies!

For most of the perennial types sowing in the winter or early spring is the norm, despite what I have said. Seed is perhaps best sown in pots or pans using a normal seed compost for the majority of species. *Meconopsis* (except *M. cambrica*) species and seed of the various woodland-loving poppies, such as *Hylomecon* and *Stylophorum*, require a moister peat-based compost, which should never be allowed to dry out otherwise all will be lost. Again sow thinly and cover the seeds lightly, topping the pot with a thin layer of fine grit. Pots can be placed in frames or in the glasshouse to await germination. Seedlings of the shade-loving types require shielding from bright sunshine, whereas the alpine species seem to demand it. All seedlings are best pricked out the moment they are large enough to handle. The longer it is left the more tricky the operation becomes, the more tangled the roots and the greater the likely losses. Seedlings should be carefully protected against the ravages of slugs and marauding insects, but also from damping off, which can sometimes devastate a fine pan of *Meconopsis* seedlings.

Sometimes seed may fail to germinate in the first season but wait for another year. There is little that can be done about this except to be patient and to avoid the temptation of throwing out the pot thinking that all is dead. During this waiting period the compost should be kept rigorously clear of any alien growth, by hand weeding.

Pots and containers are best watered from below by plunging pots up to their rims in a basin of water. This avoids the problems of washing out the compost or floating all the seeds to one side of the pot. Of course where large numbers of pots are involved this procedure is impractical and a watering can with a fine rose attached should suffice.

Seed of perennial cultivars, especially the blousy Oriental Poppies, will seldom come true to type so be prepared for a mixed and variable batch of progeny. It is always worth a gamble for one may get an exceptional and unusual form or colour which may be well worth maintaining and propagating. Poor forms and seedlings are best discarded immediately and the temptation to give the plants their parental cultivar name is best avoided at all costs and, for obvious reasons, as such practises cause confusion and bring the grower into disrepute. Where several species or cultivars of *Meconopsis* or *Papaver* are grown in close proximity expect some hybrids to result. Many of these may be extremely fine plants but to maintain the true species it may be necessary to isolate individual plants and to collect seed only from these, unless of course one prefers the hybrids.

It is the strange fact that amongst growers a plant, however beautiful, immediately takes on a new status once it becomes a success and begins to take over. It becomes less desirable or even a weed and has to be eliminated. In its place other rarer and more difficult plants are sought to fill the void and to challenge the skill of the grower. But many poppies look at their best where they self-sow amongst other flowers in the border.

Perennial poppies can be increased by division, although not those with a tuft of shoot from a single thickened taproot. Certainly this is a good method for increasing Oriental Poppies and some of the fine forms of *Meconopsis grandis* and *M. × sheldonii*. This can be attempted after flowering or in the spring as growth commences. On the whole though it is best to establish divisions well before the autumn. Division usually requires the digging up of the parent plant, although suitable slices can sometimes be removed without such an effort. Portions with some attached roots can be cut off (I use a sharp kitchen knife when my wife is not looking) and the portions planted back in the same bed or potted up. Until established, careful watering and shading will be necessary.

Oriental Poppies can also be readily propagated from root-cuttings and this method is employed commercially in order to get enough stock. Thick fleshy and healthy pieces of root are removed from the parent plant. These are cut into sections 3–4 cm (1⅕–1⅗ in) long and any fine lateral roots removed. The pieces can then be inserted upright (with the original upper end at the top) in pots or frames of silver sand or a sand-peat mixture. The cut end should lie at the surface of the pot and the whole cutting treated with a suitable water-based fungicide. Root-cuttings can be taken any time in the spring or summer and generally take four to six weeks before new shoots appear. The cuttings can then be potted on. For the average gardener this procedure is not generally necessary as ordinary division will supply all the plants one is likely to need.

PESTS AND DISEASES

Most poppies are remarkably free from the attacks of pests and diseases. Slugs and snails may attack seedlings or the emerging shoots in the spring and can be controlled with one of a number of proprietory deterrents available on the market today. Aphids (both greenfly and blackfly – especially the black bean aphid, *Aphis fabae*) can attack certain species, particularly when they are in bud. Capsid bugs may also sometimes become a problem, especially with young plants. These pests often cause distortion of the flowers and foliage or generally puckering of the leaves. A systemic insecticide provides lasting control or, if like me you distrust such chemicals, then a milder spray such as liquid derris, sprayed at regular intervals will be control enough. Some poppies (of various genera) dislike some types of systemic sprays, especially if used at a greater strength than the manufacturer advises. Yellowing foliage and distorted growth are indicators of such spray damage. Soil pests such as wireworms (click beetles) or leather jackets (crane-fly maggots) may occasionally attack the base of the plants, but this is rare in my experience.

Fungal infections of seedlings and young plants can prove a serious problem. By the time this has been noticed many of the young plants may already have succumbed. Young or mature plants of some species, particularly *Meconopsis* and *Papaver*, may suffer from downy mildew, *Peronospora* species, which can be fatal to young seedlings; it is often revealed as yellow blotches on the leaves, with grey mould beneath. Treatment with fungicides can be effective, but many poppy seedlings and young plants are easily damaged by chemical sprays, even when used at the manufacturers' recommended application rate. Better still is to try and control such problems by ensuring that pots and composts are completely sterile in the first instance, that seeds are sown thinly and young plants kept well spaced and with ample ventilation. They must not, of course, become dessicated.

AS CUT FLOWERS

Poppies are often said to make poor cut flowers and this is certainly true of those which are quick to drop their petals. However, a number of different types are sold as cut flowers in Europe. These include the large and flamboyant Oriental Poppies (*Papaver bracteatum* and *P. orientalis*), the Iceland Poppy (*P. nudicaule*) and the Tulip Poppy (*Hunnemania fumariifolia*). Others also make good cut flowers: the Californian Poppies (*Eschscholzia californica*) and the Plumed Poppies (*Macleaya cordata* and *M. microcarpa*). Most poppies 'bleed' badly when cut and soon wilt. This can be overcome by sealing the wounds by burning the ends with a match or lighter, or better still by placing the cut ends into boiling water for a few seconds. This process keeps the stems turgid and upright and prevents wilting. Poppies are best cut just before the buds burst open for they are great fun to watch unfold, will last longer in a vase and, furthermore, are less likely to get bruised in transit. If cut too immature the buds may fail to open, so that the right stage has to be carefully judged.

Classification

Wallace Roy Ernst (1962) outlined the classification of the Poppy Family in his extensive *Comparative Morphology of the Papaveraceae*. In this the family is divided into four subfamilies based upon critical details of the floral morphology and fruit characteristics. Although this is fairly technical I have included the main details here for sake of completeness.

1. Subfamily Chelidonioideae. A very diverse subfamily with nine genera and some 20–30 species. They mostly possess simple multicellular hairs (but branched in *Bocconia* and *Macleaya*). The ovary consists of two wholly united carpels and the fruit-capsules dehisce into two valves along their entire length, either from the top or from the bottom; the capsules have particularly well-developed dorsal traces (veins). The seeds are often arillate. Genera: *Bocconia, Chelidonium, Dicranostigma, Eomecon, Glaucium, Hylomecon, Macleaya, Sanguinaria, Stylophorum*.

2. Subfamily Eschscholzioideae. A smaller and more uniform subfamily with only three genera and about 17 species. The hairs are unicellular. The ovary consists of two wholly fused carpels, as in the previous subfamily, and the fruit-capsules also have well-developed dorsal traces and dehisce violently into two valves from the base to the top. Genera: *Dendromecon, Eschscholzia, Hunnemannia*.

3. Subfamily Papaveroideae. The largest subfamily with nine genera and probably in excess of 150 species. Most possess multicellular hairs, often in many rows. The ovary consists of three or more wholly united carpels and the fruit-capsules have poorly developed or no dorsal traces and dehisce by pores or valves, in the latter instance generally from the top downwards. In addition the ovary and fruit generally have a pronounced stigmatic area, which reaches its most pronounced manifestation in the radiating stigmatic rays seen in the true poppies, *Papaver*. Genera: *Arctomecon, Argemone, Canbya, Cathcartia, Meconopsis, Papaver, Roemeria, Romneya, Stylomecon*.

4. Subfamily Platystemonoideae. A small and very distinct subfamily with four genera and 15 species. The hairs are multicellular, often borne in many rows. The ovary consists of a number (often four or more) of carpels held closed together and fused only towards the base, each with its own discrete stigma. The fruit-capsule consists of a bunch of follicles which pull apart at maturity and split along the line of the placenta, not into valves. Genera: *Hesperomecon, Meconella, Platystemon, Platystigma*.

In addition I have included in this book two further and fairly closely related genera, *Hypecoum* and *Pteridophyllum*. Most authorities have varied in their treatment of these two over the years, some placing them together with *Corydalis*, *Dicentra* and *Fumaria* into the Papaveraceae, whilst others split off all these genera into a distinct family, the Fumariaceae. However, *Hypecoum* and *Pteridophyllum* have rather intermediate characters between these two families and conform rather unhappily with both and for this reason are sometimes accorded a family of their own, the Hypecoaceae. As if this were not enough *Pteridophyllum* is also accorded a family of its own, the Pteridophyllaceae, by some authorities. Now I have put all this in not so much as to confuse the reader but to stress the point that plant families are not always as clear cut as they may often appear to be and that genera do sometimes occur with intermediate characters, or ones that simply do not fit comfortably into a particular family. Both *Hypecoum* and *Pteridophyllum* have small, rather poppy-like flowers with four petals, but there are only four stamens. The fruit is a narrow two-valved capsule. In both genera the inner petals are somewhat larger than the outer and in the case of *Hypecoum* are generally three-lobed. Although *Hypecoum* has dissected foliage very similar to many members of the Papaveraceae, *Pteridophyllum* stands distinct with its neat, pinnate and rather fern-like, leaves.

RELATED FAMILIES

The most closely related family, as already seen, is the fumitory family, Fumariaceae. Despite obvious similarities in the foliage and fruit characters between these two families, the flowers of the Fumariaceae look very different and are more complex structures all together. The species are annual or perennial herbs, sometimes climbing by leaf-tendrils, and produce a watery sap when cut. The inflorescence is usually racemose and the flowers often nodding or half-nodding. There are two, often tiny and persistent, sepals and four petals. One or both of the outer petals are pouched or spurred at the base and are generally partially united to the smaller inner petals. The six stamens are fused together into two bundles of three, with the filaments extending backwards into the pouched base (bases) of the outer petals where they secrete nectar. Well-known genera in gardens include the weedy fumitories, *Fumaria*, *Corydalis* and the Dutchman's breeches or bleeding hearts, *Dicentra*.

The cabbage or mustard family, Cruciferae, is also regarded by many authorities to be closely related to the Papaveraceae. The two are not likely to be confused. Members of the Cruciferae generally have rather small flowers with four persistent sepals and four petals, often forming a cross-shape, and six stamens. Many species have more complex hairs, often medi-fixed or stellate (starry). The ovary consists of two fused carpels, which are often partitioned by a false-septum or membrane. The fruit varies enormously in shape and details, although some come close to the simple linear siliqua-like structures found in certain genera of the Papaveraceae, such as *Chelidonium* and *Dicranostigma*.

DISTRIBUTION

The genus *Papaver*, by far the largest in the family, is distributed primarily in Europe, western and central Asia with a cluster of closely related species in Arctic regions, northern Asia and Japan; there is a single species in the south-western USA and one in southern Africa. *Glaucium, Hypecoum* and *Roemeria* are distributed from Europe to central Asia, whereas *Chelidonium* stretches right across from Europe to Japan.

Exclusively Asiatic genera are *Cathcartia, Dicranostigma, Eomecon, Hylomecon, Macleaya, Meconopsis* (with one species in western Europe) and *Pteridophyllum*. Interestingly, apart from a few species of *Papaver* and one *Stylophorum*, no other genera are shared in common between Asia and North America.

However, western North America, especially California and the neigh-bouring territories, are particularly rich in Papaveraceae, with the following genera represented: *Arctomecon, Argemone, Canbya, Dendromecon, Eschscholzia, Hesperomecon, Hunnemannia, Meconella, Platystemon* and *Stylomecon. Sanguinaria* and one species of *Stylophorum* (*S. diphyllum*) are found in the cooler woodlands of North America, away from the west coast, indeed they are the only members of the Papaveraceae to be found on the eastern side of the continent.

Argemone stretches southwards from the southern United States into Mexico and Central and South America, but *Bocconia* is the only genus exclusively restricted to South America.

Key to Genera

(★ exclusively New World genera)

1. Flowers without petals, small and borne in larger terminal panicles 2
   Flowers with obvious petals, often large and showy, solitary or in
   umbels, racemes or panicles 3

2. Leaves palmately-lobed and -veined; plants herbaceous: **Macleaya**
   Leaves pinnately-lobed and -veined; plants shrubby or
   sub-shrubby: **Bocconia**

3. Leaves mainly opposite or whorled 4
   Leaves alternate or all basal 5

4. Stamens 6–12; carpels mostly 3, united; petals soon deciduous,
   3–4 mm, (¼ in) long: **Meconella★**
   Stamens numerous; carpels 6–25, beaded, separating at maturity;
   petals persistent, 6–20 mm, (¼–⅘ in) long: **Platystemon★**

5. Plants shrubby, at least at the base 6
   Plants annual, biennial or perennial, never shrubby 8

6. Plants very prickly, both in leaf and fruit: **Argemone fruitcosa★**
   Plants not prickly at all 7

7. Flowers yellow, 5–7.5 cm (2–3 in) across; leaves unlobed,
   entire: **Dendromecon**★
   Flowers white, 10–13 cm (4–5½ in) across; leaves lobed: **Romneya**★

8. Leaves cut into numerous linear segments; sap watery 9
   Leaves not as above; sap latex-like, white, yellow or orange usually . . .11

9. Petals 3-lobed, the inner pair smaller than the outer; flowers often
   weakly zygomorphic: **Hypecoum**
   Petals entire, generally more or less equal in size; flowers never
   zygomorphic 10

10. Sepals united, hood-like: **Eschscholzia**★
    Sepals free, not hood-like: **Hunnemania**★

11. Leaves orbicular, lobed or scalloped; flowers white 12
    Leaves not as above; flowers various colours 13

12. Flowers solitary, scapose; petals 6+; leaves lobed: **Sanguinaria**★
    Flowers in long-stemmed umbels; petals usually 4; leaves
    scalloped: **Eomecon**

13. Leaves pinnately-lobed, frond-like, with broad
    segments: **Pteridophyllum**
    Leaves entire or variously lobed but never frond-like 14

14. Fruit-capsule 3-valved; leaves all basal: **Platystigma**★
    Fruit-capsule not as above; leaves basal or along stems 15

15. Fruit-capsules linear, siliqua-like, generally splitting lengthwise
    when ripe 16
    Fruit-capsules globose to oblong or elliptical, generally dehiscing
    by pores or slits in the upper third when ripe 22

16. Stem-leaves amplexicaule (clasping), unstalked; flowers yellow
    or orange 17
    Stem-leaves not amplexicaule, generally stalked; flowers yellow,
    orange, red or violet 18

17. Stigma 2-lobed; fruit-capsule with a horny apex: **Dicranostigma**
    Stigma not 2-lobed; fruit-capsule with a horny apex (like a small
    arrowhead):   **Glaucium**

18. Flowers red or violet; fruit-capsule long and linear: **Roemeria**
    Flowers yellow or orange; fruit-capsule short-cylindrical to elliptical
    in outline 19

19. Flowers often solitary; stems unbranched: **Hylomecon**
    Flowers clustered or several on each stem from the upper leaf-axils;
    stems often branched 20

20. Leaves circular in outline, palmately-lobed: **Cathcartia**
    Leaves trifoliate to pinnate 21

21. Flowers rather small, 15–25 mm (⅗–1 in) across, with narrow non-
    overlapping petals; style very short; bracts absent: ***Chelidonium***
    Flowers larger, at least 30 mm (1⅕ in) across, with broader, partly
    overlapping petals; style obvious; bracts present: ***Stylophorum***

22. Plants tiny, less than 3 cm (2⅕ in) tall; stamens 6–9:   ***Canbya*★**
    Plants at least 8 cm (3 in) tall; stamens usually numerous 23

23. Plant decidedly spiny or prickly 24
    Plants smooth or hairy, sometimes roughly so but not prickly 25

24. Sepals 3, horned; petals white, yellow or golden, occasionally
    lavender: ***Argemone*★**
    Sepals 2, not horned; petals usually blue or yellow, occasionally pink
    or purple: ***Meconopsis***

25. Style absent; ovary topped by stigmatic disc, flat, convex or
    somewhat concave: ***Papaver***
    Style present; ovary not as above 26

26. Annuals with dimorphic leaves; flowers orange-red, rather
    flat: ***Stylomecon***
    Perennials without dimorphic leaves; flowers various colours but if
    red then cup-shaped or lantern-shaped 27

27. Sepals 3; petals 6, white or yellow; plants of semi-desert
    regions: ***Arctomecon*★**
    Sepals 2; petals 4–10, white, yellow, blue, purple or red; plants of
    moist mountains and woodland: ***Meconopsis***

I
Subfamily
Chelidonioideae

The Tree Celandines
Bocconia

The genus *Bocconia* is little known in our gardens except as a synonym for the two species of Plumed Poppy, *Macleaya*. The prime reason for this is that the species are plants of the subtropics and tropics of the New World, especially from Mexico and Peru and are not suitable for temperate gardens. The genus was described by Linnaeus in 1753 and for some years it included both the Old World species as well as *B. cordata* from China and Japan. In 1826 Robert Brown, recognising differences between the Old and New World species, separated the latter into a new genus, *Macleaya*. *Bocconia* is named after the Sicilian botanist Paolo Bocconi (1633–1703).

Bocconia contains nine species which look superficially similar to *Macleaya*, especially in the character of the inflorescence, but the plants are shrubs or subshrubs, not herbaceous perennials. The main differences are to be found in the leaves, which are entire to pinnate (depending on the species), but with distinctive pinnate veins. Other differences can be seen in the fruit-capsule which, unlike *Macleaya*, opens from the base upwards.

As in *Macleaya* the latex of *Bocconia* is orange and juicy and is used locally for the treating of warts and other skin disorders, but also sometimes as a dye plant.

These are excellent and effective plants for subtropical and tropical gardens, although not seen nearly as much as they really deserve. They thrive best in a light, well-drained soil with plenty of moisture during the growing season and ample mulches. An open sunny position is ideal and plants should be given ample space in which to develop.

Plants can be propagated from seed sown in heat in the spring or from cuttings as described under *Macleaya*. Away from tropical and subtropical gardens they are handsome plants for large glasshouses and conservatories with a minimum temperature of 18°C (65°F).

For *Bocconia cordata* and *B. microcarpa* see under *Macleaya*, p. 44.

Bocconia arborea S. Wats.

A small tree to 7 m (22 ft) tall with spongy bark. The leaves are pinnately lobed and clustered at the branch tips, the lobes sharply toothed, often downy beneath. The flowers are borne in branched racemes up to 20 cm (8 in) long. This species, the largest in the genus, comes from Central America and flowers in July and August.

Bocconia frutescens L.
(Syn. *B. glauca* Salisb.; *B. sinuatifolia* Stokes)
TREE CELANDINE

An evergreen shrub 1–2 m (3–6 ft) tall with stout, rather stiff, erect stems, softly hairy when young. The leaves are up to 35 cm (14 in) long and pinnately lobed, short-stalked and with a rounded or somewhat truncated base; they are smooth and bluish green above but paler and somewhat hairy beneath. The greenish flowers are borne in large diffuse, rather feathery, panicles, each flower with 14–16 stamens usually; as in *Macleaya* the flowers are small, the sepals only 9–10 mm (⅖ in) long, and petalless. *Bocconia frutescens* is a native of the West Indies and Mexico and has been in cultivation since 1739. It flowers in September and October. This species has become naturalised in Java.

Leaves of *Bocconia frutescens* (left) and *Macleaya microcarpa* (right) showing the basic differences between the two genera

Bocconia integrifolia Humb. & Bonpl.
ENTIRE–LEAVED TREE CELANDINE

Very distinct from *B. frutescens*, being a much-branched shrub to 5 m (17 ft) tall, though often less, the young branches covered in a rather mealy down. The oblong to elliptical leaves have a serrated margin but are unlobed, green above but with a contrasting white-mealy reverse. The greenish flowers are borne in a rather dense panicle, each flower with about ten stamens.

Bocconia integrifolia has been in cultivation since 1822 and is a native of South America, particularly Bolivia, Colombia and Peru.

The Greater Celandine
Chelidonium

The genus *Chelidonium* is familiar to all those interested in the flora of western Europe, for it is a widespread native in the region. There is only one species in the genus, *C. majus*, often called the Greater Celandine, though quite different to the Lesser Celandine, *Ranunculus ficaria*. The species in fact has a wide distribution from western Europe to Asia. The name *Chelidonium* was used by Dioscoridis, from the Greek *Chelidon*, the swallow; it was said that the plant came into flower with the coming of the swallow, drying up upon its departure in the autumn.

In gardens it is often dismissed as a 'weed' or 'wildling' of little interest. However, this is being wholly unfair to a plant that is extremely useful in dark, damp corners of the garden or for areas left to encourage a wild-flower garden. It is a plant of quiet charm and elegance and I would not be without it somewhere in my own garden. At the same time the Greater Celandine is one of those plants that needs little attention and is quite happy left to itself. Once established there is no need for further attention. Some will complain that it seeds around all to freely but this is a sign of success and it is little trouble to remove excess seedlings or to transplant them to other places where they may be acceptable.

The genus *Coreanomecon* Nakai, described from Korea is a synonym of *Chelidonium*.

Chelidonium majus L.   [Pl. 1]
GREATER CELANDINE, SWALLOW WORT

A tufted perennial herb with pale brittle stems which exude an acrid, saffron-coloured sap when cut; stems branched from close to the base, sparsely hairy, to 60–90 cm (24–36 in) tall in vigorous plants. The leaves are mostly in a loose basal rosette; they are up to 20 cm (8 in) long and once or twice pinnately-lobed, the segments oval, coarsely toothed and generally a rather pale bluish-green; stem leaves similar but smaller and generally less divided. The small yellow flowers, 18–25 mm (⅔–1 in) across, are borne in lax umbel-like clusters just above the foliage; sepals two; petals four, oblong, not overlapping and widely spreading; stamens yellow. The narrow fruit-pods, 3–5 cm (1⅕–2 in) long, are more or less straight and smooth, splitting from the base to the top when ripe by two valves. The seeds are black and shiny with a small white aril at one end; this latter is attractive to ants who carry the seeds away and so effect dispersal to other areas.

Chelidonium majus is primarily a plant of shady and damp habitats, hedgerows, woodlands and the bases of rocks, walls or old buildings, generally at rather low altitudes and flowering from May to July, occasionally later. It has so long been associated with humans that its precise natural distribution is uncertain, although it is undoubtedly native to many parts of Europe. However, it has long been cultivated as a medicinal herb and its use as such goes far back to both the ancient Chinese and Greek civilisations. Like many similar herbs it was believed to cure a whole range of diverse disorders including warts, gout and scrofula (a kind of tuberculosis). The plant, particularly the bright orange sap, contains a number of potentially harmful alkaloids including chelidonine, protopine, and sanguinarine, so its use could be hazardous to say the least.

Plants are generally rather short-lived in the garden, but there are always seedlings around to replace their parents. The common wild form is rather leggy and, for those who prefer a plant of more distinction, there is a double-flowered form available, 'Flore Pleno' [**Pl. 2**] or 'Plenum'. Despite its name this double form has semi-double rather than fully double flowers. There are various forms of it about, some with distinctly larger and darker blooms, and these are well worth seeking out. Most appear to come true from seed.

Another handsome form is var. *laciniatum* [**Pl. 3**] (*Chelidonium laciniatum Miller*) which boasts handsome cut foliage with deeply incised segments, more striking than the type. This plant also has the benefit of being more compact overall. The flowers are single but are noticeably fringed along their margins. Var. *laciniatum* has been known for many years – it was noted first in the Heidelberg garden of the Sprenger apothecaries in 1590 and has been cultivated ever since. Such cut-leaved forms can be found in parts of western Europe as well as western Russia. Crosses between *C. majus* 'Flore Pleno' and var. *laciniatum* produce plants with intermediate leaf characters and semi-double flowers – these are often listed in catalogues as *laciniatum* 'Flore Pleno', though they should not be confused with *C. majus* 'Flore Pleno' or 'Plenum' as it is also listed.

In addition there are other forms recorded. These include 'Variegatum' with variegated foliage, which was certainly known and shown by J. Salter of the Versailles Nursery in Hammersmith, London, in 1862, but has not apparently been seen since.

Chelidonium majus var. *grandiflorum* (*Chelidonium grandiflorum* DC.) is similar to the typical plant but is distinguished, as its name implies, by having larger flowers, said to be 35 mm (2 in) across, but also by having shorter fruit-capsules and broader bracts. This variety is native to Central Asia to

Siberia and north-western China and would certainly be well worth acquiring. However, it does not appear to be in cultivation at the present time, at least not in the West. This large-flowered variety must look very similar to the genus *Stylophorum* (see key on p. 27).

The Eastern Horned Poppies
Dicranostigma

The genus *Dicranostigma* contains three species native to the Himalaya and western China. Superficially they closely resemble the true Horned Poppies, *Glaucium*, but differ in their two-lobed stigmas and shorter more elliptical-shaped fruit-capsules without the horned apex characteristic of *Glaucium*.

In the garden they are plants for well-drained sunny sites but with ample moisture during the summer, reflecting the monsoon-soaked terrain from which the species hail. They can be raised quite readily from seed sown either under cover or outdoors. Unlike those of most members of the poppy family, seedlings transplant fairly readily.

Dicranostigma franchetianum (Prain) Fedde
ANNUAL DICRANOSTIGMA

A grey-green annual, occasionally perennial to 1 m (3 ft) tall, sometimes more, with erect branched, smooth stems. The mealy leaves are mostly basal oblong in outline, to 20 cm (8 in) long, pinnately-lobed, the upper lobes larger and more crowded than the lower; upper leaves sparse and smaller. The solitary orange-yellow, half-nodding flowers are cup-shaped, 3–4 cm (1⅕–1⅗ in) across, often borne in profusion, sepals two, mealy; petals four, oval, scarcely overlapping one another; stamens numerous, yellow with pale filaments. The fruit-capsule is smooth, cylindrical-oblong and tapered, 8–14 cm (3–5½ in) long.

Dicranostigma franchetianum is a native of south-west China, Sichuan and northern Yunnan, where it inhabits rocky and sandy habitats and river banks in rather open sites, at 2,200–4,100 m (7,200–13,450 ft) altitude, flowering from June to August.

There is a good illustration of this attractive species in *Curtis's Botanical Magazine* (tab. 9409). *D. franchetianum* was formerly more commonly seen in gardens but it is now relatively rare, although I have recently seen some fine patches of it in field trials in Holland. Unfortunately the flowers are short-lived and are of little use for cutting. However, it is a hardy annual plant that produces many flowers throughout the summer and for this reason alone is worth growing. Seed needs to be collected diligently as I do not know of it self-sowing in the garden. Plants will occasionally survive into the second year or, if sown late, may behave as a biennial. A moist light soil in sun or partial shade suits it well.

Dicranostigma franchetianum

Dicranostigma lactucoides Hook. f. & Th.   [Pl. 4]
(Syn. *Stylophorum lactucoides* (Baill.) Hook. f. & Th.)
HIMALAYAN HORNED POPPY

A biennial or short-lived perennial that looks like a small *Glaucium*. Stems branched from close to the base, almost leafless, bristly, to 40–60 cm (16–24 in) tall. Plants form attractive flattish leaf-rosettes up to 30–40 cm (12–16 in) across. The leaves are oblanceolate in outline, rather fleshy, grey- or bluish-green and somewhat scurfy, pinnately-lobed with the lobes becoming decreasingly smaller towards the short-stalked base; segments rounded to oblong, slightly toothed. The solitary yellow or orange-yellow flowers, 3–4 cm (1⅕–1⅗ in) across, are saucer-shaped; sepals two, scurfy; petals four, elliptical to oval, not overlapping. The fruit-capsule is elliptical-cylindrical and softly-hairy, 4–6 cm (1⅗–2⅖ in) long.

This attractive little species comes from the remoter regions of the Indian and Nepalese Himalaya and southern Tibet (Xizang), at 3,200–4,500 m (10,500–14,800 ft), where it inhabits high mountain moraines, screes and other rocky places, particularly favouring river banks in very exposed sunny situations, flowering there from July to September.

Dicranostigma lactucoides has been introduced into cultivation on a number of occasions during the past 50 years; the seeds primarily originating from Nepal. The species is quite hardy in our gardens but tends to be short-lived. It is certainly resentful of too much winter wet, which causes the base of the plant to rot. This can be overcome by growing plants in an extremely well-drained gritty soil – it makes a fine plant for a large scree garden – and by protecting young plants by a piece of glass during the winter months. I have found it best to sow the seeds under cover, pricking out seedlings whilst they are still very small into individual pots. Young plants can be planted outside in June and will occasionally produce a few flowers in their first season. I have never known it self-sow in my own garden, though others may have been been fortunate. Seed is normally produced in quantity, so it is surprising that this species is not more often seen.

Dicranostigma leptopodum (Maxim.) Fedde

This species is very like *D. franchetianum* but a smaller plant with rather small flowers and very narrow fruits. However, it has to be admitted that these two species are connected by intermediates in the wild, the whole forming a rather complex pattern of variability. Future researchers may well find it impossible to maintain them as distinct species.

A native of Gansu (Kansu) Province, China. Doubtfully in cultivation at the present time.

The Snow Poppy
Eomecon

The name *Eomecon* comes from the Greek *heoros*, eastern, and *mekon*, poppy, for this is a distinctive poppy from eastern China. The genus contains just one species, a woodlander thriving in moist leafy soils in dappled shade, which is grown as much for the simplicity of its elegant white flowers, as for its handsome scalloped leaves.

The leaf-shape and the branched flower stems, which are leafless but bear a number of small bracts, serve to distinguish this genus from all other members of the Papaveraceae.

Eomecon chionanthum

Eomecon chionanthum Hance [Pl. 5]
SNOW POPPY or DAWN POPPY

A rhizomatous perennial with far-reaching underground stolons, oozing orange-red sap when cut. The leaves are basal, heart-shaped to kidney-shaped, with the margin neatly scalloped into a series of short rounded lobes, palmately-veined and carried well above the ground on long stalks, which are rather fleshy, hairless, grey-green with a flush of lilac but paler beneath, to 10–15 cm (4–6 in) across, sometimes larger. The flowering scapes, which rise erect to 40 cm (16 in) tall, are branched above into a spreading cyme, each branch with a small scale-like bract at its base. The flowers themselves are white with a central boss of yellow anthers, 3–4 cm (1⅕–1⅗ in) across, with four oval petals that spread widely apart; buds oval with a pointed apex, smooth; sepals two, soon falling when the flowers expand.

Eomecon requires similar conditions in the garden to *Stylophorum* although it behaves quite differently. When well-suited it runs about underground and there is no telling where the next shoot might arise. Whereas this will undoubtedly annoy the neat-minded gardener, to me this is one of its charms. Suffice it to say that it would be unwise to plant the Snow Poppy close to other less vigorous plants for fear of swamping them, and do avoid planting it as I once did on a peat bank – it looked lovely but little else was left by the time it had occupied the entire bed. Amongst strong herbaceous neighbours or shrubs in a woodland setting it can look most enchanting. The flowers are fleetingly produced during May and June but after they are gone the handsome leaves, in many ways the best feature of this plant, carry on until browned by the first frosts of autumn.

The Snow Poppy is hardy in all but the coldest districts providing it is given a reasonably sheltered site. Plants can be propagated from seed but the more usual method is to lift some of the rhizomes in the summer, when they can be easily identified.

Amongst the gaudier and more brazen races of poppy this one makes a pleasant and subtler contrast and for that reason it is often dismissed as a 'planter's plant'. This is generally taken to mean that none but the most dedicated gardener would dream of growing it or, indeed, would want to but this surely would be wholly unjustified.

The Horned Poppies
Glaucium

The Yellow Horned-Poppy, *Glaucium flavum*, is a familiar coastal plant in parts of Britain and the Mediterranean, as well as in the Atlantic Islands, around the Black Sea and the Caspian, sometimes occurring inland.

This species was well-known to Gerard who called it *Papaver cornutum flore luteo* or the 'Yellow horned Poppie' in his *Herbal* (1597), and stated that it 'groweth upon the sands and banks of the sea'.

Gerard also attributed the horned poppy with medicinal powers. 'The root of horned Poppies boiled in water unto the consumption of the one halfe, and drunke, provoketh urine, and openeth the stopping of the liver' and 'The juice mixed with meale and honey, ruindisieth old rotten and filthy ulcers'.

The genus *Glaucium* Miller contains some 20 species distributed in Europe, south-western and central Asia. The genus derives its names from the grey or glaucous foliage characteristic of many of the species. As Miller states in the *Gardener's Dictionary*: '[It] is so called from the Greek because the leaves of this plant are of sea green colour; it is call'd the Horned Poppy, because it is a species of Poppy, having husks resembling horns.'

Indeed the fruit characters serve to distinguish *Glaucium* from all other genera in the Papaveraceae. The fruit-capsules are cylindrical, linear, straight or curved and very long, up to 30 cm (12 in) in length, and distinctly capped by a two-lobed stigma, like a tiny Dutch-cap. When ripe the capsule splits into two valves from apex to base, or vice versa, and contains numerous seeds.

Glauciums can be annual, biennial or perennial herbs, often forming a distinctive, though lax, basal rosette of leaves. Most produce yellow sap when cut. Both the branched stems and leaves are usually glaucous, glabrous or hairy, the latter often giving the foliage a typical scurfy or mealy appearance. The upper stem leaves are nearly always unstalked and clasp the stem with a broad base. The solitary flowers are lateral or terminal, often yellow but also orange or various shades of red; sepals two, soon falling; petals four, somewhat overlapping, sometimes with a pale or dark basal blotch; stamens numerous.

Horned poppies are attractive ornamental species for the garden. In addition they are sometimes cultivated for the oil extracted from the seeds, which can be used for illumination, soap-making and for various medicinal purposes.

In gardens they are easy plants for a sunny well-drained site. Miller states that 'they delight most in a warm light soil, but will grow in almost any soil, if it be not over-dunged'. Miller lists four sorts:

- *Glaucium flore luteo*, Yellow Horned Poppie (= *Glaucium flavum*)
- *Glaucium flore violacea*, Blue-flower'd Horned Poppie (= *Roemeria violacea*)
- *Glaucium hirsutum, flore Phoenicio*, Hairy Horned Poppie, with a deep scarlet flower (= *Glaucium corniculatum*)
- *Glaucium glabrum, flore Phoenicio*, Smooth Horned Poppie, with deep scarlet flower (= probably *Glaucium grandiflorum*).

Interestingly, these are the commonest species grown in our gardens today, although there are some equally tempting species little known in cultivation or, indeed, not in cultivation at all.

Most horned poppies are rather short-lived in the garden. Grown on rich soils they tend to form large plants that flower and die. On poorer, drier soils they look more in character and often go on for several years. They have a single thick, rather tough, woody taproot and cannot be divided and absolutely hate disturbance once established. They can, however, be readily raised from seed, although both G. *flavum* and G. *corniculatum* will self-sow in some gardens. Seed can be sown under cover in the early spring, the resultant seedling pricked out when large enough to handle and placed in individual pots in a light airy place in frame or glasshouse. It is a mistake to let seedlings become too large before pricking out as it is then all too easy to damage the delicate young taproot. Plants can be planted out in mid-summer, certainly before they become pot-bound and starved, so that they can build up a good sized leaf-rosette by the autumn. If they become too pot-bound, plants often remain small and seem incapable of growing to their expected size. Planted in heavy wet soils they tend, in my experience at least, to rot off during the winter months.

Horned poppies generally dislike being crowded in the flower border. They need space to look their best and to thrive. They look very fine along

a gravel path or driveway or against an old wall, where their attractive shape
and colouration can provide an interesting contrast to other plantings. Along
a beach in southern Greece I once saw some startlingly good, large-flowered
forms of G. *flavum* growing with the Sea Stock, *Matthiola sinuata* (all grey
and pink) and drifts of *Linun pubescens*, backed by banks of *Lavandula stoechas*
and *Cistus salviifolia*; how gorgeous to recreate such a medley in one's own
garden.

Key to Species

1. Sepals dark grey or blackish, smooth: *G. acutidentatum*
   Sepals grey- or bluish-green, often hairy, scurfy or warted,
   occasionally smooth 2

2. Fruit-capsule splitting from the bottom to the top....................3
   Fruit-capsule splitting from the top to the bottom....................4

3. Stems with only 1–2 leaves; petals yellow, sometimes with a white
   blotch; biennial or perennial: *G. squamigerum*
   Stems leafy; petals yellow or orange, with a dark basal blotch;
   annual: *G. elegans*

4. Ovary and fruit-capsules white-hairy 5
   Ovary and fruit-capsule smooth to warted, occasionally with a few
   bristles..6

5. Flower buds 2.5–4 cm (1–1⅗ in) long; fruit-stalk longer than the
   subtending leaf; flowers 5–8 cm (2–3 in) across: *G. grandiflorum*
   Flower buds 1–2 cm (⅖–⅘ in) long; fruit stalk generally shorter than the
   subtending leaf; flowers 3–5 cm (1–2 in) across, occasionally
   larger: *G. corniculatum*

6. Fruit-capsule, thin, 2–3 mm (1/12–⅛ in) wide, often slightly constricted
   between the seeds, smooth: *G. leiocarpum*
   Fruit-capsule thicker, 3–5 mm (⅛–⅕ in) wide, not constricted between
   the seeds, bristly, warted or occasionally smooth 7

7. Pedicels long, often more than 10 cm (4 in); fruit-capsule smooth or
   with scattered bristles: *G. fimbrilligerum*
   Pedicels short, rarely more than 10 cm (4 in) long; fruit-capsule
   warted: *G. flavum*

Glaucium acutidentatum Hausskn. & Bornm.

This little-known species has the stature and general appearance of G. *flavum*
but the basal leaves are more deeply pinnately-lobed; it is biennial or a short-
lived perennial. The sepals are very distinctive and readily separate this
species from the others, being quite smooth and dark grey or blackish in
colour, often with a bluish bloom like a plum. The flowers are an orange-
buff colour, the petals without a basal blotch. The fruit-capsules are erect

and straight, and are quite smooth, without any sign of warts (tubercles).

An attractive horned poppy endemic to Cappadocia in Turkey, where it inhabits dry hillslopes and rocky places between 950–980 m (3,100–3,200 ft) altitude, flowering from June to September.

Glaucium cappadocicum Boiss

Another Turkish species rarely seen in our gardens. In many ways it is similar to G. *acutidentatum*, but is a rather smaller plant, 30–50 cm (12–20 in) tall, apparently always biennial. The leaf-lobes are more noticeably toothed and the sepals smooth and green. The flowers are yellow, 4–5 cm (1⅗–2 in) across and are followed by glabrous, curved fruit-capsules, not more than 10 cm (4 in) in length.

G. *cappadocicum* grows in similar habitats to G. *acutidentatum* and is endemic to the region of the Upper Euphrates in Cappadocia, from where the species gets its name.

Glaucium corniculatum (L.) J.H. Rudolph   [Pl. 6]
(Syn. *Chelidonium corniculatum* L.; *Glaucium grandiflorum* sensu Hayek, non Boiss. & Huet, G. *phoeniceum* Crantz; G. *rubrum* Smith)
RED HORNED POPPY

This is generally annual, rarely biennial, 7–30 cm (3–12 in) tall and with erect or ascending stems that are covered in rough hairs. The basal leaves, up to 20 cm (8 in) long, are pinnately-lobed into oblong lobes that are rather sharply toothed; all the leaves are glaucous and covered in short hairs. The flowers are relatively small, generally 3–5 cm (1⅕–2 in) across, bright red or orange in the typical form, each petal with a basal violet blotch, but sometimes with a pale blotch; sepals glabrous or somewhat bristly. The fruit-capsule is generally 10–15 cm, (4–6 in) long, although up to 20 cm (8 in) has been recorded, and is straight or somewhat curved, but characteristically covered in short, often appressed, hairs.

G. *corniculatum* is native to the Mediterranean Basin, southern Europe, extending to the Atlantic Islands and eastwards to the Caucasus and Iran. It inhabits cultivated, fallow and waste ground or dry hillslopes up to 1,800 m (5,900 ft) altitude, flowering from March to June. This is a reasonably common plant in gardens, often found under the name G. *phoeniceum*, a synonym. Its striking blue-grey foliage makes it a useful and decorative plant for a grey- or silver-border and in many ways the foliage is more appealing than the flowers, which are rather sparsely produced throughout the summer months.

This is Gerard's '*Papaver cornutum flore rubro*' of which he states: '[It] . . . groweth not wilde in England . . . found this red horned poppie in the kingdomes of Aragon and Castile in Spain, and the fields near unto common paths. They grow in my garden very plentifully.'

Botanically G. *corniculatum* is considered to be especially variable in its flower colour. Var. *tricolor* (Bernh. ex Spreng.) Ledeb. (syn. *G. tricolor* Bernh.) is a name given to plants with larger, red or orange flowers in which the basal dark blotch is outlined in white. It comes from the eastern side of the species range, including Cyprus and Turkey. Var. *flaviflorum* DC. has yellow flowers and is also found in the east. This variety can be readily mistaken for *G. flavum* at a glance, but its annual habit and hairy fruit-capsules are good clues to its true identity. Unlike *G. flavum* it tends to be an inland plant of hills and low mountains. Despite these formal varieties the variation in flower colour and the presence or absence of petal blotches is by no means clear cut, but this does provide interesting potential for garden 'improvement and selection'.

Glaucium elegans Fisch. & Mey.
(Syn. *G. pumilum* Boiss.; *G. tenue* Regel & Schmalh.)
ANNUAL HORNED POPPY

An annual species to 30 cm (12 in) tall, though often less, with slender leafy stems that branch from the base. The basal leaves are borne in a small rosette and are pinnately lobed and stalked, whereas the stem leaves are much smaller and irregularly lobed and clasp the stem with unstalked bases. The small flowers are yellow or red, occasionally bicolored, 2–3.5 cm (⅘–1⅖ in) across. The fruit-capsule is very thin, curved or, more often, twisted, generally 6–10 cm (2⅖–4 in) long.

    This rather dainty little horned poppy is a native of Central Asia from the Caucasus to the Tien Shan Mountains, as well as Iran and Afghanistan, being a plant of rocky slopes, screes and river banks, especially in the lower montane zone where it can be found in flower from April until June.

    G. elegans is an attractive little annual, sometimes seen in cultivation, but certainly worth seeking out if one happens to be an avid collector of the less run-of-the-mill annuals grown in our gardens.

Glaucium fibrilligerum Boiss.
(Syn. *G. fimbrilliferum* B. Fedtsch.; *G. vitellinum* B. Fedtsch.)

A biennial species to 60 cm (24 in) tall, with rather robust, branching stems. The basal leaves are borne in a large rosette and are pinnately lobed and usually smooth; stems leaves smaller and half-clasping. The flowers are yellow, with unspotted petals, 4–5 cm (1⅗–2 in) across. The fruit-capsule is somewhat curved, up to 25 cm (10 in) in length and generally sparsely covered in whitish bristles.

    This is a plant from Central Asia, being found from the Tien Shan and the Pamir Mountains to Iran and Afghanistan. It is primarily a plant of the lower montane belt, growing along pebbly river beds, on rocky and clayey slopes and screes, flowering from May to July. It is probably not in cultivation at the present time.

Glaucium flavum Crantz [Pl. 7]
(Syn. *G. luteum* Scop.)
YELLOW HORNED POPPY

This familiar species is a robust, rather cabbage-like, glaucous biennial or perennial to 60 cm (24 in) tall, sometimes taller, with branched, thick stems. The fleshy leaves, up to 30 cm (12 in) long, form a large rosette, the basal stalked and pinnately lobed, with broad oblong, rather undulate lobes, laxly covered in scurfy hairs; stem leaves unstalked and clasping the stem with broad basal lobes. The flowers, 6–9 cm (2⅖–3⅗ in) across are yellow, generally without a dark basal blotch; sepals glaucous and bristly. The fruit-capsule is very long and curved, to 30 cm (12 in), occasionally longer, hairless but adorned with small wart-like processes along its entire length.

G. *flavum* is the most widespread species of horned poppy, being found from southern Britain and the Atlantic Islands through the Mediterranean Basin to the shores of the Black Sea and the Transcaucasian region. Typically it is a plant of sandy and pebbly seashores, but it can sometimes be found inland; flowering from May to August, occasionally later.

Theophrastus records that the root 'has the property of purging the belly, and the leaf is used for removing ulcers from sheep's eyes'. Dioscoridis recommends a decoction obtained from the root 'to cure sciaticas, and liver griefs and to help such as piss thick, or cobweb-like matter'.

The Yellow Horned Poppy has been cultivated in gardens for many centuries and in a good form can be a long-lived perennial. In most instances though, it has to be replaced every three or four years.

Yellow is the typical colour and forms with a dark brown basal blotch to the petals can be found in Greece and Turkey. These latter are very handsome plants with very grey foliage and exceptionally large, somewhat frilled flowers; they can be ascribed to var. *fulvum* 'Aurantiacum' [Pl. 8], a form with pure orange flowers.

The horned poppies offer a potential hybridiser some very interesting and variable material. A more long-lived perennial habit and larger red or yellow flowers would certainly attract many gardeners. In gardens G. *flavum* and its close cousin G. *leiocarpum* flower from July to September.

Glaucium grandiflorum Boiss. & Huet. [Pl. 9]

An attractive species related to G. *corniculatum* but superior in its larger flowers, 5–8 cm (2–3 in) across, which are dark orange to crimson with a dark violet-black basal blotch to each petal. The plant is 30–50 cm (12–20 in) tall, usually with greener leaves and hairy fruit-capsules 10–15 cm (4–6 in) long; the fruit-stalks are longer than their subtending leaf (shorter in G. *corniculatum*).

G. *grandiflorum* is native to Turkey eastwards to the southern Caucasus, Syria and Iran, and southwards into Sinai, where it is a plant of sandy and stony places. This highly attractive species is rarely seen in our gardens. It certainly merits a wider following and deserves to be reintroduced as seed from the wild.

Glaucium leiocarpum Boiss.

(syn. G. *flavum* var.*leiocarpum* (Boiss.) Stoj. & Stef.; G. *oxylobum* Boiss. & Bukse)

EASTERN HORNED POPPY

This is very similar to G. *flavum*, but a slighter more elegant plant. The flowers can be deep yellow, or occasionally reddish or tawny-yellow and the sepals practically glabrous. The chief differences lie in the fruit-capsules, which are not more than 20 cm (8 in) long (often only 8–12 cm (3–5 in)), smooth or warted only at the apex and often somewhat constricted between the seeds.

G. *leiocarpum* replaces typical G. *flavum* in much of the eastern Mediterranean, being found from Crete and the Balkans eastwards to Iran. It inhabits dry stony slopes and seashores, rarely at any altitude.

Occasionally identifiable in cultivation but so confused with G. *flavum* that its presence is generally overlooked. Some authorities treat it as a variety of G. *flavum*.

Glaucium squamigerum Kar. & Kir.

A little-known perennial or biennial species from the Asian Mountains distinguished by its few, minute stem leaves, small yellow flowers, 2.5–3.5 cm (1–1⅖ in) across, and unusual scaly fruit-capsule. Together with G. *elegans* it is the only other species in this account in which the fruit-capsule splits from the base to the top and not the other way round.

G. *squamigerum* is a Central Asian species and is to be found in the upper montane belt from the Tien Shan to the Pamir in the CIS (Commonwealth of Independent States; from Uzbekistan, Kazakstan and Kirghizia). It is a plant of river beds, rocky slopes and screes, sometimes on bare clay soils, and flowering from May until August. Apparently not in cultivation outside the CIS.

The Forest Poppy
Hylomecon

This delightful little forest-dweller is one of the first poppies to come into flower in the spring, an excellent woodland garden plant but succeeding in any moist, semi-shaded spot in the garden.

As currently understood, the genus *Hylomecon* contains just a single species, H. *japonicum*, although the *Flora USSR* distinguishes the Asiatic mainland plant as a separate species (H. *vernalis*) from the Japanese one. In reality H. *japonicum* is quite variable in both flower and leaf characters and it would be difficult to uphold two distinct species.

Hylomecon comes close to both *Chelidonium* and *Stylophorum*, differing from both in its unbranched stems. From *Chelidonium* it also differs in its

solitary rather than umbellate flowers and in the presence of bracts. In
Stylophorum the flowers are generally clustered and bear bracts as well as
bracteoles. In growth *Hylomecon* is also distinct, forming a slow-spreading
clump by means of short rhizomes just beneath the soil surface. In both
Chelidonium and *Stylophorum* growth radiates upwards from a basal rosette
of leaves.

Hylomecon japonicum (Miq.) Prantl & Kündig   [Pl. 10]
(syn. *Chelidonium japonicum* Thunb.; *C. uniflorum* Sieb. & Zucc.,
Hylomecon vernalis Maxim; *H. japonica* Bush; *Stylophorum japonicum*
Miq.)
FOREST POPPY

A spreading rhizomatous perennial to 30 cm (12 in) tall, rarely more; stems
erect and unbranched, slightly hairy at first. The leaves are pinnate, generally
with five leaflets but sometimes three or seven, the leaflets more or less equal,
lanceolate-oblong to almost rhombic, soft, deep green and with a sharply
and irregularly toothed margin; basal leaves long-stalked, to 25 cm (12 in)
long, the stem leaves generally only two or three, short-stalked or sessile;
bracts present. The erect flower buds are pear-shaped but rather pointed,
smooth or, more often, hairy. The bright yellow flowers, 3.5–5 cm
(1⅖–2 in) across, are upright and are borne singly on slender stalks, bowl-
shaped at first but becoming rather flat as the petals expand; sepals usually
two, soon falling; petals four, very occasionally five or six, rounded; stamens
many, yellow, about one third the length of the petals. The fruit-capsule is a
slender, erect, siliqua, 2–8 cm (1–3 in) long, hairless and opening by two
valves from just below the apex when ripe.

   H. japonicum inhabits leafy soils in moist, shaded woodland in north-
eastern China, including Manchuria, Korea and Japan where it flowers
during April and May. It was introduced into cultivation in Europe round
about 1870.

   In Japan a form with more pointed leaflets and very finely toothed along
the margins has been distinguished as var. *subintegra* Fedde. However, it is
the more normal coarsely toothed form that is seen in gardens.

   There is no doubt that this is one of the most charming and colourful
poppies for the woodland garden. The species is fully hardy. The flowers
generally appear in May and June and, although somewhat fleeting, are
produced in quantity on a vigorous plant. The species is sometimes accused
of being invasive but I have never found it to be so and, in any case, plants
are fairly shallow-rooted and excess growth can be easily removed.

   Hylomecon thrives best in a humusy soil and certainly responds to top-
dressing of leaf-mould or compost. In drier sunny positions it will linger on
but will rarely thrive or flower well, preferring the dappled shade of trees
and shrubs. It is also an excellent little plant for the peat border, though here
it may perhaps become invasive.

   Plants can be easily propagated from seed, which can be sown outdoors
in April. However, division of the parent plant provides a more ready means

of increase; divisions can be made in the early spring just before growth commences or, indeed, immediately after flowering. It is as well to mark plants as they have often disappeared below ground by late summer.

It is pleasant associated with other woodland members of the poppy family such as *Eomecon chionantha*, *Sanguinaria canadensis*, *Meconopsis chelidonifolia*, *Cathcartia villosa* or *Stylophorum diphyllum*. Together, these will provide interesting flowers and foliage from spring to late summer.

The Plumed Poppies
Macleaya

Of all the various members of the Poppy Family the genus *Macleaya* is the most unpoppy-like in both leaf and flower. The genus contains only two, rather similar, species that are stout perennials with stiff erect stems, broad, lobed leaves and large misty panicles of countless tiny flowers.

Macleaya is an Old World genus restricted to China and Japan. The genus is named in honour of Alexander Macleay (1767–1848), one-time secretary of the Linnean Society in London, but later Colonial Secretary for New South Wales. *Macleaya* is readily distinguished by its tall herbaceous stems and alternately arranged palmate leaves with their distinct palmate vein pattern (venation). The large inflorescence is a widely branching panicle with many small flowers which are without petals. There are four small sepals and a cluster of up to 30 stamens. The small elliptical, somewhat fleshy, fruit-capsule splits from the apex downwards and contains between one and six seeds.

The juice of plumed poppies is orange and will stain the skin, rather like iodine. Indeed in China the juice is used as an antiseptic treatment for cuts and blisters and may well have other medical uses.

Macleaya was at one time included in the New World genus *Bocconia*, but today most authorities recognise two separate and quite distinct genera. *Bocconia* differs in being a genus of shrubs or subshrubs mostly with pinnate leaves, although they may occasionally be unlobed. What is important is the fact that the leaf-veins are pinnately arranged. In addition the fruit capsule opens from the base upwards and the seeds are adorned with a conspicuous cup-like aril.

The two species of plumed poppies are bold and handsome plants in the garden, fully hardy and thriving on a variety of soils, although preferring a deep moist loam in a sunny position; they dislike very dry soils or exposed positions where the foliage can be easily bruised. Being tall they are suitable subjects for the back of a deep herbaceous border. However, isolated from other plants and given a border to themselves a grouping of several plants can be a very attractive feature, the striking leaves a foil to the feathery panicles of flower, which are borne in mid-summer. I have seen them used to good effect in this way as a group planting on the edge of a large lawn. Generally speaking these are not plants for the small garden, but for large gardens and parks they can provide a trouble-free feature. The stems can be cut down in the late autumn after frost has destroyed the foliage and then, in the spring, a generous mulch of well-rotted manure or compost will assure vigorous shoots for the following summer. When the clumps get too large and congested they can be dug up and divided; this can be undertaken in the autumn or the early spring.

Macleayas can also be propagated by the removal of suckers without disturbing the parent plant, or by cuttings. Cuttings can be taken in early summer by cutting up the stem into one node pieces, each with a large leaf attached – discard any damaged leaves or the smaller, upper ones. These pieces can be treated with a suitable hormone rooting agent and then inserted (right way up) into pots filled with a mixture of equal parts peat and sand, and placed in a propagating frame or on a mist bench. Once rooted the cuttings should be quickly potted on and kept growing by feeding and repotting so that they have time to form a substantial root system by the autumn. Their chances of surviving their first winter are thus greatly improved and the young plants can be planted out the following spring. Plants can also be propagated very successfully from root cuttings taken in the winter; only thick healthy roots should be used and these can be easily prized away from the parent plant. It usually takes two years to get flowering-sized plants from cuttings and for the average garden, where few plants are required, simple division of the parent plant is probably the simplest and quickest method to maintain stock. Seed, which is freely produced, can be sown and will give satisfactory, although slow, results. However, named cultivars should not be increased by this method as the resultant offspring are certain to vary. It is critical when raising any perennials from seed that poor forms (in vigour, foliage details or flower colour) be rogued out and destroyed, otherwise inferior forms will find their way into our gardens.

Macleaya cordata (Willd.)R. Br.
(Syn. *Bocconia cordata* Willd.; *B. yedoensis* Carr.)
PLUMED POPPY

A stout stoloniferous perennial with erect stems 1.5–2.5 m (5–8 ft) tall, forming fairly dense clumps. The large sculptured leaves are alternate, heart-shaped, with rounded and toothed lobes, greyish green above, but paler greyish white beneath and with prominent veining. The tiny flowers are borne in large feathery panicles, the overall colour effect being buff or creamy-white. Each flower has a cluster of 25–30 stamens and the fruit-capsules usually contain four to six seeds at maturity.

M. *cordata* is a native of eastern China and Japan, where it is a plant of woodlands, gullies and scrub, generally in the mountains and flowering in June and July. It was introduced into cultivation in 1795 as *Bocconia cordata* and featured early in *Curtis's Botanical Magazine* (tab. 1905).

Today the finest form of this species in cultivation is 'Flamingo', which is a handsome and bold cultivar with attractively pink-flushed leaves and flowers of rich pinkish buff. It, like the straight species, is widely available at nurseries and garden centres.

Macleaya × *kewensis* Turrill

This is a supposed hybrid between *M. cordata* and *M. microcarpa*, little seen in gardens, but with more or less intermediate characters.

Macleaya microcarpa (Maxim.) Fedde   [Pl. 11]
(Syn. *Bocconia microcarpa* Maxim.)

Very similar in both habit and stature to *M. cordata*. It differs primarily in its flowers, which have only 8–12 stamens and in its one-seeded fruit-capsules. The flower panicles are very attractive and have an overall bronzy flush; they appear rather ahead of those of *M. cordata*.

Macleaya microcarpa is a native of China and was introduced into cultivation in 1896. This species is often confused in gardens with its cousin, but the differences in flower and fruit details should serve to distinguish them fairly readily. The finest form in cultivation is the widely available 'Kelways Coral Plume', an especially handsome plant with deep pink flushed flower panicles. 'Coral Plume' has paler flowers.

Bloodroot
Sanguinaria

This North American genus contains a single species that is one of the least poppy-like members of the Papaveraceae. At the same time it is quite one of the loveliest and most sought-after species in the entire family.

The genus gets its name from *sanguis* – blood, a reference to the copious orange–red juice that exudes from most parts of the plant when it is cut; hence the common name of Bloodroot or Red Puccoon.

Sanguinaria canadensis L   [Pl. 12]
(Syn. *S. grandiflora* Rosc.; *S. stenopetala* Steud.; *S. vernalis* Salisb.; *S. virginiana* Gaertn.)
BLOODROOT

Bloodroot is a herbaceous perennial that dies away completely in the autumn. In the spring (generally in April) the new growth appears: folded leaves with solitary flowers appearing from within the leaf fold. As the flowers fade the leaves expand gradually to their full extent.

Sanguinaria canadensis

The rootstock consists of a branched, thick, fleshy rhizome, which lies horizontally quite close to the soil surface. The rhizomes give rise to a number of single-leaved buds. The leaves, when expanded, are more or less heart-shaped, with long stalks and a shallowly lobed and scalloped margin, to 20 cm (8 in) across, bluish-green above and smooth and paler beneath. The solitary white flower arises from within the fold of the leaf and quickly expands to 35–40 mm (1⅖–1⅗ in), the two sepals soon fall away; there are eight oblong petals (occasionally 12), the four outer narrower than the four inner; stamens numerous. The fruit consists of a narrow erect capsule borne on a stalk up to 15 cm (6 in) long.

S. canadensis is native to eastern North America from about North Dakota and Oklahoma eastwards in both Canada and the USA, where it occurs in woodland and on rocky slopes, generally at low altitudes.

Bloodroot is a generally easy garden plant thriving in a variety of soils but preferring a moist leafy soil, especially if it is on the slightly acid or neutral side. Sun or partial shade will suit it equally well providing the soil does not dry out severely during the summer. It is undoubtedly a delightful plant for the woodland garden where its charming anemone-like flowers can enliven a spring glade or peat bank. Even after flowering, the handsome leaves can be a useful feature with other woodlanders.

The wild form, with single flowers, is an elegant little plant and despite the fact that the flowers are over all too soon it is well worth growing. The double-flowered form 'Plena' is more often seen in gardens with its fully double flowers with numerous strikingly white petals, which expand to form a globe. Although the purist in me wants to dismiss double freaks from my own garden I have to admit to a genuine soft spot for this little marvel – the double flowers have poise and an elegance unparalleled in the poppy family and, furthermore, are considerably longer lasting than its single-flowered counterpart.

In recent times a pretty pale pink form (which perhaps should be given the cultivar name 'Rosea') has emerged, with both the young foliage and the flowers suffused with pink. Although slow-growing this exciting introduction is likely to prove very popular once it becomes more widely available. Pink-flowered cultivars with the names 'Amy' and 'Peter Harrison' are also known but how these all differ I am not sure.

Sanguinaria is generally a rather slow-growing plant in gardens and patience is required until a good-sized clump has built up. Plants creep slowly through the soil and on the whole resent disturbance. An annual top-dressing of bonemeal and leaf-mould is decidely beneficial, especially as rhizomes can sometimes become exposed at the soil surface. Seed is rarely available and division of the rhizome affords the best means of propagation. When to lift and divide the rhizomes is debatable and authorities are not generally agreed on the best time. Despite this I and several friends have had success both in the autumn, once the leaves have died down, and in the early spring (March) before growth commences. To avoid lifting a whole prized clump it is perhaps best to uncover one side and remove pieces of rhizome – as much as is required. The pieces used should be healthy and undamaged, each with a bud or two. These pieces of rhizome should be carefully cleaned of old compost and dead leaf-remains and replanted as quickly as possible in a similar site or in a nursery bed, just covered with a sifted mixture of peat or leaf-mould and sharp grit. The success rate can be very good.

Old established clumps will eventually start to 'go back' and generally lose vigour due to both soil impoverishment and congestion of the rhizomes. Lifting then becomes essential. A fork placed well under the clump and gently lifted will bring up the mass of rhizomes without causing too much damage. This can then be teased apart and the healthy pieces replanted once the site has been enlivened with new compost. Newly planted pieces will often flower but take time to build up again into a good clump.

Bloodroot is most effective as a multi-flowered clump. This is how it is seen in its native North American woodlands where the plant can sometimes blanket the ground in pristine profusion.

In cultivation it is more fickle, delighting in some gardens, but moody and unpredictable in others and sometimes declining without apparent course. It is, however, worth every bit of attention to force it to thrive.

The Celandine Poppies
Stylophorum

The genus *Stylophorum*, as currently understood, contains three species, two native to China and one to North America. They are juicy woodlanders with rather bristly stems, with lobed or divided leaves and yellow, four-petalled poppy flowers. They are elegant woodlanders for cool, moist shaded places in the garden, excelling, as would be expected, in the woodland glade, amongst shrubs or in the peat border. The oblong fruit capsules are bristly or hairy and release their seeds by splitting lengthwise into a number of valves. As the generic name implies, the ovary is endowed with a prominent, rather thick style.

The yellow woodland poppies are much confused in gardens and indeed the closely related Japanese Wood Poppy, *Hylomecon japonicum*, has been placed in the past in both *Stylophorum* and *Chelidonium*. *Stylophorum* differs from *Hylomecon* in having bracteoles and flowers several on a common stem, each long-stalked. In *Chelidonium* the stems are freely branched but without bracts or bracteoles and the flowers are small. In *Hylomecon* the flowers are solitary on unbranched stems and there are bracts present.

In the garden environment all the species in these genera require very similar conditions and are generally relatively easy to cultivate. Their merit is in the coolness of their attractive, yet subtle, foliage and their somewhat fleeting, yellow, flowers.

The species of *Stylophorum* can be propagated from seed or *S. diphyllum* by division of the parent plant. Seed can be sown in pots in the early spring under cover, pricking the seedlings out once they have developed their first or second true leaves. They are less temperamental with regard to transplanting in their seedling stage than some poppies, although somewhat brittle. However, they greatly dislike strong sunlight or becoming too dry. An airy, partly shaded frame is ideal for the young plants, which can be put out in the garden in early summer. *S. diphyllum* can be easily divided, either after flowering or in the early spring just before growth commences. Good sized pieces of root will soon re-establish themselves.

Stylophorum diphyllum (Michx.) Nutt.   [Pl. 13]
(Syn. *Chelidonium diphyllum* Michx.; *S. petiolatum* Nutt.)
CELANDINE POPPY

This is a tufted perennial, 30–40 cm (12–16 in) tall, with downy stems and leaves. The basal leaves form a lax-rosette from which arise a number of branched stems leafy in the upper part but bare below. The leaves are bluish-green, pinnately-lobed, with five to seven oblong, blunt-toothed lobes, each lobe looking rather like a thin oak-leaf. The stem leaves are similar but shorter stalked, the upper most much reduced and bract-like. The golden-yellow poppy flowers, 3–5 cm (1–2 in) across are borne on slender stalks

Stylophorum diphyllum

(pedicels) to 7 cm (3 in) long, several of these arising together on the stem; petals usually four, rounded, spreading widely to form a shallow bowl-shape. The fruit-capsules are erect at first but nodding when ripe, oblong to spindle-shaped and beset with spreading hairs, many-seeded.

S. diphyllum is to be found at low altitudes in shaded woodland in eastern North America, relishing in cool glades and deep leaf-litter, along with other woodland treasures such as trilliums and cypripediums and bloodroot (*Sanguinaria*). In gardens it has been cultivated since 1854 and is the most satisfactory of the three stylophorums, both in habit and colour. Plants flower between May and July, occasionally throwing a few blooms later in the year. In favoured gardens it will self-sow, in others it is shy and slow to increase. It is never as invasive as *S. lasiocarpum* or indeed its distant cousin *Chelidonium majus*.

Stylophorum japonicum. See *Hylomecon japonicum* (p. 43).

Stylophorum lasiocarpum (Olivier) Fedde   [Pl. 14]
(Syn. *Chelidonium lasiocarpum* Olivier)
CHINESE CELANDINE POPPY

This interesting Asian species is generally biennial in habit, although plants may sometimes linger into a third or fourth year. It looks rather like an enlarged Greater Celandine, *Chelidonium majus*, reaching to 45 cm (18 in) tall in flower. Plants are rather brittle and ooze a reddish sap when cut. The leaves are mostly crowded into a basal rosette from which arise one or several branched flowering stems with several leaves in the upper half. The leaves are very different from *S. diphyllum* with a larger sharply lobed and toothed terminal leaflet with several smaller leaflets (up to five pairs) below, decreasing in size down the stalk, green above, but with a whitish bloom beneath; upper leaves similar though short-stalked. The flowers are rather pale yellow, cupped, 3–4 cm (1⅕–1⅗ in) across, several arising together on long slender hairy stalks toward the top of the stems; petals usually four, ovate and somewhat overlapping. The narrow oblong-shaped fruit capsule is covered in soft hairs.

   S. lasiocarpum is a woodland species native to central and eastern China. In gardens it is an easy, accommodating plant, though not often seen. Like its cousins it is a plant for moist, shaded sites and in my garden, at least, seeds around profusely. The resultant seedlings transfer to other quarters without too much difficulty. This plant is rather brittle and the stems and leaves can be easily bruised if it is in too exposed a site. It flowers from May to July, occasionally later.

Stylophorum sutchuenense (Franch.) Fedde
(Syn. *Chelidonium sutchuenense* Franch.)

This is the least well known of the three species but nonetheless attractive. Plants have a similar habit to *S. lasiocarpum* but generally have a solitary stem that is leafy in the lower part, not bare. The most obvious difference is seen in the distinctive shaggy red hairs that cover the stems and leaves, especially beneath. The yellow flowers, 3–4 cm (1⅕–1⅗ in) across are borne on slender stalks, 4–5 cm (1⅗–2 in) long, and arise in a cluster from the uppermost leaves. The fruit-capsule is narrowly oval and hairy.

   S. sutchuenense, another woodland species, is native to western China.

II
Subfamily
Eschscholzioideae

The Tree Poppies
Dendromecon

Dendromecon is one of the few truly shrubby members of the poppy family, with woody stems and an evergreen habit; the Latin name literally means tree poppy, from *dendro* tree and *mekon* poppy. If it were only hardier it would certainly be a very popular shrub in our gardens with its mass of bright yellow poppy flowers produced during the summer. However, this fine shrub comes from the hot regions of California and although it will survive in a sunny warm position, in more northerly climes it will succumb all to readily to severe winter weather. But, this should not deter one from trying it in more favourable gardens.

Most authorities recognise two species in the genus *Dendromecon*, *D. harfordii* and the better known *D. rigida*. However, both species show considerable variability and at least one authority has proposed a more fragmentary revision consisting of some twenty species. The more orthodox interpretation is followed here.

Dendromecon is clearly closely allied to that better known Californian genus, *Romneya*, which can be easily distinguished by its subshrubby habit, far larger white flowers and lobed or toothed leaves; in *Dendromecon* the leaves are always entire.

Of the two species only *D. rigida* is available in the trade in Britain and seed is sometimes offered in catalogues. It is a plant for a 'hot spot' against a sheltered sunny wall. A deep well-drained loamy soil, with added mortar rubble or a similar aggregate to lighten it further, is essential and during cold winter weather some form of protection may help ensure survival – straw or hessian wrapped around the plant should afford the best protection. In most regions though, a sunny conservatory will certainly afford a more sure means of success. Propagation from cuttings is possible during the summer; cuttings should be of firm, well-ripened, young shoots and consist of two- or three-node pieces and placed in a sandy compost in moderate heat, although one should not expect a high success rate.

Dendromecon harfordii Kell. [Pl. 15–16]

An evergreen shrub to 3 m (10 ft) tall with erect or somewhat arched stems, rather crowded with leaves. The leaves, 3–10 cm (2–4 in) long are elliptical to oval with a blunt, rounded apex. The yellow poppy flowers, 5–7 cm (2–3 in) across, are borne singly on short lateral stalks towards the short tips.

D. *harfordii* is restricted to the islands of Santa Cruz and Santa Rosa off the coast of California and was first described in 1873. It was introduced into cultivation in the USA as late as 1933, where it is still grown to this day. In Britain it is not in general cultivation, however, it is represented here by var. *rhamnoides* (Greene) Munz (syn. D. *rhamnoides* Greene; D. *arborea* Greene). In this interesting variety the leaves are longer, to 12.5 cm (5 in) and a paler grey-green with a sharply tapered apex. The leaves are generally less crowded than the type form.

Although this variety seems to be somewhat hardier in temperate gardens, it is unfortunately rarely seen outside America. It arrived in cultivation in Britain in 1963, introduced by a former Director of the Royal Horticultural Society's Garden at Wisley, Frank P. Knight. It is a great pity that this plant is not more often seen in our gardens as it is certainly a finer species than D. *rigida*. In California, at least, it has deservedly found favour in parks and gardens, but then it is quite at home in those sun-drenched environs. I am told by friends in California that it is easy to propagate from seed or cuttings and is a finer garden plant than D. *rigida*, so perhaps more attention should be paid to it in European gardens. It would thrive especially well in those favoured gardens of the Mediterranean region.

Var. *rhamnoides* does not overlap in distribution with the typical plant, var. *harfordii*, being found farther south on the islands of Santa Catalina and Santa Clemente.

Dendromecon rigida Benth. [Pl. 17]

THE TREE POPPY

An evergreen shrub to 3 m (10 ft) tall, sometimes more, with slender, woody, branched stems; young stems smooth, grey-green and only slowly becoming woody. Leaves rather leathery, grey-green, narrowly lanceolate to almost elliptical, 2.5–7.5 cm (1–3 in) long, pointed and entire, short-stalked or unstalked. Flowers borne singly and laterally towards the shoot tips on slender stalks, bright yellow, 5–7.5 cm (2–3 in) across, fragrant; petals four, somewhat overlapping, forming a cup shape, the margin somewhat toothed.

D. *rigida* is a Californian native and was first discovered there in the wild by that great North American plant explorer David Douglas. However,

Dendromecon rigidum

it was left to William Lobb to introduce it into cultivation in 1854. It is found on the mainland (unlike *D. harfordii*) from Shasta County southwards to northern Baja California.

This fine shrub comes and goes from cultivation in Britain at the whim of the climate. Being tender, it is unlikely to survive for long outdoors unprotected. However, during a succession of mild winters it will thrive well enough and specimens more than 4.5 m (15 ft) tall have been recorded against a hot house wall in the south of England. Its apparent frailty in our gardens should not deter it from being tried, for young plants are vigorous and soon come into flower. The wise gardener will assure its survival by taking cuttings each season for overwintering in a frost-free environment. A shrub in full bloom is a very fine sight.

The Californian Poppies
Eschscholzia

The Californian Poppy, *Eschscholzia californica*, is well known and has been cultivated in European gardens since 1790. The wild forms have flowers in shades of white, cream, yellow and orange, but in cultivation pink, red, crimson, bronze, apricot, salmon and bicoloured forms exist, as well as those with frilled semi-double flowers. *E. californica* is an easy and adaptable garden flower and has always been a popular summer annual because of its showy blooms produced over a long flowering season. This particular species is the state flower of California, where it can sometimes be found in dazzling numbers in the spring and early summer.

The genus *Eschscholzia* contains about ten species in all which are restricted to western North America, centred on California. They are primarily plants of dry sandy and stony regions, grassy places, deserts and semi-deserts. The species can be readily recognised by their silky-petalled flowers, finely cut, rather ferny looking foliage and long slender fruit-capsules. However, the most obvious character, and one that clearly separates this from other genera, is the one piece calyx that abscisses at the base and pops off the top of the expanding petals like a tiny pointed cap. This endearing habit was a great source of fascination and amusement to me as a child and to watch the petals unfurl is rather like watching the miracle of the expanding butterfly that has recently emerged from the chrysalis.

The species can be annual or short-lived perennial herbs and when cut ooze a colourless juice. The alternate leaves are generally hairless and ternately divided into numerous fine dissections. The solitary flowers arise on slender leafy or scapose stems and are erect in bud; sepals two but wholly united to form a smooth cap which detaches itself in one piece as the flowers open; petals four, occasionally six or eight, folded round each other in bud, often yellow, sometimes white, cream or orange; stamens numerous; ovary cylindrical, dilated at the base to form a funnel-shaped torus, above with a four to six lobed stigma, the lobes linear and diverging. The fruit-capsule is linear-cylindrical, ribbed, two-valved, explosive when ripe to expel the seeds, with the two valves usually curling spirally.

The genus is named in honour of Dr J.F. Eschscholz (1793–1831) who was surgeon and naturalist on the Russian expeditions to the Pacific Coast of North America in 1816 and 1824.

In cultivation Californian poppies present few difficulties. They thrive in a wide variety of soils providing they are not waterlogged, though preferring light well-drained ones and full sun. Seed is best sown where the plants are required to flower, taking care not to sow too thickly. This can be undertaken in the autumn (at least with *E. californica*) for a late spring and early summer flowering the following year or, more usually, in the spring (March–April) for flowers that will bloom through the summer and early autumn. They are particularly attractive associated with other annuals such as *Clarkia* and *Godetia* or for a more subtle effect with annual grasses such as *Briza maxima* or *Lagurus ovatus*. For an interesting, if rather gaudy, display try sowing some of the self-colours with *Papaver commutatum* 'Ladybird', *P. pavonina* or with one of the annual lupins such as *Lupinus varius*. They can look splendid scattered along a wide gravel path or driveway where they will often self-sow. Dead-heading, the removal of young fruits, will certainly help to prolong the flowering season.

E. californica makes a useful, though not particularly long-lived, cut flower. The buds should be picked just before they burst open and the stems generally hold up well in water.

The named cultivars of *E. californica* would make a very bold bedding display to rival marigolds, salvias and busy-lizzies, but for some reason they have seldom been used in such a way, probably because, unlike the others, they are not so easily raised in trays or pots for bedding out and generally resent too much disturbance.

The perennial sorts will often over-winter, especially if the weather is mild, to flower early in the following season. If they don't then they are easy to raise from seed once again or, indeed, they may self-sow themselves.

It is a great pity that *E. californica*, magnificent though it undoubtedly is, should so dominate this genus in cultivation. Several of the other species deserve our attention. Perhaps they will acquire favour when easy annuals (for direct sowing) once more come into favour.

Key to Species

1. Flower buds with a rim-like disk immediately beneath: **E. californica**
   Flower buds without a rim-like disk immediately beneath 2

2. Plants scapose with all the leaves at the base of the plant 3
   Plants not scapose, with leafy stems 6

3. Cotyledons bifid; petals yellow but often with an orange
   base: **E. mexicana**
   Cotyledons entire; petals yellow or orange 4

4. Leaves with few long sub-parallel divisions; flowers pale
   yellow: **E. lobbii**
   Leaves with many short, non-sub-parallel, divisions; flowers bright
   yellow or orange 5

5. Sepal-cap with a long drawn out point; seeds bur-like: **E. caespitosa**
   Sepal-cap acute, but not drawn out into a point; seeds
   pitted: **E. glyptosperma**

6. Leaves and sepals hoary with curly white hairs: **E. lemmonii**
   Leaves not as above, usually glabrous 7

7. Flowers small, the petals only 3–8 mm (⅛–⅓ in) long 8
   Flowers larger, the petals 10–30 mm (⅖–1⅕ in) long 9

8. Petals 3–6 mm (⅛–¼ in) long: *E. minutiflora*
   Petals 7–8 mm (⅓ in) long: *E. covillei*

9. Sepals 4–10 mm (⅙–⅖ in) long; petals 5–15 mm (⅕–⅖ in) long,
   yellow, often with an orange base: *E. ramosa*
   Sepals 10–18 mm (⅖–⅔ in) long; petals 10–30 mm (⅖–1⅕ in) long;
   yellow or orange 10

10. Leaves mostly 3-ternate, with blunt segments; flowers yellow or
    orange: *E. caespitosa*
    Leaves mostly 4-ternate, with pointed segments; flowers
    yellow: *E. parishii*

Eschscholzia caespitosa Benth.   [Pl. 23]
TUFTED CALIFORNIAN POPPY

A small annual to 14–20 cm (5½–8 in) tall with the leaves crowded into a
basal tuft, though sometimes present on short stems, with the erect flower-
scapes greatly exceeding the leaves. The leaves are grey-green and finely
divided into numerous linear blunt lobes, not more than 8–9 mm (⅓ in) long
usually, glabrous or slightly bristly; the leaves vary considerably in length.
The flowers, 30–45 mm (1⅕–1⅘ in) across, open widely and are a pleasant
bright yellow; sepal-cap 10–18 mm (⅖–⅔ in) long, long-pointed; petals
rounded, somewhat overlapping. The fruit-capsule is 5–8 cm (2–3 in) long.
  E. caespitosa inhabits dry grassy and bushy flats and slopes to about 1,000 m
(3,300 ft) altitude, growing in sandy places as well as grassland or chaparral.
It is common in California from the South Coast Ranges to Los Angeles
County where it is generally to be found in flower during April and May,
occasionally later.
  This pretty little annual poppy is occasionally available in the seed trade
but is certainly listed by some society seed lists. It is a very pleasing plant
for the front of a border in patches or, if you prefer, for edging. The form
generally available has been named 'Sundew' and has scented lemon-yellow
flowers more subtle than most of the other eschscholzias and it will repay by
flowering in abundance right through the summer.
  Various wild varieties of *E. caespitosa* are recognised. Of these perhaps the
most distinct is subsp. *kernensis* Munz, which has leafier stems and larger deep
orange flowers and capsules 2.5–4 mm (¹⁄₁₀–⅙ in) thick. It is native to Kern
County and the Tejon Pass region of California, growing on heavy clay soils.

Eschscholzia californica Cham.   [Pl. 18–21]
CALIFORNIAN POPPY

This familiar garden poppy is a very variable plant in the wild. It can be an
annual or perennial up to 60 cm (24 in) tall, usually glabrous and branched
from close to the base. The grey- or blue-green leaves are divided into
numerous linear to narrow-oblong, blunt lobes, the basal leaves up to 20 cm
(8 in) long, sometimes longer, the stem leaves similar though smaller and

short-stalked. The solitary terminal flowers form a wide funnel-shape, 4.5–7 cm (2–3 in) across when fully expanded, the torus unlike that of all other species with two rims, an outer spreading disk-like rim and an inner erect transparent one; sepal-cap pointed, 1–4 cm (⅖–⅘ in) long; petals fan-shaped, satiny, cream to yellow or orange, rarely white in the wild. The fruit-capsule is 3–8 cm (1–3 in) long.

This species is widespread in California and southern Oregon in both the valleys and foothills up to 2,000 m (6,600 ft) altitude, growing in grassy or sandy places (it is common in the western Mojave Desert), rocky areas, along roadsides and embankments or invading areas that have been burnt. It flowers in the wild from February to September depending on the area and altitude.

E. Californica is very variable in the wild. In California some 50 subspecies have been described in the past, though most of these cannot stand up to close scrutiny and further research is required. Plants are often perennial but in the south of California and in Baja California an annual form (often called subsp. *peninsularis* (Greene) Munz) predominates. Perennial forms found growing on sand-dunes in California, with rough puberulent leaves and prostrate stems, have been called var. *maritima* (Greene) Jepson (syn. *E. maritima* Greene). Another type widespread inland from the Columbia River to southern California has very glaucous foliage and large deep orange flowers in the spring, followed by smaller pale yellow flowers later in the year. This plant is variously called var. *crocea* (Benth.) Jepson or var. *douglasii* (Benth.) Gray (syn. *E. douglasii* Benth.).

The species *sensu lato* is readily identified by the disk-like outer rim of the torus, which no other species possesses. In bud this appears as a disk outside and at the base of the calyx and persists into the fruiting stage. Like most Californian poppies the flowers open in bright weather but wrap up when it is dull or wet, the petals protecting the stamens within.

E. californica has been long in cultivation and many forms have been bred and selected. From the original yellow, cream and orange introductions have come plants with white, pink, orange, deep red, scarlet, apricot, salmon, bronze, bicolours such as pink or bronze on the outside and cream on the inside, as well as others with semi-double or frilled petals. In many ways the simple elegance and self colours of the wild type are hard to beat and some of the modern strains are almost offensive to the eye.

Seeds merchants offer a small selection of named cultivars or more often a mixture of colours such as Harlequin Hybrids and Ballerina, Double Ballerina Mixed, Monach Mixed or Thai Silk Series. The last comes in various shades of deep pink but the others are mixtures of most of the colours already listed.

The following list includes most of the cultivars that have been available in the past 30 years:

'Alba' – single, creamy-white
'Alba Flore Pleno' – semi-double, creamy-white
'Aurantiaca' – single, orange

'Caniculata' – single with fluted petals, various colours
'Carmine King' – single, carmine red
'Cherry Ripe' – cerise-pink
'Chrome Queen' – single, apricot
'Crimson Carmine' – single, carmine-red
'Crocea' – single, orange with a paler reverse
'Dalli' – semi-double, scarlet with a gold centre
'Dazzler' – crimson-scarlet
'Douglasii' – single, pure yellow
'Eastern Queen' – salmon-apricot, rose-red on the reverse
'Enchantress' – semi-double, rose-pink
'Fireflame' – single, orange-scarlet
'Flambeau' – semi-double, orange-scarlet
'Geisha' – single, orange with a red reverse
'Mandarin' – orange with a reddish reverse
'Mauve Beauty' – rosy-purple
'Mikado' – scarlet
'Milky White' – single, cream [**Pl. 22**]
'Orange King' – orange
'Orange Queen' – orange with a paler reverse
'Purple Robe' – single, rosy-purple with a white centre [**Pl. 22**]
'Purple-Violet' – rosy-violet
'Rajah' – purple-carmine
'Ramona White' – cream with a pink reverse
'Rosea' – cream flushed pink, with a pale rose reverse
'Sulphur Yellow' – pale lemon-yellow
'Sunlight' – pale lemon yellow
'Toreador' – semi-double, orange with a red reverse

Eschscholzia covillei Greene
(Syn. *E. minutiflora* var. *darwinensis* Jones)

Very similar to *E. minutiflora*, but with somewhat larger flowers, the petals 7–8 mm (⅓ in) long (not 3–6 mm (⅛–¼ in)). This plant is restricted to the northern Mojave Desert area of California. It is not, to my knowledge, in cultivation.

Eschscholzia glyptosperma Greene   [**Pl. 24**]
DESERT POPPY

A small tufted glaucous annual with scapose flowers and leaves crowded into a dense basal tuft. The leaves are much dissected into numerous linear segments; all the leaves are about the same size. The flowers are sharply pointed in bud, not drawn out into a point (apiculum) as in *E. caespitosa* and are bright yellow 2–4 cm (⅘–1⅗ in) across usually and borne well above the foliage. The seeds are deeply pitted, unlike those of *E. caespitosa*, which are covered in a rough, meshed network.

E. glyptosperma inhabits the arid regions of the Mojave Desert extending from California into Utah and Arizona. It grows in sandy and stony places, Creosote Bush scrub and other bushy places, to about 1,600 m (5,200 ft) altitude.

This interesting desert species is not in cultivation but it would be a pretty acquisition with the general size and constitution of *E. caespitosa* and *E. lobbii*.

Eschscholzia lemmonii Greene   [Pl. 25]

A distinctive plant to 30 cm (12 in) tall, with branched, somewhat leafy, stems and finely dissected leaves covered with curly white hairs giving the plant a hoary appearance. The flowers are orange, 3–4 cm (1⅕–1⅗ in) across, the sepal-cap hoary like the foliage. The fruit-capsule is 3–6 cm (1–2½ in) long.

This unusual Californian poppy is not cultivated in gardens, though its unusual hoary foliage and orange flowers would certainly be an asset. *E. lemmonii* is restricted in California to the San Carlos Range and the environs of San Luis Obispo County.

Eschscholzia lemmonii

Eschscholzia lobbii Greene [Pl. 26]
FRYING PANS

This is a small scapose annual with basal tufts of leaves. The leaves are rather distinctive, grey-green, but with comparatively few linear-lanceolate to linear, well-shaped segments. The flowers are pale yellow, like buttercups, 1.5–2.5 cm (⅗–1 in) across, borne well above the foliage or slender glabrous stalks; sepal cap abruptly narrowing to a short pointed apex; petals oval to semi-orbicular. The distinctive seeds are bur-like, being adorned with short pointed appendages.

E. *lobbii* inhabits the gravelly and clay foothills as well as the open valleys of California's North Coast Ranges and the Sacramento Valley, flowering during March and April, but not growing above about 650 m (2,100 ft) altitude.

This is a very pleasant annual in the garden to be treated in much the same way as E. *caespitosa*. The two species are much confused but the few long leaf-divisions of E. *lobbii* together with its bur-like, rather than almost smooth, seeds are sufficient to separate them. E. *lobbii* in fact replaces E. *caespitosa* in the northern part of California.

Eschscholzia mexicana Greene
MEXICAN GOLD

A scapose annual species, with leaves crowded in basal tufts. The leaves are dissected into numerous, narrow, blunt divisions. The flowers, 15–35 mm (⅗–1⅖ in) across are deep yellow, often with an orange base to the petals; in bud the sepals are smooth and abruptly contracted into a short, acute, apical point.

E. *mexicana* inhabits sandy and gravelly places in Baja California and the Sonora region of Mexico, to Colorado, southern Utah and western Texas, where it flowers early in the year, from February to May.

This species is much confused with E. *caespitosa* and its presence in cultivation is doubtful. In the seedling stage the two species can be readily distinguished; the cotyledons of E. *mexicana* are deeply cleft, those of E. *caespitosa*, and indeed E. *glyptosperma*, are entire. Incidentally the cotyledons of the well-known E. *californica* are also deeply cleft.

Eschscholzia minutiflora S. Wats.
SMALL-FLOWERED CALIFORNIAN POPPY

A greenish or somewhat greyish annual with leafy, ascending stems. The leaves are finely dissected and thickish, with linear to narrow-oblong lobes. The distinctive small flowers, only 6–10 mm (¼–⅖ in) across are borne on short stalks; buds only 4–6 mm (⅙–¼ in) long, with a short abrupt point. The capsule is 3–5 cm (1⅕–2 in) long.

A rather weedy species of little garden merit, common in sandy and gravelly places from southern California and Baja California through the Mojave and Colorado Deserts to Utah, Arizona and the north-western Sonoran Desert, generally at low altitudes but reach to 1,250 m (4,100 ft).

The closely related *E. covillei* Greene apparently differs only in its somewhat larger petals, 7–8 mm (⅓ in) long, rather than 3–6 mm (⅜–¼ in). It also has a different chromosome count, n = 12 as opposed to n = 18. This little-known species inhabits the northern regions of the Mojave Desert.

Eschscholzia parishii Greene   [Pl. 27]

A glabrous annual species to 35 cm (14 in) tall, branched from close to the base. Most of the leaves are crowded at the base of the plant, being finely dissected into numerous linear, acutely-pointed lobes; stem leaves few, scattered and reduced. The flowers are yellow, 2.5–4.5 cm (1–1⅘ in) across and are conspicuous in bud with their long-pointed sepal-cap, 13–16 mm (½–⅔ in) long overall. The fruit-capsule is 5–7 cm (2–3 in) long.

This interesting plant is at once separated from the other species by its sharply pointed, rather than blunt, leaf-segments and the long slender tip to the flowerbuds. It hails from northern Baja California, to California's Mojave Desert and the Colorado Desert, being a plant of dry rocky and stony places, particularly Creosote Bush scrub below 1,250 m (4,100 ft) altitude.

Not in cultivation.

Eschscholzia ramosa Greene
(syn. *E. elegans* Greene; *E. wrigleyana* Millsp. & Nutt.)

A leafy annual species rather like a large version of *E. minutiflora*, to 40 cm (16 in) tall, with branched stems. The strongly glaucous, glabrous leaves are finely dissected into numerous linear segments; stem leaves similar to the basal but short-stalked. The yellow flowers, 15–25 mm (⅗–1 in) across, often have an orange base to the petals; sepal-cap 4–10 mm (⅙–⅖ in), abruptly contracted to a short apical point. The fruit-capsules are 4–7 cm (1⅗–3 in) long.

An attractive species that really should be in cultivation. The flowers are not large but are produced in abundance and contrast delightfully with the distinctly blue-grey foliage. *E. ramosa* is native to the islands off the Californian Pacific Coast – to Ensenada, Isla Guadalupe and the Channel Islands. It is a plant of rocky and sparsely grassy habitats, flowering from March to May.

The Tulip Poppy
Hunnemannia

This little-known genus with its extraordinary name contains a single species, *H. fumariifolia*. The genus is in fact named in honour of the English botanist and plant explorer John Hunneman, who died in 1839.

Hunnemannia look very like a Californian poppy, *Eschscholzia*, differing primarily in possessing separate sepals and a broadly lobed stigma.

Hunnemannia fumariifolia Sweet

TULIP POPPY

The plant is essentially a perennial with slender, erect stems to 60 cm (24 in) sometimes taller, which become gradually woody below. The finely divided, ferny leaves, 5–10 cm (2–4 in) long, are thrice ternate with numerous linear,

Hunnemannia fumariifolia

grey-green segments; the leaves are stalked, the stalk (petiole) clearly keeled beneath. The solitary flowers are bright golden-yellow, 5–7 cm (2–3 in) across, broad cups with four rounded, overlapping petals; the two sepals, which are closely united in bud, soon fall away the moment the flowers begin to open; stamens numerous, rather short and spreading away from the ovary; anthers orange. The linear, siliqua-like fruit-pod is many seeded and closely resembles that of *Escscholzia*, splitting from the apex to the base.

H. fumariifolia is native to the highlands of Mexico where it inhabits rocky and stony habitats, and roadsides mainly at 1,500–2,000 m (4,900–6,600 ft) altitude. It is sometimes called the Mexican Tulip Poppy.

The Tulip Poppy is a choice perennial commonly grown in gardens as a half-hardy annual. Plants flower readily from seed in their first year. They are best sown where they are to flower; thin sowing is essential to get the best from this plant and to avoid excessive thinning at the seedling stage. Plants thrive best in a well-drained, rather light, soil in a sunny position, flowering from July to October from an April sowing. For earlier flowering an autumn sowing is possible in mild districts, although seedlings should be protected from severe weather. Alternatively, seed can be sown under cover during the late winter. Any average seed compost will suffice and to avoid pricking out, (not always easy with this species) try sowing two to three seeds in individual pots. A temperature of 10–15°C (50–60°F) is ideal. Plants should be well hardened off before planting out in the late spring. During exceptionally mild winters mature plants may survive in the open, but they cannot be relied upon to do so. In any event plants are so readily raised from seed that this is not so important.

In California, where *H. fumariifolia* is commonly cultivated, the species has become locally naturalised.

In cultivation, especially large-flowered forms have been selected and these make particularly good 'annual fillers' for the flower border; many annual 'poppies' can be used in this way and it is rather surprising that this is not attempted more often. Colourful annuals of many sorts are invaluable fillers in new herbaceous borders or for a quick display of summer colour in recently constructed gardens. The annual border, a common feature of gardens earlier in the century, is now alas a rare sight – they have much to recommend them and can provide a very interesting feature in the garden.

H. fumariifolia makes a useful cut flower, picked the moment the blooms open. The blooms are rather longer lasting in water than those of most other poppies. Grown in a well-lit position it also makes an attractive pot plant indoors, especially for sunny conservatories.

III
Subfamily
Papaveroideae

The Desert Poppies
Arctomecon

A small genus of three species restricted to the south-west USA where they inhabit very dry sandy and stony habitats. The species have extremely hairy leaves and stalks and this hairiness has given the genus its name (from the Greek *arcto*, bear and *mecon*, poppy). Although the plants are small the flowers are relatively large, with two to three sepals, four or six petals and numerous stamens. The fruit is a three- to six-valved capsule. The hairiness of the plants alone is enough to distinguish this genus from the other Papaveraceae in the region. However, their perennial habit and persistent corollas are also noteworthy features. Only one species is worthy of consideration here in any detail.

Arctomecon merriamii Cov.
DESERT POPPY, BEAR POPPY

A perennial herb to 30 cm (1 in) tall, occasionally taller, with a stout taproot; stem often somewhat branched close to the base. The leaves are mostly basal, grey- or blue-green, 2.5–7.5 cm (1–3 in) long, wedge-shaped and with a coarsely toothed apex, and covered in long brownish hairs, giving the leaf-tufts a distinctly silky appearance. The solitary white flowers, 4.5–7 cm (2–3 in) across, are nodding in bud and borne on long, slender, hairy scape-like stalks (peduncles); sepals three, shaggily-hairy; petals six, obcordate and somewhat overlapping one another, drying and persisting around the developing capsule; stamens numerous. The fruit-capsule is three- to six-valved, 2.5–3.5 cm (1–2 in) long, and contains shiny black seeds.

   A. merriamii is native to southern California and neighbouring Nevada, where it inhabits rocky and sandy places, often in Creosote Bush Scrub, generally between 850–1,400 m (2,800–4,600 ft) altitude and flowering during April and May.

This highly attractive species is said to be rare in the wild and it clearly inhabits extremely harsh conditions – it grows, for instance, in the Death Valley region. I can find no record of it having been in cultivation, but its hairiness and perennial nature would almost certainly make it a difficult plant to overwinter in the open garden, except for those who garden in hot, dry conditions. However, its tufted nature and attractive flowers would make it a fine subject for the alpine house where conditions might perhaps be controlled to its liking. Such plants make an interesting challenge for dedicated enthusiasts of 'rare and tricky' plants in cultivation.

The other two species are equally handsome, but little known: *A. californica* can be distinguished by its yellow flowers borne several to each stem, each with three sepals and six petals (West Nevada to the Mojave Desert and north-west Arizona, where it was first discovered in 1941). *A. humilis* is similar, but the flowers have only two sepals and four petals (north-west Arizona and the adjacent parts of Utah).

Arctomecon californica

The Prickly Poppies
Argemone

No other genus in the poppy family has created, over the years, quite so much confusion amongst botanists and gardeners. A plethora of names exists and many species and subordinate taxa have been described to confuse and to tantalise.

As it is known today *Argemone* can be said to contain some 28 species, which are restricted to North and South America and the Hawaiian Islands, the greatest number being concentrated in the south-western USA and Central America.

The majority of species are annual or perennial herbs, although one is a shrub. They are readily distinguished from other poppies by their stiff stems, prickly leaves and prickly fruit-capsules, although these features are very variable between the different species of *Argemone*. When cut, the stems generally ooze a white, yellow or orange sap. The leaves are alternate along the stems and usually noticeably pinnately-lobed, besides the prickly margins the leaves may also bear further prickles along the veins on one or both surfaces. The flowers are erect in bud and are large, 3–15 cm (1–6 in) across, and showy, generally solitary; sepals usually three, occasionally two or four to six, smooth bristly or prickly, each sepal terminating in a spine-tipped horn; petals four or six, white, cream, yellow or occasionally lavender or purple; stamens generally numerous but sometimes as few as 20, with linear anthers. The fruit-capsule is erect and is composed of three to seven fused carpels, rounded to oblong or egg-shaped, sparsely to densely spiny, sometimes smooth, parting at the top into a number of short valves when ripe; valve number equal to the number of carpels, hence three to seven; style short or absent.

As in *Papaver* the capsule details are of critical importance in separating the species. Other useful characters are the presence or absence of prickles on the stems and the surface of the leaves as well as the size and shape of the sepal-horns.

Argemone is a very homogenous group and there is a pronounced morphological similarity between the species. This means that it is not possible to divide the genus into different sections or other types of division. This is in contrast to genera such as *Papaver* and *Meconopsis*, which show a great range of morphological characters. This would indicate to the botanist that *Argemone* is of rather recent origin, evolutionarily speaking.

Their large showy flowers and the ease of cultivation of most of the species would, one might suppose, mean that they are widely grown in gardens. However, this is not so and at the present time only a few species are available, although others can be found within the confines of botanic gardens and private collections. Many of the species are handsome and bold plants. There is something incongruous about plants that are so robustly defensive in their stiff stems and prickly nature should produce such large and seemingly delicate flowers with their thin-textured and satiny petals. Yet it is this combination that is so attractive, just as in many cacti and other defensive plants able to produce from amongst their spiny masses wonderful blooms of delicate and transient beauty.

The Mexican Poppy *Argemone mexicana* is by far the best-known species and it has been cultivated for many centuries, primarily as a medicinal plant. The name *Argemone* comes from the Greek for cataract of the eye, *argema*, for it was supposed that the juice of the plant was capable of curing such afflictions. *A. mexicana* was well known to Gerard as *Papaver spinosum* or the prickly poppy. Of it Miller states: 'Argemone – because it purges away the mistiness of the eyes. It is called the Infernal Fig, because the Capsule pretty much resembles a fig; and Infernal, from its Asperity.'

Miller clearly did not think much of *A. mexicana* as a garden plant for he says: 'This is an annual plant, which is very common in most parts of the West Indies, and is by the Spaniards call'd Fico de Inferno, or the Devil's Fig; there is no great beauty or use of this plant amongst us, that I know of . . . I have been informed that Gum bouge [Gamboge] is made from the Juice of this Plant.'

As good garden plants I can hardly do better than quote Graham Rice (*Garden Flowers from Seed* by Christopher Lloyd and Graham Rice): 'The prickly poppies fall among the unsung heros of the huge poppy family. Hardly anyone grows them, but their long succession of flowers makes them one of the most desirable of plants for well-drained, sunny but not inhospitable borders.'

Plants are best treated as half-hardy annuals, although the perennial types will over winter if the weather has been kind. Seed can be sown in April in pots rather than seed trays as the seedlings get away better if they are not disturbed unduly; cellular trays will of course do just as well. Sow two to three seeds to a pot and thin these to the strongest in due course. Alternatively seed can be sown where the plants are to flower, especially in mild districts where late frosts are uncommon.

The prickly poppies thrive best in a light, well-drained soil in a sunny sheltered position and are especially showy during hot dry periods in the summer. Seed is set in quantity, but beware, the fruit-capsules are extremely prickly and vicious when ripe so wear a pair of gloves when collecting seed. *A. mexicana* will often seed around in gardens but the more handsome white-flowered *A. platyceras* and *A. albiflora* seldom do so in my experience. Scan the seed lists for these last two species and for *A. grandiflora*, *A. squarrosa* and *A. sanguinea*, for they are all worth seeking out and to add to the hosts of delightful poppies grown in our gardens.

The most comprehensive revision of the genus was undertaken by Gerald Ownbey at the Department of Botany, University of Minnesota, Minneapolis and published in two parts. Firstly, a 'Monograph of the Genus Argemone for North America' (*Memoirs of the Torrey Botanical Club* 21(1), 1958) and secondly 'The Genus Argemone in South America and Hawaii' (*Brittonia* 13, 1961).

Although a number of species clearly have great horticultural appeal, others (perhaps a half of the total) are rather less desirable or distinctly 'weedy' – only the more appealing are included here.

A. mexicana was undoubtedly the first species to be cultivated in Europe. Its date of introduction is said to be 1592, however, its first reference in literature was that of Bauhin in *Phytopinax*, 1596, followed closely by Gerard in 1597. Gerard had received seed of it from St Johns Island in the West Indies.

The next species brought to Europe was *A. albiflora*, which Lamarck (1793) distinguished as a white-flowered variety of *A. mexicana*. It was certainly cultivated in Denmark by 1812 and in England by 1820, where it enjoyed great popularity for a number of years. Other species followed: *A. ochroleuca*, *A. grandiflora* and in 1877 Joseph Dalton Hooker introduced *A. polyanthemos* from Colorado (under the name *A. hispida* it was featured in *Curtis's Botanical Magazine* t. 6402, 1878).

Argemones appear to have been popular in Europe in the period 1827–40 but declined thereafter for some obscure reason or other. In their native countries, particularly in North America, they have never met with great enthusiasm in gardens.

In the Americas the various species of *Argemone* have been traditionally used for their medicinal properties. In Latin America, in particular, the juice extracted from stems and seeds have been employed for a wide variety of different ailments. In Puerto Rico, it is recorded, seed of *A. mexicana* are used as a purgative and the juice of the plants is said to be beneficial in treating various eye conditions. *Argemone* contains a cocktail of different alkaloids. Surprisingly these have never been thoroughly investigated which is very strange considering the modern trends towards 'natural medicines'.

Key to Species

1. Flowers yellow, occasionally golden or bronze 2
   Flowers white, pink or lavender. 6

2. Plant shrubby; leaves close, small and holly-like: **A. fruticosa**
   Plants annuals or herbaceous perennials; leaves not as above 3

3. Flowers relatively small, 3–6 cm (1⅕–2½ in) across; stamens not
   more than 75. 4
   Flowers larger, 7–10 cm (3–4 in) across; stamens at least 150 5

4. Flowers pale lemon-yellow, oblong in bud; fruit-capsule always
   prickly: **A. ochroleuca**
   Flowers bright yellow, rounded in bud; fruit-capsule smooth or
   prickly: **A. mexicana**

5. Petals yellow to gold or bronze; filaments red to purplish: **A. aenea**
   Petals always bright yellow; filaments lemon-yellow: **A. superba**

6. Petals pink or lavender 7
   Petals white. 9

7. Lower leaves lobed for less than two thirds the distance to the midrib; upper leaves clasping the stem: **A. polyanthemos**
Lower leaves lobed almost to the midrib; upper leaves not clasping the stem 8

8. Stamens about 80; stem and leaf surfaces prickly as well as finely hairy: **A. rosea**
Stamens 150 or more; stem and leaf surface sparsely prickly, not hairy: **A. sanguinea**

9. Leaves with shallow rounded lobes, not long-spine-pointed; flowers often separated from the nearest leaf by a short stalk: **A. munita**
Leaves shallowly to deeply lobed, the lobes angular, often acute and with a long spine-tip; flowers often immediately subtended by one or several leaves 10

10. Sepal-horns flattened or angular in cross-section 11
Sepal-horns rounded in cross-section 12

11. Leaf-surface prickly on the main veins, as well as minutely bristly between the veins; fruit-capsule spines compound (with smaller spines on the base of the main ones): **A. squarrosa**
Leaf-surface sparsely prickly along the main veins, otherwise smooth; fruit-capsule with simple spines: **A. platyceras**

12. Prickles of flower buds at right-angles to the surface; leaves lobed almost to the midrib: **A. sanguinea**
Prickles of flower buds ascending; leaves generally not lobed more than two thirds the way to the midrib 13

13. Sepal-horns 3–6 mm (⅛–¼ in) long **A. albiflora**
Sepal-horns 6–15 mm (¼–⅗ in) long 14

14. Flower buds smooth or with very few spines; upper leaves not clasping the stem; fruit-capsules sparsely spiny: **A. grandiflora**
Flower buds always prickly; upper leaves clasping the stem; fruit-capsules generally rather densely spiny 15

15. Flower buds 18–28 mm (¾–1⅛ in) long; flowers 10–12 cm (4–5 in) across; stamens about 100: **A. hunnemannii**
Flower buds 15–22 mm (⅗–⅞ in) long; flowers 7–10 cm (3–4 in) across; stamens 150 or more: **A. polyanthemos**

Argemone aenea G.B. Ownb.

An annual or short-lived perennial with bright yellow latex when cut, the stems solitary or few, 30–80 cm (1–32 in) tall, prickly. The grey-green leaves have bluish veins and are pinnately-lobed, the upper less markedly so than the lower; lobes with prickle-tipped teeth, generally prickly on the main veins beneath, less so or smooth above. The buds are moderately prickly, oblong in outline; sepal-horns, 7–12 mm (¼–½ in) long, round in cross-section, smooth or with a few prickles at the base. The flowers are deep yellow or gold, sometimes almost bronze, 7–10 cm (3–4 in) across, each usually subtended by two small leaf-like bracts; petals rounded; stamens about 150, with purplish or red filaments and yellow flushed purple anthers; stigma purple. The elliptical to oblong fruit-capsule is armed with stout spines.

A. aenea has a scattered distribution in southern and western Texas and the neighbouring part of northern Mexico. In these regions it inhabits dry, often sandy habitats, on plains and hills, but also in fields and along roadsides from sea level to about 1,450 m (4,800 ft) altitude, flowering from February to May.

This interesting and attractive species is not in cultivation. It finds its closest ally in *A. superba*, which differs primarily in its smaller, rounder flowerbuds and pale yellow filaments. In addition the petals are pure yellow, never golden or bronzed.

Argemone albiflora Hornem.
(syn. *A. alba* of cultivation)

An attractive annual or biennial to 1 m (3 ft) tall, though often less; stems much-branched and usually moderately prickly, oozing a yellow latex when cut. The leaves can be greyish-green or plain green and are pinnately-lobed, the lower cut almost to the midrib, the uppermost more shallowly-lobed and clasping the stem with broad bases; margins spine-toothed, with the undersurface of the leaf prickly on the main veins but the upper surface generally quite smooth. The elliptical or rounded flowerbuds are prickly; sepal-horns rather short, 3–6 mm (⅛–¼ in) long, rounded in cross-section, smooth. The flowers vary in size from 5–10 cm (2–4 in) and are pure white, generally with one or two leaf-like bracts close beneath; stamens 150 or more, with yellowish filaments and yellow anthers; stigma purple. The fruit-capsule is elliptical to oblong and stoutly spiny.

This species is found over a wide area in the USA from Mississippi to North Carolina, southwards to Florida and Texas, but it has become naturalised in surrounding areas, generally as an escape from cultivation. It inhabits a variety of soils from sand dunes and beaches to fields, field boundaries, wasteland and roadsides, generally at low altitudes and flowering from about late March to June, sometimes later.

A. albiflora has been cultivated in Europe for almost 200 years, being found in literature of the time as *A. alba*, an invalid name. This is undoubtedly a very fine and attractive species, certainly one of the best of the white-flowered 'group', and can generally be distinguished by the combination of smooth upper leaf-surface, clasping upper leaves and short-horned flowerbuds.

In cultivation, flowers with more than the usual complement of five petals quite frequently occur, these often numbering eight.

The Texan population, which can be distinguished by its fruit-capsules that bear a mixture of stout spines and smaller prickles, is distinguished as subsp. *texana* G.B. Ownb.

Unfortunately, many plants grown under this name (*A. albiflora*) generally prove to be *A. platyceras* – at least in Britain.

Argemone fruticosa Thurber ex Gray
(syn. *A. fruticosa* Mueller)
SHRUBBY PRICKLY POPPY

This species is not in cultivation, but it is so distinctive and unusual amongst the prickly poppies that some mention of it must be made.

The plant is a shrub to 2 m (7 ft) tall with rigid woody stems becoming bare of foliage below; young stems glaucous, somewhat prickly but densely covered in leaves. The holly-like leaves are leathery, markedly glaucous, oblong, not more than 3.5 cm (1⅖ in) long and armed along the margin with rigid spines. The flowers, 5–10 cm (2–4 in) across, are yellow, often rather pale and immediately subtended by several leaves. The fruit-capsule is broad egg-shaped and densely armed with stout spines.

A rare and little-known species restricted to the Coahuila region of Mexico where it inhabits rocky mountain slopes and canyons at 1,700–1,900 m (5,600–6,200 ft), flowering from May to August.

This is undoubtedly a very interesting species and it would be well worthwhile bringing it into cultivation. However, it is very unlikely to prove hardy in frost-affected regions.

Argemone grandiflora Sweet

This is another of the white-flowered prickly poppies but in its typical form it is quite distinct with its smooth glaucous, often red-tinged stems, smooth leaves (apart from the prickly margins) entirely smooth flower buds and fruit-capsule with just a few scattered spines. The leaves are more or less glaucous but are delightfully highlighted by pale, almost white, veins. The six-petalled flowers are large, 6–10 cm (2½–4 in) across, white and satiny, with contrasting bright yellow anthers and purple stigma.

This is certainly a very fine plant that surely deserves a greater audience in our gardens. It is a lovely foil for other, more delicate annuals such as the flaxes, viscaria or phacelias; or for those who opt for grey and white, try growing it with *Omphalodes linifolia*. Although the individual flowers do not last very long, as with most of the other prickly poppies, they are produced in succession over a long season. The cultivar 'White Lustre' is a particularly fine form well worth seeking out.

A. grandiflora has been cultivated since the 1820s, being first described from a cultivated plant. In his original description Sweet* states: 'For the opportunity afforded us of giving a figure of this grand plant, we are obliged to the kindness of Robert Barclay Esq. of Bury Hill, in whose superb collection it was raised this spring, from seed received from Mexico.'

---

* Described and figured in Sweet's *British Flower Garden* 3, t. 266 (1829).

In the wild, *A. grandiflora* occupies a variety of habitats from disturbed soils, roadsides and wastelands, to the hills and mountains, though not above 1,850 m (6,100 ft) altitude. Its distribution is confined to east-central Mexico from Hidalgo to Tamaulipas, where it flowers practically throughout the year.

Farther to the north in Mexico forms with somewhat prickly stems and leaves with prickles beneath are distinguished as subsp. *armata* G.B. Ownb.

Argemone hunnemannii Otto & Dietr.
(syn. *A. platyceras* var. *chilensis* Prain; *A. p.* var. *hunnemannii* (Otto & Dietr.) Fedde)
CHILEAN PRICKLY POPPY

This species, which surprisingly is not in cultivation, is unusual in being the only South American prickly poppy with white flowers. It is confined to Chile at rather low altitudes – at least it has not been recorded much above 600 m (2,000 ft).

A. *hunnemannii* clearly comes close to *A. polyanthemos* in general appearance and differs primarily in its larger buds (18–28 mm (⅔–1⅛ in) long as opposed to 15–22 mm (⅗–⅞ in)) and flowers that are often 10–12 cm (4–5 in) across. The armature of the fruit-capsule is clearly different; in *A. hunnemannii* the spines are spreading to erect and rather slender, whereas in *A. polyanthemos* they are stouter, spreading or often somewhat recurved.

Argemone mexicana L.   [Pl. 28]
(syn. *Papaver spinosum* Bauhin; *A. spinosa* Moench; *A. versicolor* Salisb.; *A. mucronata* Dum.; *A. mexicana* var. *typica* Prain; *A. m.* var. *ochroleuca* Britton; *Ectrus mexicanus* Nieuwland)
MEXICAN POPPY

This is undoubtedly the best-known and most widespread species of *Argemone*. In the wild it is native to Central America and the West Indies but it has had a long association in cultivation and today it has become a widespread weed in tropical and subtropical regions of the world. It is especially prevalent around seaports and has no doubt been transported from port to port over many years. The seeds have a long viability and are able to endure many years before germinating. Its spread is perhaps not so surprising as it, unlike most of its brethren, is very much a coastal or island species.

Gerard (1597) remarked of this species that it was 'so full of sharpe and venemous prickles, that whosoever had one of them in his throte, doubtless it would send him packing to heaven or to hell'.

A. *mexicana* has attracted a host of common names of which the following are probably only a sample: Bird-in-the-bush, Donkey Thistle, Bermuda Thistle, Flowering Thistle, Gamboge Thistle, Gold Thistle of Peru, Infernal Fig, Jamaican Thistle, Mexican Thistle, Mexican Prickly Poppy, Mexican Thorn Poppy, Queen Thistle and Stinking Thistle.

The species is a variable annual to 1 m (3 ft) tall, though often less, the stout stem generally branched close to the base, smooth to sparsely prickly.

The leaves are grey-green with whitish blotches (bloom) over the conspicuous veins, the lower leaves deeply pinnately-lobed, the upper less so and clasping the stem with rather narrow bases; lobes with slender spine-teeth, the upper and lower surfaces smooth or somewhat prickly on the main veins. The buds are oblong, smooth or with a few prickles; sepal-horns 5–10 mm (⅕–⅖ in) long, round in cross-section, spine-tipped, otherwise smooth. The flowers are bright yellow, very occasionally pale yellow, 4–6 cm (1⅗–2⅖ in) across, closely subtended by one or two leaf-like bracts; petals six, obovate usually; stamens few, 30–50, with pale yellow filaments and deeper anthers; stigma purple. The fruit-capsule is oblong to elliptical, to 20 mm (⅘ in) long, smooth or spiny.

The Mexican poppy is native to Central America and the West Indies, south to Guatemala and Nicaragua and northwards to Texas and Florida, but it is widely naturalised outside this region. It is found most often on cultivated waste and disturbed land, field boundaries, roadsides and sea-shores, up to about 1,600 m (5,250 ft) altitude. *A. mexicana* is a prolific seeder and can be found in flower almost throughout the year.

This familiar species can be readily recognised by its bright yellow flowers and relatively few stamens. Forms with wholly smooth leaves, stems buds and fruits are assigned to forma *leiocarpa* (Greene) G.B. Ownb. (syn. *A. leiocarpa* Greene; *A. mexicana* var. *leiocarpa* Prain; *A. alba* var. *leiocarpa* Fedde). The smooth character of var. *leiocarpa* are maintained in cultivation even when it is grown in association with the more usual prickly form. It is believed that it first originated on the island of Key West but has since been introduced to other islands and Florida, as well as areas of South America and West Africa.

The fact that this rather charming poppy is so often dismissed as a troublesome weed in some parts of the world should not put one off growing it in the garden, for it is a handsome, floriferous plant that repays by producing flowers over a long season.

The closely related *A. ochroleuca* can be readily distinguished by its pale lemon flowers, consistently spiny fruit-capsules and oblong, rather than almost rounded, flowerbuds. In addition differences can be observed in the stigmatic lobes, which are spreading in *A. ochroleuca*, but closely appressed to the style at anthesis in *A. mexicana*.

There are undoubtedly a number of forms of *A. mexicana* in cultivation, some with well-marked leaves that recall *Silybum marianum*, a widely grown decorative thistle with handsome leaf-rosettes. Other forms have deep, yellow or tangerine flowers. The only named cultivar is 'Yellow Lustre' which produces luscious bowl-shaped flowers of polished chrome yellow; it is undoubtedly the best form for the garden.

Argemone munita Dur. & Hilg.   [Pl. 29–30]

This is an extremely variable, white-flowered, prickly poppy from the south-western United States of America and neighbouring Baja California (Mexico).

A. munita is an annual or perennial herb to 1 m (3 ft) tall, though often very much shorter; stems moderately to densely branched, often purplish, sparsely to densely prickly. The leaves, especially the lower, are pinnately-lobed, the lobes reaching only halfway to the midrib, rounded, prickly along the margin, sparsely to densely prickly on both the upper and lower surfaces; lower leaves stalked but the upper broader and shorter and clasping the stem with broad bases. The flowerbuds are oblong to elliptic-oblong with prickles at right-angles to the surface; sepal-horns 6–8 mm (¼–⅓ in) long, usually round in cross-section, smooth to prickly. The flowers, 5–10 cm (2–4 in) across but sometimes larger, are white and with a distinct, though short, stem between the flower and the nearest leaf; petals six, obovate; stamens numerous, at least 150, with pale yellow filaments and yellow anthers; stigma purple. The fruit-capsule is elliptical to lanceolate in outline, 9–15 mm (⅖–⅗ in) long and armed with simple spines or a dense mixture of spines and lesser prickles.

A. *munita* is native to California and Baja California, Arizona, Nevada and Utah, where it commonly grows on sandy, gravelly or rocky soils, especially in semi-desert regions, to 2,600 m (8,500 ft) altitude. Flowering in the wild from April until September.

This species is readily recognised by its shallow and blunt leaf-lobes and by the fact that the flowers are separated from the uppermost leaf by a short interval of at least 3–4 mm (⅙ in). Even so this is an extremely variable species. In his monograph of the North American species (1958) Gerald Ownbey gives three subspecies as well as intermediate forms. Of these the most widespread is subsp. *rotundata* (Rydb.) G.B. Ownb. (syn. A. *rotundata* Rydb.; A. *hispida* Torrey; A. *mexicana* var. *hispida* Wats.; A. *platyceras* var. *hispida* Prain). This subspecies, which is the usual one seen in cultivation, has densely prickly stems, leaves and flowerbuds and the stems are noticeably glaucous with an attractive purple flush. Subspecies *rotundata* covers most of the range of the species except for the coastal and subcoastal regions of California and Baja California, which is occupied by subsp. *munita*, a far less prickly species in all its main features.

Ownbey points out that an interesting relationship exists between A. *munita* and fire. Areas recently burnt often produce a flush of plants as seed that has lain dormant in the soil is clearly triggered into germination by the heat; the increased germination of many western American plants by exposure to heat is well documented.

Argemone ochroleuca Sweet [Pl. 31]
(syn. A. *mexicana* var. *ochroleuca* Lindl.; A. *ochroleuca* var. *barclayana* Prain; A. *sulphurea* Sweet ex London)
PALE MEXICAN POPPY

This handsome prickly poppy is very closely related to A. *mexicana* and differs primarily in its pale lemon-yellow flowers and more elongated flowerbuds. In addition the capsules are more lanceolate and always spiny (never smooth) and the stigmatic lobes are clearly spreading when the flower opens (in A. *mexicana* they are pressed close to the surface of the style).

A. *ochroleuca* has a distinctly more inland distribution than A. *mexicana*, being found primarily in central and western Mexico and Baja California where it is a weed of hills, cultivated and wasteland, plains and roadsides, flowering almost throughout the year in favoured localities. Unlike *A. mexicana* it has not become a widespread tropical and subtropical weed around the world, although it is naturalised in Australia. Reports of it from South America refer to *A. subfusiformis*, which is found in Argentina, Bolivia, Chile, Ecuador and Peru. This latter species is not, as far as I am aware, in cultivation.

A. ochroleuca is an attractive species in the garden. The subtle combination of greyish leaves and pale yellow flowers, often produced in profusion, give the plant a distinctive character. In gardens both *A. ochroleuca* and *A. mexicana* are highly self-compatible and crosses appear to be rare; in fact most cultivated forms of *A. mexicana* have 2n = 56 chromosomes, where those of *A. ochroleuca* are 2n = 28.

Narrow-petalled forms of *A. ochroleuca* are afforded the rank of subsp. *stenopetala* (Prain) G.B. Ownb. (syn. *A. intermedia* var. *stenopetala* Prain). Both subspecies can be found together in the wild and are only distinguishable in bud and flower. The buds are not more than 12 mm ($\frac{1}{2}$ in) long and the flowers smaller, only 3–5 cm (1–2 in) across, with narrow–elliptical rather than rounded petals.

Argemone platyceras Link & Otto   [Pl. 32]
CHICALOTE OR CRESTED POPPY

This is perhaps the finest of the white prickly poppies in cultivation and the one most often seen in gardens. It has been cultivated in European gardens since the 1820s and it was from plants flowered in Berlin in 1829 and 1830 that the original description and drawing were prepared.

Taxonomically this species has been much muddled with other white-flowered species from Mexico and the south-western United States but such things need not concern us unduly here. *A. platyceras* is in fact distinctive in its sparsely and weakly prickly leaves (except for the margin) and stems, flattened sepal horns and densely prickly fruit-capsules. The leaves generally have a few scattered prickles on the upper and lower surface, although they can be wholly smooth. The large white flowers, 10–14 cm (4–6 in) across are pure satiny white but often open with a faint lemony flush. The stamens vary from pale yellow to lavender, both in the filaments and anthers; the stigma is generally purplish. The fruit-capsule is completely covered by slender spines, so densely so as to almost conceal the surface of the capsule.

This is a handsome plant, more robust than *A. mexicana* and, in gardens at least, often attaining 90 cm (36 in) in height. The foliage is deeply and sharply lobed, grey-green but often with an overtone of blue. The flowers, although smaller, are reminiscent of those of its Californian and Mexican cousin *Romneya*.

Although perennial *A. platyceras* is best grown as an annual for it is unlikely to overwinter satisfactorily in any but the mildest of districts. In any event seed is easily raised and plants flower in early summer from an early spring sowing under glass. Purple-flowered forms sometimes seen in horticultural literature, more correctly refer to *A. polyanthemos* I believe, although the colour is decidedly more lavender than purple.

A. platyceras inhabits hills and mountain slopes, often on rocky or volcanic soils, cultivated and fallow fields and wasteland at quite high elevations, 1,850–3,200 m (6,100–10,500 ft). It is widespread in Mexico from Vera Cruz to southern Hidalgo, Oaxaca and Michoacan, as well as the state of Mexico itself.

A. hispida Gray (syn. *A. platyceras* var. *hispida* Prain) is a distinct species which A. Gray stated was 'The greatest ornament of the vegetation of Colorado, where it occurs in open grassy or stony places in great profusion, flowering for three months of the year'. It is readily distinguished by its more densely prickly stems, by the leaf-surfaces which, besides being prickly, are covered all over in tiny crisped hairs. The flowers are rather smaller, generally 7–10 cm (3–4 in) across. *A. hispida* does not overlap in distribution in the wild with *A. platyceras*, being confined to the USA from Colorado to Wyoming and New Mexico.

Argemone polyanthemos (Fedde) G.B. Ownb.

(syn. *A. intermedia* var. *polyanthemos* Fedde, *A. intermedia* Eastwood)
PLAINS PRICKLY POPPY

This is another of the large white-flowered persuasion closely related to both *A. albiflora* and *A. grandiflora*.

The species was introduced into cultivation in England in 1877 from seed collected by Joseph Dalton Hooker in Colorado. A plant grown at Kew was figured in *Curtis's Botanical Magazine* in 1878 (as *A. hispida* Gray).

In the wild *A. polyanthemos* is restricted to the Great Plains from the eastern flanks of the Rockies from south-west Dakota to Wyoming, New Mexico and Texas. It is a plant of sandy and gravelly soils, inhabiting fields, roadsides and waste ground as well as the foothills, generally at rather low elevations but to over 2,200 m (7,200 ft) in Colorado and New Mexico; flowering from April to August depending on location.

Plants are annual or biennial, often only 40 cm (16 in) tall but sometimes attaining 80 cm (32 in). The leaves are markedly glaucous and succulent, the lower more deeply lobed than the upper, which clasp the stem, somewhat prickly on the veins beneath but completely smooth above. The flowerbuds are oblong and moderately prickly, the sepal-horns 6–10 mm (¼–⅖ in) long, round in cross-section. The flowers, 6–10 cm (2–4 in) across, are generally white but occasionally lavender, with yellow stamens and purple stigma.

This species differs from *A. albiflora* in its longer sepal-horns (only 3–6 mm (⅛–¼ in) long in the latter) and narrower and longer fruit-capsules. Undoubtedly the two are very closely related and some authorities would surely merge the two, albeit as subspecies or varieties of the same species. The two overlap in part of their ranges in the wild.

The dwarfer habit of *A. polyanthemos* would make it a fine garden plant, especially in its rarer lavender-flowered form. Yet this species does not appear to be at all common in cultivation at the present time; indeed I do not know of authenticated material in cultivation. This is sad because this and several other fine *Argemone* species are very accessible and could surely be brought into cultivation without too much difficulty. Sometimes our efforts to bring in ever rare and more unusual plants into cultivation makes us, I believe, overlook the simple beauty of some of these easy-to-grow plants. Perhaps a rekindled vogue for annual borders in the garden might propel such species back to our attention.

Argemone rosea Hook.
(syn. *A. mexicana* var. *rosea* (Hook.) Reiche; *A. platyceras* var. *chilensis* Prain; *A. platyceras* var. *hispido-rosea* Fedde)
ROSE PRICKLY POPPY

Although not in cultivation *A. rosea* merits a mention. It is restricted to a relatively small area in Coquimto Province, Chile.

The species is an annual with stems, leaves and flower buds densely covered with prickly bristles. The leaves are deeply and narrowly pinnately-lobed and sharply spine-toothed; upper leaves much reduced but not clasping the stem. The flowerbuds have small horns, only 2–4 mm (¼ in) long, and finely pointed. The flowers are 6–10 cm (2–4 in) across and lavender (reports of white-flowered forms have not, to my knowledge, been substantiated); stamens about 80 and stigma purple.

Argemone sanguinea Greene
(syn. *A. mexicana* var. *rosea* Coulter ex Greene; *A. platyceras* var. *rosea* Coulter; *A. purpurea* Rose ex Pringle)

This is yet another species unaccountably not in cultivation at the present time. It is, in many ways similar to *A. albiflora* and certainly in its lavender-coloured forms is distinctive enough. However, it often occurs with white flowers and these are more difficult to separate. In *A. sanguinea* the sepal-horns are clearly larger, 5–10 mm (⅕–⅖ in) long (not 3–6 mm (⅛–¼ in)) and generally with a few prickles in the lower part. The fruit-capsules of *A. sanguinea* are usually three-to five-parted (carpellate), whilst those of *A. albiflora* are four- to seven-parted; the capsular spines are stouter and often recurved in *A. sanguinea*.

A. sanguinea comes from southern Texas and the neighbouring regions of northern Mexico. It is a plant of the chaparral, of fields and field-margins, wasteland and disturbed ground and along roadways from sea level to about 1,600 m (5,250 ft) altitude, flowering primarily from February to June.

Argemone squarrosa Greene

This species is very similar in general appearance to *A. platyceras*, however, it is a far more prickly plant overall. Both stem and leaves are generally moderately prickly, the leaf-prickles confined to the main veins but the areas in between covered in tiny bristles. The pure white flowers are 10–12 cm (4–5 in) across usually and bear yellow stamens and a purple stigma. The fruit-capsules are densely spiny and are unusual in that the main spines are compound with lesser spines borne on their basal half; this is in contrast to the simple spines of the fruit-capsules of *A. platyceras*. In addition the stamens of *A. platyceras* are often reddish-lavender or lavender and this can provide a quick means of distinction.

A. *squarrosa* is primarily a prairie species, being found there and in the surrounding foothills (often sandy soils) from Kansas and Oklahoma to south-eastern Colorado and New Mexico, generally between 1,000–1,850 m (3,300–6,100 ft) altitude. It can be found in flower between May and September.

In cultivation it is generally present as subsp. *glabrata* G.B. Ownb. which differs only in having little or no fine bristles between the main leaf-veins, or indeed on the flowerbuds or fruit-capsules. This subspecies is confined to western Texas and south-eastern New Mexico.

In cultivation subsp. *glabrata* is often, and perhaps not surprisingly, confused with *A. platyceras*. If the stamens are pink or purplish rather than yellow then the plant will certainly prove to be the latter. However, the fruit-capsule characters are perhaps more convincing. In subsp. *glabrata* the main spines will certainly be compound (as described above) and 8–15 mm (⅓–⅗ in) long; in *A. platyceras* they are simple and no more than 10 mm (⅖ in) in length.

Argemone superba G.B. Ownb.

This bright and cheerful species was described in 1958 from material collected west of Ciudad del Maiz in Mexico by Gerald Ownbey and F. Ownbey. The species comes very close to *A. aenea* in leaf characters and in the character of the flower buds and fruit-capsules. The prime differences lie in the plain bright yellow flowers of *A. superba*, with no hint of gold or bronze, in the yellow rather than red or purple stamen filaments and in the narrower stigma – only 2.5–3 mm (⅛ in) wide. These differences seem rather slight in many respects and further investigations may well show that the two elements could be easily encompassed within a single species, perhaps at subspecific or varietal level.

The two in fact do not overlap in distribution in the wild, that of *A. aenea* being to the north and east of *A. superba* and separated in Mexico by the Sierra Madre Oriental.

This fine species would be a fine introduction into our gardens. Both it and *A. aenea* are unlikely to be confused with the other yellow-flowered species in cultivation (namely *A. mexicana* and *A. ochroleuca*) on account of their larger flowers and far more numerous stamens.

The Pygmy Poppies
Canbya

If *Romneya* has claim to have the largest flowers in the poppy family then the members of the little American genus *Canbya* certainly have the smallest. There are only two species, both desert ephemeral annuals of little interest to the gardener but of more than passing interest to the botanist.

The genus is named in honour of the American amateur botanist William Marriott Canby, who was born in 1813.

Apart from their small size (neither species is more than 5 cm (2 in) tall) the genus is characterised by its thick, tufted leaves, three sepals, persistent corolla of six petals and by having relatively few stamens (not usually more than 15). The dried and shrivelled petals cling on around the base of the developing fruit, a feature little seen in the poppy family as a whole.

Canbya aurea S. Wats.
YELLOW PYGMY POPPY

A tufted annual 2.5–5 cm (1–2 in) tall, forming discreet little cushions of leaves. The leaves are linear to narrow-elliptical, not more than 12 mm (½ in) long. The tiny flowers have six golden petals, scarcely 3 mm (⅛ in) long, and 3–15 stamens.

Cathcartia villosa

C. aurea inhabits sandy and stony places, often in sagebrush, in eastern Oregon and north-western Nevada as well as northern Mexico, where it can be found in flower during May and June.

Canbya candida Parry ex A. Gray   [Pl. 33]
WHITE PYGMY POPPY

This species is even more minute than its cousin *C. aurea*, being rarely more than 2.5 cm (1 in) tall, with narrow, rather thick leaves up to 6 mm (¼ in) in length; both leaves and stems are borne in small tufts. The solitary flowers are borne on thread-like stalks and have six white petals, about 3 mm (½ in) long, and only six to nine stamens.

   C. candida inhabits sandy dry places in the western Mojave Desert in California, flowering during April and May, occasionally earlier.

The Woodland Poppy
Cathcartia

The genus *Cathcartia* was described in 1851 by William Jackson Hooker based on a single species *C. villosa*, which had been discovered in Sikkim by his son, Joseph Dalton Hooker, in 1849.

   In 1934 George Taylor transferred the species to *Meconopsis* and most people have since followed Taylor's conclusion. However, the presence of rounded, palmately lobed and veined leaves, a sessile stigma and a slender fruit-capsule that splits almost to the base are so distinctive compared to the other members of *Meconopsis* that it would seem far better to place the species in a distinct genus. The *Flora of Bhutan* (1(2), 1984) followed this line, which I wholly agree with.

Cathcartia villosa Hook. f. ex Hook.   [Pl. 34]
(Syn. *Meconopsis villosa* (Hook. f. ex Hook.) G. Taylor)
HIMALAYAN WOODLAND POPPY

Another rather modest species but handsome enough in foliage and flower to make it acceptable for the woodland garden. Indeed *C. villosa* deserves to be more widely grown in gardens for it is not a difficult species to cultivate.

   The species is an herbaceous perennial with leafy stems and a rather short rootstock covered in persistent leaf-bases and reddish bristles. The long-stalked, bristly basal leaves are oval or rounded in outline and partly cut into three to five lobed segments. The upper leaves are similar in size and shape but short-stalked. The slender bristly stems rise to about 60 cm (24 in) and each bears one to five semi-nodding flowers, borne on slender stalks from the upper leaf-axils. The flowers are yellow, 4–5 cm (1½–2 in) across, with four rounded, somewhat overlapping petals and a central boss of golden or yellow stamens – the anthers become brown on ageing. The fruit-capsule is almost cylindrical, up to 8.5 cm (3½ in) long, smooth and, rather unusually splits for more than a half of its length into four to seven valves.

C. villosa is a native of the Himalaya from the Mt. Everest region of Nepal eastwards to Bhutan, at altitudes of 2,900–4,480 m (9,500–14,700 ft). It is a plant of woodland glades and banks, of stream margins and rock crevices. I have observed it on several occasions in both the upper reaches of the Arun and Tamur valleys in east Nepal. There it often forms large patchy colonies in woodland where sunlight filters on occasion and in areas subjected to heavy summer monsoon rains.

This species was discovered by Joseph Dalton Hooker in 1849 in Sikkim. Seed sent home by Hooker flowered at the Royal Botanic Gardens, Kew, two years later.

C. villosa is one of my personal favourites. It can in no way be considered brash, but the attractive and rather distinctive leaves and handsome flowers make it a charmer for the woodland garden or for a semi-shaded place amongst shrubs. It is a species that requires a moist soil and will tolerate an almost totally shaded position providing that it is not too dry. A few central leaves always remain at ground level during the winter to mark the position of the plants.

Seed is generally produced in quantity but tends to germinate rather sparingly in my experience. Furthermore, seedlings should be pricked out with care as losses can be expected if they are roughly handled. Young plants seem to resent too much disturbance and once planted out are best left to their own devices. Established plants generally flower in their second season and will go on for many years. Large plants can be divided in the spring but I would rather leave them alone and grow new plants from seed than risk loosing mature plants. An annual top-dressing of compost or leaf-mould, placed around the plants is highly beneficial.

The related *C. smithiana* Hand.-Mazz. (syn. *Meconopsis smithiana* (Hand.-Mazz.) G. Taylor) from south-west China and Upper Burma is not in cultivation. It can be distinguished by having distinctly three-lobed leaves and a more rounded, hairy ovary.

The Blue Poppies
Meconopsis

Of all the varied members of the poppy family, none has created such excitement and intrigue as the famous blue poppies. No other genus in the Papaveraceae has plants with blue flowers and, for this alone, they have long stolen the hearts of gardeners.

One can perhaps judge the feeling of disbelief when the first blue poppies were reported from the wild and the general astonishment when the first unfurled its translucent petals in cultivation. The most famous of the blue poppies is undoubtedly *Meconopsis betonicifolia*, which first flowered in cultivation in 1924 under the name *M. baileyi*. Seldom has a plant gained such popularity so rapidly in cultivation and today, despite the fact that this glorious species has been in our gardens for more than 60 years, it is as popular as ever. However, this was by no means the first of the blue poppies to be introduced into cultivation: *M. wallichii* first flowered in 1852, *M. grandis* in 1895, *M. horridula* in 1904, *M. latifolia* in 1908 and *M. quintuplinervia* in 1914–15. Of these *M. grandis* closely rivals *M. betonicifolia* for the size and blueness of its flowers, as well as ease of cultivation.

It is wrong to think of *Meconopsis* as containing only blue-flowered species, for those with yellow, violet, purple, red and occasionally white flowers are well represented. The genus in fact contains some 43 species, all but one being natives of the Himalaya and western China. The exception is the Welsh Poppy, *M. cambrica*, which is confined to western Ireland and Wales, southwards through western France to northern Spain.

The genus was established by L.A.G. Viguier, Montpellier, in 1814, based upon Linnaeus's *Papaver cambricum*, which was transferred to the new genus. *Meconopsis* was distinguished from the closely similar *Papaver* primarily by the presence of a short style and the absence of a sessile stigmatic disc on top of the ovary. While these features serve to distinguish the majority of subsequent species of *Meconopsis* from *Papaver* several species in the former genus have no appreciable style but, at the same time, do not possess any sign of a disc. Thus the two largest genera in the poppy family are distinguished by very fine details. However, species do not always conform to generic boundaries as simply as the taxonomist would wish. In *Meconopsis* two species, *M. discigera* and *M. torquata*, bear fruits with a short style as well as a well developed (but non-stigmatic) disc. This disc is generally regarded by taxonomists as a derived character with no direct relationship to *Papaver*. Curiously, in most of the regions inhabited by *Meconopsis* there are few species of *Papaver* – they are concentrated primarily in Europe and western Asia with species also represented in North America, Africa and Australia. In gardens the two genera are unlikely to be muddled, even at a casual glance.

The Mexican Poppies or prickly poppies, *Argemone*, confined to the New World, are also very closely related to *Meconopsis*. They can be readily distinguished by their very prickly stems and leaves, and the presence of three sepals, rather than two, per flower, each adorned with a 'horn' at the apex.

The main problem facing the taxonomist and horticulturist with *Meconopsis* is the position of *M. cambrica* itself and the delimitation of the individual species.

It is indeed curious to have *M. cambrica* restricted to western Europe whilst the rest of the species occur a great distance away to the east. There are features of habit, pollen and seed structure, as well as cytology in *M. cambrica* that are rather at variance with other members of the genus, though none of these are obvious without a detailed study (see Ernst, 1962). There are, as a result, good reasons perhaps to separate this species from the others and give it a genus to itself. Herein lies a tricky dilemma for the taxonomist, for *Meconopsis* is based upon *M. cambrica* and if the genus has to be split then all the other species would have to move to a new genus; as no existing name is available one would need to be created. To do so would be to excite the wrath of the horticultural world and serve no great purpose except to gain the perpetrator, however well-intentioned, a certain degree of notoriety.

Amongst the species there are those that are readily recognised and easily defined. However, as in many similarly sized genera, some of the species show a good deal of variation and even some overlap in their overall characters as seen in the wild and this can serve to blur specific boundaries. This is most prominent between species like *M. napaulensis* and *M. paniculata* and within species such as *M. grandis* and *M. horridula* where there is a great deal of variation between populations or, indeed, sometimes within a single population.

In cultivation the problem is often of a different nature for, in many instances, only a few forms represent most species rather than the whole span of possible variations. The problem in certain groups has been the propensity towards hybridisation (especially between *M. napaulensis*, *M. paniculata* and *M. regia*) so that the species identities become blurred, or worse, lost all together.

The first serious studies of *Meconopsis* were undertaken by David Prain whose paper of 1896, published in the *Journal of the Asiatic Society of Bengal*, was the first detailed study of the genus. This was followed by a more comprehensive account in the *Annals of Botany* in 1906. Prain made a further revision in 1915 when he recognised some 43 species within *Meconopsis* (in *Bulletin of Miscellaneous Information Kew* – now *The Kew Bulletin*). Frank Kingdon-Ward, who had observed many species in their native habitats, proposed various amendments to Prain's classification, which he published in the *Gardener's Chronicle* during 1926. However, the most comprehensive and far reaching study was George Taylor's monograph *The Genus Meconopsis*, which was first published in 1934 and has remained the devotee's bible on the subject ever since. The only other significant work on the genus is James L.S. Cobb's *Meconopsis* published by Christopher Helm in 1989. Whereas this work can in no way be described as a monograph of the genus and adds little to our understanding of the taxonomy and botany of the species, it is at the same time, the most comprehensive and useful work on the cultivation of this beautiful group of plants.

Meconopsis are perennials, some being long-lived and flowering year after year, whilst others are monocarpic, dying once they have flowered and seeded. The long-lived perennial species may form a taproot crowded by a tuft of shoots or the rootstock may be more diverse, plants spreading by means of a branching, generally slender underground rhizome giving rise to shoots at interval and resulting in a spreading patch. The monocarpic species generally form a solitary rosette of leaves, which can in some reach 60 cm (24 in) or more across. The leaf-rosettes may be permanent or they may wither down to a resistant central bud in the autumn. Stems, when present, bear few to many alternate leaves, the uppermost sometimes arranged in a whorl. Monocarpic species may flower in their second season or take a number of years to reach flowering size.

Leaves are very variable within the genus and range from simple undivided and untoothed types to those that are deeply cut into a number of lobes or divided into separate leaflets. Many species ooze a yellowish sap when cut. The leaves can be smooth or variously adorned with simple or branched hairs or bristles.

Flowers are borne on simple (leafless) scapes, in racemes or in more complex terminal panicles forming a stout inflorescence. The sepals are generally two (very occasionally three or four) and soon fall once the buds open. There are most commonly four petals per flower, but this may vary up to ten, especially in cultivated plants. There are numerous stamens, which have slender stalks (filaments). Fruit-capsules vary in shape from globose to oblong to narrowly cylindrical and may be smooth, hairy or bristly, dehiscing by means of valves in the upper part, these sometimes splitting almost to the base of the capsule. Mature capsules, which are nearly always erect, bear numerous seeds.

Cultivation

Meconopsis species range from those that can be considered easy to grow to those that are difficult or indeed have proved almost impossible over the years. They are often regarded as connoisseur's plants and as such they have attracted an aura of exclusivity they do not altogether warrant.

These are beautiful plants and one sight of a border with patches of blue, red, pink or yellow meconopsis is enough to send any keen gardeners scurrying home to try and grow some for themselves. With the exception of the Welsh Poppy, *M. cambrica*, which can be readily grown in most temperate gardens providing the soil is not too dry, the remainder, which are exclusively Asian in origin, need more careful treatment.

To understand the cultural requirements of meconopsis it is wise to examine their habitat conditions in the wild. The species are all to be found in mountain regions, particularly the Himalaya and the mountains of western China. They are plants of woodland, scrub, alpine meadows, screes, moraines or cliffs, often, though not exclusively, growing on acid or neutral soils. In these regions most of the precipitation falls as monsoon rain during the summer months, whilst during the winter any precipitation will normally be as snow. This means that during the winter months, when temperatures can drop well below freezing, plants are often protected beneath a blanket of snow and will be dormant as well as relatively dry. In the spring, as the snow melts and the temperatures increase, the plants come into growth. In the early summer (late May and June) the monsoon rains arrive and they persist right through the peak growing and flowering season only easing off in the autumn when plants are in seed and beginning to die down or cease growing for the year. The season of highest temperatures therefore coincides with maximum rainfall. In our gardens such conditions can rarely be found and the situation is often reversed with the winters being mild and wet and with a great reduction in rainfall in the summer period. This is why in northern Britain and in north-west North America (the region around Vancouver and Seattle for instance) where the winters are more reliably cold and there is a good deal of rainfall during the summer, meconopsis thrive far better than elsewhere – the conditions are more akin to their native habitats.

However, this should not put anyone off attempting to grow at least one or two species in their gardens. Walk round a large garden such as the Royal Botanic Gardens at Kew, the Saville Gardens at Winsor or indeed a host of southern gardens in the early summer and you are almost certain to find several different species in bloom. In such places more care needs to be taken over their culture with plenty of rich humus added to the soil and liberal mulches provided during the summer to keep the moisture level high around the base of the plants.

For those growing meconopsis for the first time there are several species and their cultivars that can be considered reasonably easy to grow – *M. betonicifolia, M. cambrica, M. chelidonifolia, M. dhwojii, M. grandis, M. napaulensis, M. paniculata, M. quintuplinervia* and *M. regia* fit into this category. Of course there is an inherent danger in listing 'easy species', for in some gardens one or several may prove to be difficult for one reason or another.

Soil preparation is important. Before planting the area should be deeply dug and ample humus (compost or well-rotted manure) dug into the soil. The ideal site is a sheltered one, preferably not in a frost pocket, with dappled shade where the sunlight can filter through surrounding trees or shrubs. An open windy site with unshielded sunlight is wholly unsuitable as is a soil that at any time becomes waterlogged.

Plants are best placed in their permanent positions in the spring or early summer so that they have plenty of time to become established before the winter arrives. A generous mulch (compost, bark chippings, straw or similar) placed closely around the plants will keep the soil moist and cooler throughout the summer.

Monocarpic species such as *M. napaulensis, M. paniculata* and *M. regia* will produce huge evergreen rosettes if well grown and these can be quite a feature in themselves. They, like most of the other species, are greedy feeders and will 'consume' as much humus and manure as can be supplied. For these species, which extend up to two metres tall in flower, a sheltered site is essential, otherwise plants can be easily blown over or the handsome foliage bruised.

There is no doubt that these plants look best in groups rather than as isolated individuals in the border and, where space allows, a drift can be a most arresting sight.

For the less-hardy types (see under individual species) some form of protection in the spring will help prevent frost damage to emerging shoots and buds. For those that may be prone to rotting in winter (especially in mild wet areas) a frame light, cloche or other cover will help ward off excessive moisture. Care needs to be taken at the same time that the plants do not become too dry, otherwise they may wither from drought.

The more difficult and rarer species require more specialist treatment, unless you are fortunate enough to be in a very favourable region for their culture. The construction of special humus rich screes with integral irrigation, peat beds and misted benches has been advocated and indeed some have found these a highly successful way of growing some of the gems in the genus. For those who want to try some of these difficult poppies I can do no better than to refer them to James L.S. Cobb's excellent book *Meconopsis*, which deals with their individual cultural requirements in great detail.

Plants can be purchased from a number of different sources, especially of the easier species and cultivars. However, for those wishing to build up a good stock of plants, seed provides the readiest and cheapest means of acquiring plants. Seed should be as fresh as possible. Spring sowing is perhaps easiest, although some advocate an autumn sowing, especially for species such as *M. punicea*, which requires a cold winter before it will germinate. One problem of autumn sowing is that if the seeds germinate quickly then the tiny seedlings have to be nurtured through the winter months. It is important to remember that meconopsis seed will deteriorate if left unsown for too long and some loss of viability must be expected. If collecting home-grown seed then this can, if it is ready in time, be sown the moment it is ripe and this will give just enough time before the winter to build up strong little plants that will have a fair chance of coming through the winter, especially if they are confined to a protective frame or glasshouse.

The ideal compost for seed sowing is a moist organic compost; one dare scarcely say today that a good peat-based compost is ideal for the purpose but until really proven alternatives come along one has no alternative but to advocate their use in such instances. James Cobb recommends a '50 per cent soil-less compost or plain moss peat (sedge peat forms a hopeless skin on composts and should be avoided), 30 per cent sphagnum and 20 per cent coarse grit or expanded rock granules'.

Seed should be sown very thinly to help avoid overcrowded seedlings, which would invite problems with damping off. The seeds require light to germinate so that a very thin covering is all that is required – fine sharp grit is ideal for the purpose. Pots should be well watered from below and placed in a sheltered frame away from too strong sunlight. Seed sown in the late winter can be boosted into germination by placing the pots over a soil-warming cable or in a propagator with a range of 10–20°C (50–60°F) night to day. At all stages, before and after gemination, it is disastrous to allow the compost to dry out and this will only result in failure.

Seedlings should be pricked out as soon as they are large enough to handle and will only suffer if they are allowed to linger on in the original pot and become congested. Seedlings should be grown on as fast as possible, although different species vary a good deal in vigour, especially in their first season. The most vigorous types, such as *M. betonicifolia*, *M. napaulensis* and *M. paniculata*, should be constantly potted on to build up large plants in the shortest possible time. In this way the more vigorous species may be large enough to plant out by mid-summer. If not, they should be over-wintered in an airy frame and kept moist, although not excessively so.

Collecting home-produced seed is an enjoyable pastime. If enough is gathered then there is plenty to hand on to other gardeners or to send to seed exchanges. Meconopsis seed, like all poppy seed, should be gathered the moment the capsules begin to split, otherwise much valuable seed may be wasted. The best way is to detach the fruit-capsules and tip the contents into dry envelopes. Seed should be thoroughly dried in a cool room and any debris (chaff) removed. Care should be taken to mark the name of the plant on the packets, otherwise awful confusion results and you will not be popular around the seed exchanges! Sealed dried packets can be placed in air-tight plastic containers and placed in a fridge until the seed is required. Commercially, seed can be stored in special cabinets in a seed bank where the conditions can be carefully controlled. Under ideal conditions seed can be kept for a number of years in this way. For most of us, however, careful cleaning and storage is all we can do and, with meconopsis at least, ensuring that seed is sown reasonably quickly after harvesting.

Some species can be relied upon to produce a good annual harvest of seed, others are more tricky. During hot dry weather developing fruit may abort and no seed results, which is very unfortunate where the monocarpic species are concerned. During such periods it is as well to nurture plants and try to keep up the moisture content of the soil to ensure at least some seed set.

Perennial species such as the various forms of *M. grandis*, *M. chelidonifolia* and *M. quintuplinervia* can also be propagated by division of the parent plant. This can be undertaken in the spring as growth commences or, preferably, the moment the plants finish flowering. With the former species the easiest method is to dig up the parent plant and to slice it up carefully into one or two shoot portions. With the latter two species, which have a more spreading habit, it may only be necessary to remove the outer shoots by digging around the outside and leaving the main plant intact. Divisions should be kept moist and shaded for some weeks until it is clear that they are growing successfully.

Meconopsis suffer from few pests. Slugs and snails may attack soft young shoots or buds as they emerge in the spring and these can be easily guarded against. Aphids may sometimes infest the young leaves or inflorescences, though this is not a major problem – some systemic pesticides harm meconopsis so an organic cure is preferable.

Various fungal diseases attack meconopsis causing damping off of seedlings, root rots or worst of all crown rot (possibly bacterial in origin). Where any of these are suspected then a regular spray with a systemic fungicide (used strictly at the manufacturer's instructions) may alleviate the problem. Crown rot in established plants may indicate stresses in the plants caused by adverse soil conditions, such as waterlogging. Damaged plants are best removed and burnt.

Classification

George Taylor recognised two subgenera and a number of sections in his *An Account of the genus Meconopsis* (1934) and, with few modifications, this has remained the basis of classification ever since. The most significant difference has been the removal of two species, *M. villosa* and *M. smithiana*, to their former genus *Cathcartia*.

Subgenus Dioscogyne G. Tayl. This subgenus is characterised by the presence of a flat disk surmounting the ovary and from the centre of which arises the short style. Contains only two species, *MM. discigera, torquata*.

Subgenus Eumeconopsis (Prain) Fedde. Characterised by the absence of a disk. Most species bear a distinct style, occasionally no style is present but then the stigmatic lobes do not radiate outwards over a disk as in *Papaver*. Contains three main sections:

1. Section Cambricae (Prain) Fedde. Perennial herbs with leafy stems and a tufted, non-bristly base. Flowering stems several from each tuft; flowers yellow or orange, 4-petalled. *M. cambrica* (the only species).

2. Section Eucathcartia (Prain) G. Tayl. Perennial herbs with a tufted and bristly base. Flowers yellow, four-petalled, borne on a solitary flowering stem. *MM. chelidonifolia, oliverana.*

3. Section Polychaetia Prain. Monocarpic or polycarpic perennials – if the latter then flowers never yellow.

Subsection Eupolychaetia G. Tayl. Monocarpic perennials with a persistent leaf-rosette during the winter months.

Series Superbae Kingdon-Ward. Leaf-margin finely serrated, not lobed, with a dense silky pubescence. *MM. regia, superba.*

Series Robustae Prain. Leaves deeply lobed, generally bristly. *MM. dhwojii, gracilipes napaulensis, paniculata, wallichii.*

Subsection Cumminsia (Prain) G. Tayl. Monocarpic or polycarpic perennials without a persistent winter rosette of leaves.

Series Simplicifoliae G. Tayl. Species tend to be polycarpic, with dense, bristly, leaf-rosettes. Flowers borne on leafless scapes. *MM. punicea, simplicifolia, quintuplinervia.*

Series Grandes Prain. Species monocarpic to polycarpic, with dense leaf tufts and leafy stems with the uppermost leaves in a whorl below the flowers. *MM. betonicifolia, grandis, integrifolia.*

Series Primulinae Prain. Monocarpic perennials with a basal leaf tuft and stems with a few alternate leaves; flowers solitary or several. *M. primulina* – not in cultivation.

Series Delavayanae G. Tayl. Small tufted polycarpic perennials with few entire leaves and a branched rootstock. Flowers solitary and scapose. *M. delavayi* (the only species).

Series Aculeatae Prain. Large series of monocarpic perennials with a solitary taproot and basal rosette of leaves. Flowers borne in a well-defined leafy inflorescence or scapose (some then borne from the same leaf-rosette). *MM. aculeata, forrestii, henrici, horridula, lancifolia, latifolia, speciosa.*

Series Bellae Prain. Small tufted polycarpic perennials with finely divided leaves and solitary scapose flowers; pedicels arching over in fruit. Fruit capsule pear-shaped. *M. bella* (the only species).

Key to Species

(* rare in cultivation)

1. Leaves in a false whorl where the flowers arise (plants occasionally with one or two basal scapose flowers in addition) 2
   Leaves not as above; stems leafy or flowers all scapose 4

2. Flowers yellow; plants monocarpic: *M. integrifolia*
   Flowers blue, purple or reddish, occasionally white; plants perennial, occasionally moncarpic 3

3. Basal leaves with a truncated or somewhat heart-shaped base; fruit-capsule oblong, densely bristly: *M. betonicifolia*
   Basal leaves with a narrowed, wedge-shaped base; fruit-capsule narrow-elliptical, glabrous to somewhat bristly: *M. grandis*

4. Ovary and fruit-capsule with a broad disc at the top – below the short style: *M. discigera**
   Ovary and fruit-capsule without a disc 5

5. Flowers solitary, scapose – all the leaves basal 6
   Flowers borne in distinct racemes or panicles – stem leafy 11

6. Leaves dissected, occasionally subentire, but then some leaves with at least several lateral lobes; fruit-capsule pear-shaped, borne on a curved stalk: *M. bella**
   Leaves entire, never with lateral lobes; fruit capsule oblong to almost globose, borne on an erect stem 7

7. Flowers blood-red; petals elliptical, up 6–10 cm (2½–4 in) in length: *M. punicea**
   Flowers blue to violet-purple or pink; petals oval to almost rounded 3–5 cm (1⅕–2 in) in length.....................................8

8. Petals 6 or more; plants monocarpic to perennial (polycarpic) 9
   Petals usually 4; flowers fully nodding; plants perennial (polycarpic) ..10

9. Flowers pink; anthers yellow or brownish: *M. sherriffii**
   Flowers blue; anthers blue: *M. simplicifolia*

10. Flowers pale lavender-blue; plants spreading, with persistent, bristly, persistent leaf-bases: *M. quintuplinervia*
    Flowers violet-purple; plants tufted, not creeping, leaf-bases not bristly nor persistent: *M. delavayi**

11. Plants perennial (polycarpic); flowers, yellow, orange or red.........12
    Plants monocarpic – dying after flowering and seeding; flowers yellow, pink, red or blue, occasionally white.....................14

12. Leaves oblong, pinnately divided to the midrib; plant scarcely
    hairy, the tufted base without bristles; flowers yellow, orange or
    red (sometimes double, or semi-double):   **M. cambrica**
    Leaves rounded in outline, three to five-lobed; plant densely hairy
    to bristly, the tufted base bristly; flowers always yellow (never
    double or semi-double) 13

13. Plant tufted, not spreading by means of surface stolons; stems
    unbranched, to 60 cm (24 in) tall: **M. villosa**
    Plant spreading by means of surface stolons, patch-forming; stems
    branched, to 100 cm (40 in):   **M. chelidonifolia**

14. Plants deciduous, the leaf-rosettes dying away to a resistent bud in
    the late autumn 15
    Plants evergreen, with a large leaf-rosettes present throughout the
    winter 17

15. Leaves deeply, pinnately dissected, cut to the midrib, at least in the
    basal half: **M. aculeata**
    Leaves not dissected to deeply toothed, often with an undulate
    margin, never cut for more than one third of the distance to the
    midrib 16

16. Flowers pale blue, four-petalled; leaves broadly oval, coarsely
    toothed; leaf-spines without a dark base: **M. latifolia**
    Flowers deep blue to mauve or pale wine red; leaves elliptical to
    narrow-oblong, generally more or less untoothed; leaf-spines often
    with a dark base: **M. horridula**

17. Leaves unlobed, with a finely toothed margin; flowers yellow or
    white; stigma deep purple-black 18
    Leaves shallowly lobed to deeply pinnately dissected; flowers
    yellow, blue, red or purple; stigma greenish or whitish, occasionally
    pale purple 19

18. Flowers yellow; leaves covered in gold hairs: **M. regia★**
    Flowers white; leaves covered in greyish hairs: **M. superba★**

19. Flowers blue, red or purple 20
    Flowers yellow, occasionally white 21

20. Leaves deeply pinnately dissected, the lower segments distant along
    the slender stalk (rachis); flowers pale- to mid-sky blue   **M. wallichii**
    Leaves shallowly lobed, never cut all the way to the midrib; flowers
    pink or red   **M. napaulensis**

21. Leaves shallowly pinnately lobed, sometimes the lower lobes deeply
    separated, almost to the midrib; stigma pale purple: **M. paniculata**
    Leaves deeply pinnately lobed with rather distant division and a
    slender rachis; stigma, pale green or whitish: 22

22. Leaves densely bristly, the bristles with a purple-black base: **M. dhwojii**
    Leaves sparsely bristly, the bristles pale: **M. gracilipes★**

Meconopsis aculeata Royle

This species is closely related to *M. horridula* from which it can at once be differentiated because of its dissected leaves.

Like *M. horridula* plants are monocarpic, the leaves withering away to a resting bud in the autumn prior to flowering – generally in the second or third year. The leaves, up to 30 cm (12 in) long, are pinnately-lobed and with a stalk often equalling the blade in length; the initial lobes are further lobed or toothed, both surfaces with a sparse covering of pale straw-coloured spines. The upper stem leaves are usually unstalked. The flowers, 4.5–6 cm (2–2½ in) across, are borne in a bristly raceme up to 60 cm high, and varying in colour from pinkish- to purplish-blue. There are usually four rounded petals and a central boss of golden stamens. The stigma varies in colour from green to purple. The fruit-capsule is oblong to almost globose, densely spiny and splitting by four to six valves close to the styled apex.

M. aculeata hails from the western Himalaya (eastern Afghanistan through Kashmir to Kumaon in India). In inhabits rocky meadows, screes and boggy ground, particularly along stream margins, at altitudes from 2,500–4,375 m (8,200-14,400 ft).

This species has been in cultivation since 1864 when it first flowered at the Royal Botanic Gardens at Kew. It is undoubtedly an attractive plant with much grace and appealing silky flowers. It is perhaps less tolerant of winter wet than its cousin *M. horridula* and it may be advisable to protect plants by a cloche or frame light during this vulnerable period of the year.

Some forms in cultivation, with less dissected leaves, may be hybrids with *M. horridula* (Cobb, 1989), but recent seed introductions from Kashmir by Chris Chadwell and others have introduced authenticated wild material once more into our gardens and perhaps some interesting variation may turn up.

Although generally taprooted, plants like those of several other mono-carpic species in the genus may sometimes produce a more spreading and fibrous root-system.

There is a very charming white-flowered form in cultivation with contrasting purple anthers and stigma, although being monocarpic such forms are often difficult to establish in cultivation for any length of time.

Meconopsis bella Prain   [Pl. 37]

This is perhaps the most tantalising and prettiest little blue poppy of all. Tantalising in that, despite numerous introductions from the wild over the years, *M. bella* has proved a fickle and temperamental plant in cultivation. It can be likened to an alpine poppy (*Papaver alpinum*) in overall dimensions.

M. bella is a small perennial with a slender, carrot-like taproot, covered by the persistent leaf bases. The leaves, which in the wild die away during the winter, are all basal, and variously pinnately lobed or unlobed, with a long stalk, hairless or with a few scattered bristles. The solitary flowers are borne in succession and arise on slender, slightly bristly scapes up to 12 cm (6 in) long. The cupped flowers range from clear pale blue to pink or purplish-blue

Meconopsis bella

and are 4–5.5 cm (1½–2 in) across, with a central boss of golden anthers borne on filaments coloured like the petals. There are four, occasionally five or six, rounded, partly overlapping petals. The fruit-capsule is narrow pear-shaped and smooth, splitting by four to seven valves close to the top.

This is another Himalayan species found from central Nepal eastwards through Sikkim to Bhutan at an altitude of 3,750–5,150 m (12,300–16,900 ft). In these high remote regions it inhabits damp shaded cliff habitats or sloping meadows or banks with a low scrub of dwarf rhododendrons and other woody plants.

Most who have seen it in the wild describe it as a plant confined to deep mossy cliff crevices where its long taproot penetrates deep into the rocks. However, I have twice seen scattered colonies of it in the wild and never in that type of habitat, rather on sloping meadows where it nestled beneath dwarf shrubs in moist shaded places with the flowers poking through low ground-hugging branches. The fragile flowers, translucent and watery, were a pale to deep lavender-blue of the utmost beauty and refinement. In fact the picture in James Cobb's *Meconopsis* shows *M. bella* growing in just such a habitat.

The degree of dissection of the leaves is very variable and whereas some plants may have markedly dissected leaves, others are undissected or with few lobes. George Taylor (1934 Monograph) was unaware of forms with undissected leaves. It seems to me that this requires further investigation for plants from central Nepal (particularly the Marsyandi Valley) are of this type whereas those from the eastern Himalaya have finely dissected leaves in all the recorded samples.

Whatever their source, *M. bella* has proved very difficult – a great pity as this is a real gem of a plant. The first seed sent to Britain were dispatched by King in 1888 (the year of its discovery) from Sikkim. Since then there have been quite a few collections, but few have resulted in flowering plants. According to accounts seeds germinate reasonably well but it is difficult to get large enough plants by the autumn that will survive the winter. Older plants are prey to severe frosts and the expanding shoots vulnerable to the ravages of slugs. Plants are slow growing and often take four or more years to come into flower.

Such treasures as *M. bella* are bound to attract the grower who thrives on the challenge of growing to perfection a plant considered by many to be almost impossible to grow. The horticultural world is full of such challenging plants and, in most instances, someone will eventually master the cultivation of each. As far as *M. bella* is concerned I can do no better than refer readers to James Cobb's detailed analysis of its cultivation as outlined in his book *Meconopsis*. I have never tried growing this charmer myself and leave it to those who have the time, patience and necessary skills.

Meconopsis betonicifolia Franch. [Pl. 38–39]
(Syn. *Cathcartia betonicifolia* (Franch.) Prain; *Meconopsis baileyi* Prain; *M. betonicifolia* var. *baileyi* (Prain) Edwards)
HIMALAYAN BLUE POPPY

A perennial, sometimes monocarpic, with erect stems to 1.6 m (5 ft). The leaves are oblong, to 15 cm (6 in) long, coarsely toothed and with a distinctive truncated or somewhat heart-shaped base, the basal and lower stem leaves stalked, the upper half-clasping the stem, the upper three to four often in a close whorl (at least on the main stem) where the flowers stalks arise; all leaves covered by a scattering of rusty-coloured bristles. The flowers are sky blue to rose-lavender, 7.5–10 cm (3–4 in) across, nodding to facing sideways, few, mostly on the upper half of the plant, each borne on long bristly stalks up to 15 cm (6 in) long, though often less. The broad oval to almost rounded petals are most often four in number but sometimes five or six, often somewhat frilled or wavy and spreading widely apart to expose the prominent boss of golden-yellow anthers terminating white filaments. The oblong capsule splits by four to seven valves in the upper third and is densely bristly.

M. betonicifolia is native to the eastern Himalaya, from south-eastern Tibet (Xizang) and Upper Burma, northwards to north-western Yunnan, where it inhabits woodland, ravines and moist alpine meadows and stream margins or scrub, between 3,120 and 4,000 m (10,200–13,100 ft) altitude.

This, the commonest of the blue poppies grown in gardens, is a superb plant and worth every possible attention. Its discovery is credited to the French missionary and collector Père Delavay who found it in north-western Yunnan in 1886. Fragmentary specimens collected by Colonel Bailey from the neighbouring region of south-eastern Tibet were described by Prain in 1915 as *M. baileyi*. Prain did not connect his specimens with Franchet's *M. betonicifolia*. In the summer of 1924 Frank Kingdon-Ward, one of the most intrepid of plant-hunters, collected further and far more complete material, at the same time introducing the species into cultivation under the name *M. baileyi*. It was only later that Otto Stapf and then George Taylor realised the affinity of *M. betonicifolia* and *M. baileyi* and the fact that they represented in all probability geographical variants of a single species. The main difference is in the far more densely bristly fruit-capsule of plants from south-eastern Tibet – it is this form that is in cultivation today.

Established names often take many years to disappear and despite the fact that the correct name for this poppy is *M. betonicifolia* it can still be found in some catalogues as *M. baileyi* or Bailey's Blue Poppy.

The species is unlikely to be confused in gardens with any other except perhaps *M. grandis*. The leaves of the latter are generally larger with a distinctly tapered base and the flowers rather more substantial, the petals more cupped and less frilled. Furthermore, the fruit-capsules of *M. grandis* are long and slimmer, with or without bristles, but never as densely so as in *M. betonicifolia*.

The main confusion in gardens between these two closely allied species lies in the fact that many plants sold as *M. grandis* are in fact *M. betonicifolia*. If unsure, simply check the leaf-bases of plants – if they are tapered they are probably *M. grandis*, if somewhat heart-shaped or truncated, *M. betonicifolia*. In reality the latter sets copious seed in an average year, whereas the former rarely sets much in cultivation so that seedlings of *M. grandis* are always scarce.

M. betonicifolia varies in cultivation from a biennial to a perennial. Even when perennial it seldom survives for more than four or five years in my experience. However, it is so easy from seed, or relatively easy, that it is usually simple to ensure a supply of plants. The leaves die away completely in the late autumn, so it is wise to mark the position of plants with care less they be dug up by mistake. One of the joys of this species is to watch the new shoots arise, rusty-haired and fresh, in the spring, sometimes flushed with purple.

In the best forms the flowers are a clear sky blue, sometimes with the merest hint of lavender. Other forms are a darker blue tinged with purple. However, there is little doubt that plants grown on acid soils produce the best blue flowers, but, despite this, it is well worth seeking out a good coloured strain in the first instance.

It used to be said that this lovely species could only be grown in the cooler, moisture parts of Britain, but provided there is ample moisture in the soil and some shade from fierce sun then this simply is not so. In my Suffolk garden in a region of Britain becoming notorious for its summer droughts I can grow *M. betonicifolia* satisfactorily, not in large patches as they can in the north and west of the country, but in more modest groups. Soil preparation requires more care with plenty of added leaf-mould and compost and diligent watering during dry summer periods. I prefer to plant them in a semi-shaded position where the dappled light sets them off against other woodland novelties. The only disadvantage is that, even with much care and attention, when the air is very dry little seed is set and the plump seed pods sometimes prove to be quite empty. However, one sight of the first blue petals bursting from the flowerbuds makes every effort worthwhile.

When selecting plants from a nursery, pick healthy, vigorous-looking plants, particularly those with several side shoots – these are more likely to prove to be properly perennial. Weakly plants and those with a single shoot at the end of the growing season are likely to prove to be moncarpic and although they will flower well enough they will almost certainly die after fruiting.

Seed sown in very early spring probably ensures the best means of increase. Avoid sowing too thickly as the delicate seedlings are notorious for damping off at this vulnerable stage. Prick out as soon as they are large enough to handle and grow on as fast as possible to help ensure vigorous plants more likely to be perennial. Plant out in late summer to allow them enough time to become established before they enter winter dormancy. Seed or divisions from known polycarpic (fully perennial) forms are more likely to be long-lasting in the garden.

Seed can be sown in the late summer and autumn from freshly gathered seeds. This certainly gives a good germination but seedlings then need to be overwintered in a glasshouse or frame and unless you are very skilled some losses must be expected.

There are various forms of *M. betonicifolia* available: 'Branklyn'* and Harlow Carr Strain are both fine blue selections; var. *alba* [**Pl. 40**] has white flowers which are attractive in their own right but scarcely with beauty of the best blues, however, this is a plant worth having in a collection.

M. betonicifolia hybridises in cultivation with a number of other species. Of these by far the finest hybrids are those involving *M. grandis* as the other parent. These go under the general name of *M.* × *sheldonii* [**Pl. 61**]. The best of these are magnificent plants of great substance and long-lived in gardens given the right condition. The cross has been made a number of times; the original was raised by W.G. Sheldon in 1934 at Oxted, Surrey and this original cross is still in cultivation today and bears striking flowers of greenish-blue. The hybrids are generally sterile and need to be propagated by division or the removal of lateral shoots. The best (which have probably involved different

---

* Sometimes regarded as a form of *M.* × *sheldonii*. It should not be confused with *M. grandis* 'Branklyn' (see p. 106).

1. *Chelidonium majus*

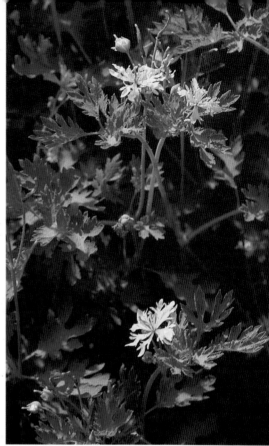

2. *Chelidonium majus* 'Flore Pieno'

3. *Chelidonium majus var. laciniatus*

4. *Dicranostigma lactucoides*

5. *Eomecon chionanthum*

6. *Glaucium corniculatum*

7. *Glaucium flavum*

8. *Glaucium flavum* var. *fulvum*

9. *Glaucium grandiflorum*

10. *Hylomecon japonicum*

11. *Macleaya microcarpa*

12. *Sanguinaria canadensis* 'Plena'

13. *Stylophorum diphyllum*

14. *Stylophorum lasiocarpum*

15. *Dendromecon harfordii*

16. *Dendromecon harfordii*

17. *Dendromecon rigida*

18. *Eschscholzia californica* in Snell Valley, Napa County, California

19. *Eschscholzia californica*

20. *Eschscholzia californica,* Riverside County

21. *Eschscholzia californica,* cultivar trials, Sahin, Zaden, Netherlands

22. *Eschscholzia californica* 'Milky White' and 'Purple Robe'

23. *Eschscholzia caespitosa,* Tolumne County, California

25. *Eschscholzia lemmonii*

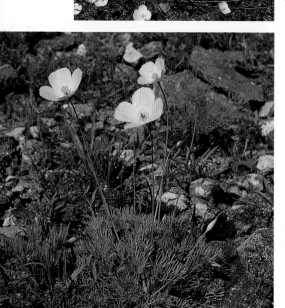

24. *Eschscholzia glyptosperma,* Kingston Range, California

26. *Eschscholzia lobbii,*
Butte County, California

28. *Argemone mexicana*

27. *Eschscholzia parishii,* Kingston
Range, California

29. *Argemone munita,* Kern County,
California

30. *Argemone munita*

31. *Argemone ochroleuca*

32. *Argemone platyceras*

33. *Canbya candida*, Riverside County, California

34. *Cathcartia villosa*

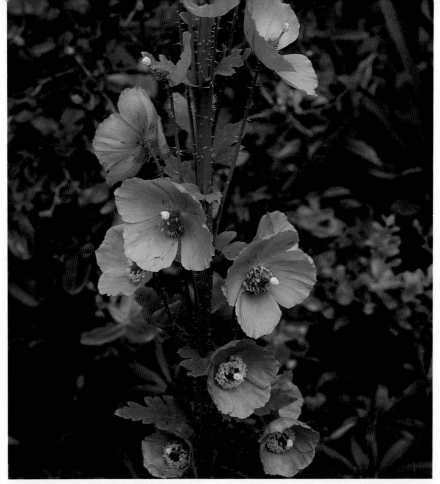

35. *Meconopsis aculeata* × *latifolia*

36. *Meconopsis* × *beamishii*

37. *Meconopsis bella*

38. *Meconopsis betonicifolia*

39. *Meconopsis betonicifolia*

41. *Meconopsis cambrica*

40. *Meconopsis betonicifolia* 'Alba'

42. *Meconopsis cambrica* 'Aurantiaca'

43. *Meconopsis cambrica* 'Aurantiaca'

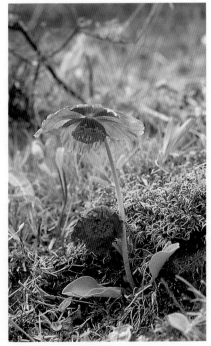

44. *Meconopsis delavayi*, Lijiang,
Yunnan, China

45. *Meconopsis delavayi*, Lijiang,
Yunnan, China

46. *Meconopsis dhwojii*　　　　**47.** *Meconopsis grandis*　　　　**48.** *Meconopsis grandis* form

49. *Meconopsis grandis* GS600

50. *Meconopsis horridula,* Upper Marsyandyi Valley, Central Nepal

51. *Meconopsis horridula* – a Chinese form in cultivation

52. *Meconopsis horridula,* Lijiang, Yunnan, China

53. *Meconopsis integrifolia,* Dai-cai-ba, north-western Yunnan, China

54. *Meconopsis latifolia*

55. *Meconopsis napaulensis*, leaf-rosette

56. *Meconopsis napaulensis*

57. *Meconopsis napaulensis*

58. *Meconopsis napaulensis × paniculata*

59. *Meconopsis paniculata*, leaf-rosette, Bumthang Valley, Bhutan

60. *Meconopsis punicea*

61. *Meconopsis × sheldonii* – a pale form of this variable cross

62. *Meconopsis* × *sheldonii* 'Slieve Donard' PG 96

63. *Meconopsis superba*

65. *Papaver alpinum* 'Summer Breeze'

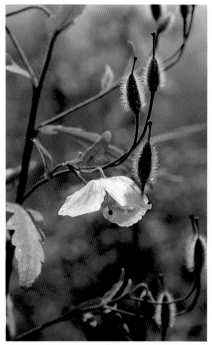

64. *Meconopsis wallichii,* Ghunsa Khola, eastern Nepal

66. *Papaver apulum*

67. *Papaver atlanticum*

68. *Papaver burseri*

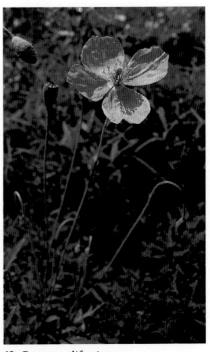

69. *Papaver californicum*

70. *Papaver commutatum* 'Ladybird'

71. *Papaver glaucum*

72. *Papaver lateritium*

73. *Papaver lateritium* 'Fireball'

74. *Papaver miyabeanum*

75. *Papaver nudicaule*

76. *Papaver orientale*

77. *Papaver orientale* 'Cedric's Pink'

78. *Papaver orientale* 'Cedric's Pink'

80. *Papaver orientale* 'Goliath' in a
cottage garden border

79. *Papaver orientale* 'Cedric's Pink' and
'Mrs Perry'

81. *Papaver orientale* 'Goliath'

82. *Papaver pavoninum*

83. *Papaver rhaeticum,* near
Barcelonette, French Alps

84. *Papaver rhaeticum* in cultivation

85. *Papaver rhoeas,* Long Melford, Suffolk, England

86. *Papaver rhoeas,* Long Melford,
    Suffolk, England

87. *Papaver rhoeas*

88. *Papaver rhoeas,* dark form from northern Cyprus

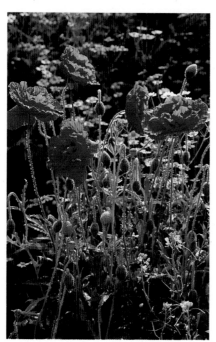

89. *Papaver rhoeas* – double-flowered form found in the wild, Suffolk, England

90. *Papaver rhoeas* – Shirley Poppy types

91. *Papaver rupifragum*

92. *Papaver somniferum*

93. *Papaver somniferum*

94. *Papaver somniferum*

95. *Papaver somniferum* – trials of peony-flowered cultivars at Sahin, Zaden, Netherlands

98. *Papaver somniferum* 'White Cloud'

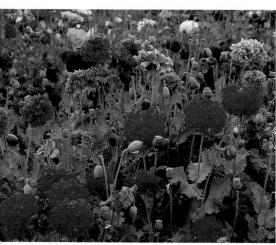

96. *Papaver somniferum* – trials of peony-flowered cultivars at Sahin, Zaden, Netherlands

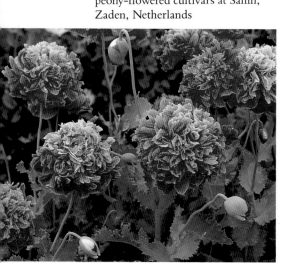

97. *Papaver somniferum* 'Salmon Peony'

99. *Papaver somniferum* – unnamed double red form

100. *Papaver spicatum*

101. *Papaver triniifolium*

102. *Roemeria refracta*

103. *Romneya trichocalyx*

104. *Romneya trichocalyx*

105. *Stylomecon heterophylla*

106. *Stylomecon heterophylla*

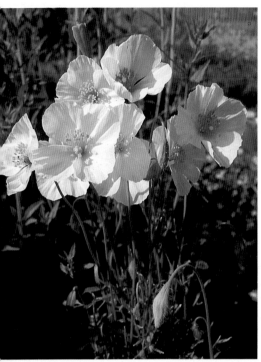

107. *Stylomecon heterophylla* 'White Satin'

108. *Meconella californica*

109. *Platystemon californicus,* Bear Valley, Colusa County, California

110. *Platystemon californicus,* Bear Valley, Coiusa County, California

111. *Platystemon californicus* – in cultivation

112. *Hypecoum imberbe,* north-eastern Cyprus

114. *Pteridophyllum racemosum*

113. *Hypecoum trilobum,* near Samarkand, Uzbekistan

forms of *M. grandis*) have various cultivar names: 'Slieve Donard' (*M. grandis* 'Prain's Variety') [**Pl. 62**] is particularly fine with rich deep blue flowers; 'Crewdson Hybrids' are somewhat paler with more delicate narrower petals, but equally effective; 'Aberchalder Form' is a pale flowered *M. × sheldonii*; 'Ormswell' is similar to ordinary *M. × sheldonii* but rarely available; 'Kingsbarns Hybrids' are fine plants of *M. × sheldonii* persuasion and the result of an unusual plant of this hybrid that produced viable seed – they are vigorous hybrids that lend themselves to vegetative propagation; 'Miss Dickson' – a rare and lovely white form.

Other hybrids include:

M. × auriculata (*M. aculeata* × *M. betonicifolia*) – not in cultivation today.
M. × coxiana (*M. betonicifolia* × *M. violacea*) – not in cultivation today.
M. × musgravei (*M. betonicifolia* × *M. superba*) – apparently fertile but not in cultivation today. It would be a very fine plant!
M. × sarsonii (*M. betonicifolia* × *M. integrifolia*). A fine fertile hybrid which can be properly perennial or monocarpic. Plants bear glorious clear sulphur-yellow flowers in the best forms. The character of the plant and leaves most closely resmemble *M. betonicifolia* and it can be propagated in a similar way. The similar looking *M. × beamishii* (*M. betonicifolia* × *M. grandis*) can be distinguished by its tapered leaf-bases and generally five to eight (not four) petals per flower.

Meconopsis cambrica (L.) Vig. [Pl. 41]
(Syn. *Papaver cambricum* L.; *P. luteum* Lam.; *Argemone cambrica* (L.) Desportes; *Cerastites cambrica* (L.) Gray; *Stylophorum cambricum* (L.) Spreng.)
WELSH POPPY

This widely grown, easy and readily available species is familiar in many gardens where it is often dismissed as weedy and unruly. However to my mind it is a real charmer, easy and free-flowering, with a good deal of elegance and poise. If it does seed around rather too freely, does this matter from a plant that is so willing to put on a show from spring until the first frosts of autumn? A shady path lined with Welsh poppies or a woodland glade where the flowers glow amongst the dappled shade is a sight worth seeing in any garden.

Plants are fully perennial, forming lax basal tufts of rather pale green leaves. These are up to 20 cm (8 in) long and variously divided into a number of lobed divisions, hairless or somewhat hairy. The flowering stems are branched and carry several leaves in the lower part, the flowers carried aloft on slender stalks up to 60 cm (24 in) tall, often less. The flowers are yellow in the ordinary form, 5–6.5 cm (2–2½ in) across and more or less erect, each with four broad petals. The narrow-oval fruit capsule has a distinctive short style, is completely smooth and opens by four to seven valves in the upper quarter.

M. cambrica is a native of western Europe, inhabiting damp and shaded rocky, wooded and grassy places in western Ireland, Wales, south-west

England, west France and north-west Spain, below 600 m (2,000 ft) altitude usually. It is widely naturalised in other parts of the region.

The Welsh poppy has been cultivated for many centuries and the wood engraving in Parkinson (1640), under the name *Argemone Cambro-Britanica lutea*, is the earliest known drawing of the species.

M. cambrica holds an isolated position in the genus, both geographically and taxonomically (see p. 83).

This species present little problems in cultivation. Seed and plants are readily available. As they come so easily from seed there is no need to resort to vegetative propagation, unless to preserve a particularly fine form. They include:

'Aurantiaca' – a form with orange flowers. [**Pl. 42–43**]
'Flore Pleno Aurantiaca' – the orange counterpart of 'Flore Pleno'.
'Flore Pleno' – a form with double yellow flowers.
'Frances Perry' – an unusual single-flowered variant with deep orange-crimson flowers which, for some reason, is seldon seen in gardens.

All these different forms will self-sow readily in gardens, especially in moist shaded areas. In dry gardens they can be more difficult to establish initially. It is wise to keep them away from rock and scree gardens to prevent them becoming a problem from seeding around.

Meconopsis chelidonifolia Bur. & Franch.

This is one of the more modest species in the genus but one that has a quiet charm all of its own. It has been likened, as its names infers, to the Greater Celandine, *Chelidonium majus*, and although larger in all its parts it does bear a superficial resemblance to that species.

M. chelidonifolia is a perennial with a branching root-system and perennating by means of lateral buds that slowly form a spreading mat. The leaves, which are rather pale green, are pinnately cut into a number of broad, lobed segments, bristly on both surfaces; the upper leaves tend to be trifoliate or trilobed whilst the basal have generally withered by flowering time. The slender branched stems rise to 90 cm (36 in) sometimes more, and are erect and arched, with the flowers borne on very slender stalks from the upper leaf-axils. The flowers are clear yellow, rather small, 2.5–3.5 cm (1–1½ in) across, and generally half-nodding. There are four rounded somewhat overlapping petals. The fruit-capsule is elliptical in outline, smooth or somewhat bristly, and splitting by five or six valves close to the apex.

This dainty species inhabits mountain thickets in western Sichuan at an altitude of 1,875–2,800 m (6,150–9,200 ft).

It was first collected by Faber on Mt. Omei in 1887, though it was not described until 1891. Seed was introduced to Britain by Ernest Henry Wilson who probably collected it close to Tatsien-lu (now Kangding), an area of great interest to plant collectors in the earlier part of the present century.

M. chelidonifolia (often misspelled '*chelonidifolia*') has never been very popular in cultivation. Admittedly it has none of the brashness of some of its cousins but, at the same time, this is a species with a delicate charm and its little dancing flowers enliven a woodland setting. Indeed this is a species for the woodland glade, in a damp humusy pocket. It has few demands, although best if the slender stems are allowed to grow through the branches of low shrubs, otherwise they tend, in my experience, to fall over.

Vegetative buds are produced at the upper leaf-axils, a feature this species shares in common only with one other – *M. lyrata*. These can be detached and can be easily grown on to produce new plants. Division of the parent plant in early spring is another means of increase, but seed is rarely produced in cultivation and plants are considered to be self-sterile.

Meconopsis delavayi (Franch.) Franch. ex Prain   [Pl. 44–45]
(Syn. *Cathcartia delavayi* Franch.)

In a genus of big and bold species with flamboyant blooms it is pleasant to be able to observe some of the smaller, but equally attractive, members. *M. delavayi* certainly fits into this latter category. The species is a perennial with a rootstock that is branched above, each short branch terminating in a small leaf-cluster that dies away during the winter months to leave a resting bud. The leaves are bluish-green, quite thick, elliptical or diamond-shaped, untoothed and abruptly narrowed below into a short stalk, not more than 15 cm (6 in) in length overall, generally less, with scattered bristles on both surfaces. The solitary flowers are a deep violet-purple and nod on leafless scapes up to 25 cm (10 in) tall. There are generally four somewhat over-lapping petals, oval to rounded, making the flower 4–6 cm (1⅗–2⅖ in) across when fully opened; anthers orange, hidden beneath the 'umbrella' of petals. The fruit-capsule is narrow oblong, smooth, and opens at the apex by three to five short valves.

M. delavayi has a very limited distribution in the wild, being restricted to north-western Yunnan, primarily to the eastern-flanks of the limestone Lijiang (Lichiang) mountains, at altitudes between 3,100 and 4,375 m (10,200–14,350 ft). In this region it inhabits primarily sloping west meadows, but can also sometimes be found on damp limestone screes.

This little gem of a species was first discovered in 1884 by Père Delavay who did most of the early collecting, and made many new discoveries, in the Lijiang mountains of north-western Yunnan. Delavay collected little live material and it was left to George Forrest a few years later to introduce many of these new species into cultivation. Forrest in fact collected seed in the wild in 1911 and it first flowered in cultivation two years later at the Royal Botanic Garden, Edinburgh. However, *M. delavayi* has never proved easy in cultivation and has always been very rare. Yet one person, R.D. Trotter of Brin House, Inverness, a fine and skilled plantsman, mastered its cultivation at one time, discovering that broken pieces of root inserted upright in a sand bed will eventually produce both roots and shoots. This is best undertaken in spring using a propagator or, at least, a little bottom heat. Despite this discovery this much cherished species has remained extremely rare in cultivation. Recent expeditions to north-western Yunnan have introduced fresh live material and some seed, so it is to be hoped that it may now stand a better chance in cultivation.

M. delavayi is a dainty delight to see in the wild; it created a feeling of great excitement when I travelled in the Lijiang region, an area so remote in the days of Delavay and Forrest, but now reasonably accessible. In the company of two fine plantsmen, Tony Schilling and Ron McBeath, I climbed over these mountain slopes for several weeks in the spring of 1987. High above the Lijiang Valley are steep, almost inaccessible mountain slopes covered with fir and rhododendron that give way in places on the eastern flanks to steep grassy meadows interspersed by scree. These meadows are full of treasures: corydalis, lilies, globe-flowers and primulas. Amongst all the joys we found scattered colonies of *M. delavayi*. Many plants bore one or two flowers, though up to eight were counted. The colour ranges from pale violet-blue to violet-purple, the flowers nodding hairbell-like or with the petals spreading widely apart to reveal the stamens beneath. The joy and excitement in seeing such a splendid little beauty so perfect in the wild can never be matched in cultivation. Long may it thrive on those distant slopes.

Meconopsis dhwojii G. Taylor   [Pl. 46]

An attractive monocarpic species with an evergreen rosette of long-stalked, pinnately-lobed leaves. The leaves, up to 30 cm (12 in) long, have rather distant lobes and are covered in bristles that have a distinctive purplish-black base; the upper stem leaves are similar, but smaller and short-stalked. The flowering stem, which can reach 1 m (3 ft) tall, is erect and branched in the upper two thirds, the lower branches bearing several flowers but the uppermost with a solitary bloom. The flowers are a soft pale yellow and cupped, often half-nodding and 4–5 cm (1–2 in) across, with four rounded petals. The anthers are orange-yellow and the stigma greenish or yellowish. The fruit-capsule is more or less elliptical in outline, covered in dense spreading bristles and splitting by five or six valves just below the styled apex.

M. dhwojii was discovered in eastern Nepal by Lall Dhwoj, an officer in the Royal Nepal Army. It is recorded to grow at altitudes of 3,850–5,625 m (12,600–18,450 ft), although the upper altitudinal limits seems too high to me for this type of species.

In cultivation *M. dhwojii* first flowered in 1932 and it has been in cultivation ever since. Plants are particularly pleasing in flower with both some lower and upper flowers opening simultaneously. The evergreen leaf-rosettes are very distinctive and are unlikely to be confused with any other species; they generally come into bloom in their second or third seasons from seed.

There seems to be no great difficulty with this species in cultivation. It comes readily from seed and grows away quite quickly if pricked out at an early stage and kept well fed and watered. Like its brethren it thrives in a rich humusy soil and has thrived with me on several occasions in a peat border, although in my Suffolk garden I cannot boast those more robust and splendid specimens one sees in northern gardens. However, it does seem to over-winter with ease and comes into flower in early summer, apparently unhindered by late spring frosts. *M. dhwojii* finds it closest ally in *M. gracilipes*, which is restricted to an area of central Nepal to the west. It differs primarily in the coarser, less finely cut, foliage without purple blotches at the base of the spines. However, despite this the two species are very closely related and further research may show them to be extremes of the same species. Both species hybridise in gardens with *M. napaulensis*.

M. × ramsdeniorum (*M. dhwojii* × *M. nepaulensis*) is a poor thing with yellow or pink flowers of little merit, and fortunately sterile. Why such hybrids are continuously named is a mystery to me; let us leave well alone and name only the very best and those proven in gardens. Many such hybrids disappear as quickly as they first appeared. To avoid such horrors in the garden the answer is not to grow species close together that hybridise freely. One can always grow a few plants in isolation purely to produce pure seed and then the species will not be threatened by hybrid progeny.

M. dhwojii is a fine species and worth a place in any garden. Being undoubtedly easier and hardier than some it well deserves a wider following.

Meconopsis discigera Prain

This species is at once distinguished from all other species of *Meconopsis* in cultivation by the disk-like process surmounting the ovary and fruit-capsules. The species is a rather slow-growing monocarpic perennial with a long thickened taproot and a dense basal rosette or leaves, the lower of which gradually withering but persisting so that the live rosette sits on top of a felted mat of dried leaves; each leaf is up to 18 cm (7 in) long, oblong to wedge-shaped, often with a three-lobed apex, although sometimes entire, the surface, particularly the petiole and midrib, densely covered in golden bristles. The bracts are similar to the leaves, but smaller and usually entire. The rather stout flowering stem rises to about 40 cm (16 in), occasionally taller, and is both grooved and bristly and carries up to 20 flowers in a narrow

Leaf and fruit capsule of *Meconopsis discigera*

raceme. The flowers vary considerably in colour from yellow, pale to mid-blue, to purple, crimson, red or whitish, each 6–8 cm (2½–3 in) across, and with their short stalks running down the stem (decurrent) in a distinctive manner; petals four; stamens with rather dark filaments and yellow anthers. The fruit–capsule, 3–4 cm (1⅕–1⅗ in) long, is oblong, ribbed and bristly and with a distinctive lobed stylar disk at the apex; this disk overlaps the top of the ovary and has a toothed margin; when ripe the capsule splits just below the stylar disk by 6–10 short valves.

M. discigera is a native of the high Himalaya from central Nepal to southern Tibet (Xizang), Sikkim and Bhutan, being a plant of rocky places, cliffs, screes and moraines between 3,500 and 4,100 m (11,500–13,450 ft) altitude; flowering from June to August. M. discigera holds a rather isolated position within the genus. The only other species with a disk-like process on top of the ovary is the little known M. torquata, which comes from an area of Tibet close to Lhasa. It differs primarily by its narrower leaves, in the petals being hairy on the outer surface and in the absence of a style.

M. discigera cannot be regarded as being in any way easy in cultivation. Over the years seed has been introduced on many occasions, although few have succeeded in flowering it well and many plants fail even to get to the flowering stage. The handsome leaf-rosette gradually increases in size (a mature rosette may be 20 cm (8 in) across) and as the lower leaves die they persist so that after several years they form a dense mat at the base of the plant, a very characteristic feature of the plant in the wild. I have seen it on several occasions in the Nepalese Himalaya and it always seems to inhabit the bleakest and most inhospitable places where most meconopsis would never dream of growing. This is almost certainly why it is so difficult to grow. Such plants are like a magnet to growers and as long as seed is available there will be those who will want to attempt to raise them. The successful cultivation of such species is not just to rear them from seed to flowering but to maintain them in cultivation thereafter. Monocarpic species such as M. discigera provide a special challenge, for unless viable seed is set all is lost.

In the autumn the rosette dies back to a large resting bud and in cultivation this is very prone to rotting during the winter. It is clear that plants must be protected from excessive moisture in the autumn and winter but, at the same time, allowed plenty of moisture during the growing season. A very well-drained soil is an absolutely essential ingredient, after all the species is basically a plant of high screes and moraines. However, getting the conditions just right in cultivation is a tricky balancing act that will test the most skilled of growers.

Meconopsis gracilipes G. Tayl.

This pretty monocarpic species is closely related to *M. dhwojii* (see under that species for general remarks). The beautiful yellow, half-nodding, cup-shaped flowers are perfectly formed. A rare plant in cultivation, flowering in three to four years from seed usually. *M. gracilipes* is endemic to the Khorlak region of central Nepal.

Meconopsis grandis Prain   [Pl. 47–48]

A stout tufted perennial rising to 60 cm (24 in) in flower, occasionally more; stems stiff and erect, usually bristly. The leaves vary from lanceolate to elliptical or oblong and are irregularly toothed along the margin, sometimes rather obscurely so, with the base of the leaf-blade tapering into the petiole; the upper leaves are unstalked, generally smaller, but more coarsely toothed;

Flower, leaf and fruit of *Meconopsis grandis* (left) and *M. betonicifolia* (right)

all leaves covered by scattered rusty-coloured bristles, the upper three to five leaves aggregated into a whorl where the flower stalks arise. Flowers rich blue, purple or wine-purple or occasionally pinkish-purple, 8–12 cm (3–5 in) across, borne on slender, bristly stalks 12–15 cm (5–6 in) long but elongating to twice or three times that length in fruit, mostly borne on the upper half of the plant, but occasionally solitary from a basal scape. The almost rounded to broadly oval petals are commonly four in number, occasionally more, and form a wide cup-shape, the individual petals scarcely frilled. The yellow anther are borne on the ends of whitish filaments. The narrow-oblong capsule may be smooth or somewhat bristly and dehisces by four to six valves in the upper quarter.

All the eulogies poured onto *M. betonicifolia* could well be used on *M. grandis*. In many ways this is the blue poppy *par excellence*. The intense blues of the finest forms, the substance and poise of the cupped flowers and the perennial nature of this stunning plant are enough to assure it a place in our gardens. That is not so often seen in our gardens is perhaps due to frequent confusion in the trade with *M. betonicifolia* and the fact that the best forms seldom set seed in cultivation. This apart though, *M. grandis* is fairly easy to propagate from side shoots or careful divisions and if the resultant plants are a little costly to purchase does it matter for such a superb poppy.

M. grandis was first discovered in the Jongri district of Sikkim in the eastern Himalaya in the 1880s. Since then its distribution has been extended to cover Nepal, east of Mt. Everest, and parts of south-eastern Tibet (Xizang) as well as Bhutan. In these regions it is a plant of open woodland, alpine thickets, rocky stream margins and yak pastures at altitudes of 3,120–5,300 m (10,200–17,400 ft).

Its introduction into cultivation is generally attributed to David Prain and it first flowered at the Edinburgh Botanic Garden in 1895. Since then *M. grandis* has been re-collected in the wild on a number of occasions; notably Ludlow and Sherriff in Bhutan and south-eastern Tibet and by various collectors, in more recent times, in eastern Nepal. I have seen it on several occasions in Nepal at altitude and nearly always close to, or in association with, yak pasturage, where it can form substantial colonies.

M. grandis is quite variable in the wild. In Nepal, for instance, the fruit-capsules can be longer, narrower and often smooth, whereas elsewhere they are shorter and often bristly. Flower colour also varies from the eastern forms, which appear to be the best blues, to those in the west, particularly Nepal, which can be a less pleasing and decidedly inferior wine-purple.

This species is closely allied to *M. betonicifolia* and the differences between these two species is outlined on p. 95. Like *M. betonicifolia* plants die down in the late autumn leaving withered leaves on the soil surface. The thick leaf buds that arise in the spring vary from pale green to purple and are densely best with pale straw- or rust-coloured hairs. The blueness of the flowers is quite breathtaking in the finest forms, but as with the other blue poppies the precise colour can be greatly affected by soil alkalinity, even when all other conditions suit the plants. More alkalinity turns the best blues more pinkish or purple; the more acid the soil the better the blue.

Plants thrive best in good rich, moist, humusy soil and are unable to tolerate too much dry hot weather. Even so, I have always managed to grow one or two forms in my dry Suffolk garden in a carefully prepared bed, though they do not increase as vigorously as in other more favoured northern gardens. Nonetheless I have managed to propagate several plants simply by shaving off side shoot with a sharp kitchen knife without having to resort to disturbing the parent plant; with care such shoots will come away with some root attached and if carefully nurtured in a shaded frame will quickly become established.

Plants are very hardy and there is no need for winter protection except possibly in early spring when severe frost may threaten the newly emerged shoots.

As with *M. betonicifolia* weak seedlings may throw all their effort into flowering in the second season and die quickly afterwards. Removal of the flowering stem (often a single-flowered scape in small plants) may sometimes force the plant into producing several side shoots for future years, but this is a bit of a gamble and does not always work, unfortunately.

It is wise to check named forms with some care as they sometimes are not what they proport to be. In any case if plants are raised from seed (some forms set some seed!) then they are unlikely to be exactly like their parents. Divisions of the finest forms is therefore the best means of assuring a succession of good plants. Some seedlings may well prove to be hybrids with *M. betonicifolia*, *M.* × *sheldonii* (p. 96).

Cultivars include:

'Alba' – a fine white form but rare in cultivation and generally difficult to acquire.

'Betty Sherriff's Dream Poppy' – one of the very best forms of *M. grandis* with deep blue, half-nodding flowers borne on strong elegant, dark stems. The discovery of this plant is well worth relating. It concerns the wife of George Sherriff (of Ludlow and Sherriff fame). I can do no better than quote from the account in the book *A Quest of Flowers* (1975) by Harold R. Fletcher, a former Reguis Keeper of the Royal Botanic Garden, Edinburgh: 'Their collecting at Shurigbe (in Bhutan) began auspiciously – and in somewhat surprising circumstances. During the night of 25 May, Betty Sherriff dreamt that her husband walked into her tent, stood beside her campbed and gave her instructions for collecting on the following day. She was to seek out below the camp a small track leading to the Me La; to follow the track for about three miles until it bifurcated; to take the right hand fork and walk some 300 yards to a large rock mass. On the far side of the rock she would see a poppy she hadn't found before. As Sherriff left the tent he turned, shook a finger at her and said: "Be sure you go." The next morning at their usual time 5.00 a.m. breakfast, when she told Hicks and Tsongpen the substance of her dream, they were both sceptical and urged her to keep to their original plan . . . But the dream and the shaking finger had been so vivid and the instructions so clear and positive, that she determined to leave the rest of the party to seek her dream poppy. She has no problems; she found the track easily; she found the mass of rock easily and behind it she found a glorious blue meconopsis which she hadn't collected before, a form of *Meconopsis grandis*. Hicks at first unbelieving, returned to the spot the next day and took several photographs'.

In the autumn Hicks in fact returned to collect seed. In cultivation this gem became known in Scottish gardens as 'Betty's Dream Poppy'.

'Branklyn' – originally a selection made from GS600 with exceptionally large, good blue flowers. It is doubtful whether plants now under this name are the same as those originally selected at Branklyn Gardens by Perth, Scotland. Distinct from *M. betonicifolia* 'Branklyn' (see p. 96).

GS600 – a selection from a collection of George Sherriff, this is a very fine blue of exceptional quality, but rarely sets seed. Well worth acquiring. [**Pl. 49**]

'Keillour Crimson' – plants originally from a Nepalese collection with dark purple flowers, scarcely the eye-catcher of the blue forms. Rarely available.

'Miss Jebbs' – a dwarf variant with deep blue flowers. Occasionally available.

'Nepal Form' – vigorous plants with bluish-purple flowers. Occasionally sets seed, but plants generally available in the trade.

'Prain's Form' (sometimes called 'Keillour Crimson') – deep purple flowers.

'Sikkim Form' – a rather unsatisfactory form with pale leaves and rather small purplish-blue flowers. It has one advantage in being early in flower.

Meconopsis horridula Hook.f. & Th.   [**Pl. 50–52**]
(Syn. *M. racemosa* Maxim; *M. rudis* (Prain) Prain; *M. prattii* (Prain) Prain; *M. prainiana* Kingdon-Ward; *M. calciphila* Kingdon-Ward).
PRICKLY BLUE POPPY

A monocarpic plant with a narrow, somewhat fleshy taproot; height of flowering plant very variable from 20 cm (18 in) to 1 m (3 ft). Basal leaves in an untidy rosette, elliptical to narrow-oblong up to 25 cm (10 in) long,

Fruit capsules of *Meconopsis horridula*

narrowed below into the petiole, the margin untoothed to somewhat lobed, the whole surface beset with sharp yellowish or purplish spines, which often arise from a purple, wart-like base; upper leaves smaller and bract-like. Stems and pedicels spiny. The flowers are pale to deep blue, lilac-blue or reddish-blue, very occasionally white, 5–7.5 cm (2–3 in), facing sideways or half-nodding, each borne on a stalk up to 22 cm (9 in) long, though often less. The oval to almost rounded petals vary in number from four to eight and overlap one another, forming a broad cup shape. The dark-stalked stamens bear greyish-black anthers that are coated with yellow or orange-yellow pollen. The narrow-oblong capsule has a long apical style and is covered in spreading, often straw-coloured, spines.

Few species of *Meconopsis* show quite as much variation as this one. In its finest forms *M. horridula* is a plant of the utmost beauty and if it were only perennial and not monocarpic it would, assuredly, be more often seen in our gardens. I have seen it in the wild on a number of occasions both in the Nepalese Himalaya and in Yunnan, China. It is one of those plants I would walk a thousand miles just to see, for it has few rivals amongst all the many races of poppies. In the wild this species inhabits the highest and remotest regions, rocky and grassy meadows, screes and low rhododendron or willow scrub, at altitudes from 3,100 to 5,940 m (10,200–19,500 ft), being found in some localities almost at the upper altitudinal limit for vegetation; in fact the 1921 Mt Everest Expedition collected it at 19,000 ft (5,790 m). At such high elevations plants are reduced and very dwarf, sometimes only 10–15 cm (4–6 in) tall in flower. *M. horridula* is distributed from western Nepal eastwards throughout the central and eastern Himalaya, to south-eastern Tibet (Xizang) and western China (western Kansu to Sichuan and north-western Yunnan).

M. horridula is particularly variable in leaf characteristics and in the details of the inflorescence. The leaves may have smooth or scalloped margins, the surface sparsely to densely bristly with the bristles sometimes arising from a blackish wart-like base. All the flowers may arise on leafless scapes from the leaf- rosette or, at the other extreme, may all be disposed along a long narrow raceme; every condition between these extremes can be observed in the wild. With so much possible variation it is not perhaps surprising that the species should have acquired a rather cumbersome synonymy over the years. George Taylor in his monograph, recognising the polymorphic character of this species, placed all the names under Hooker and Thomson's *M. horridula*.

The great variation found within *M. horridula* makes it of particular interest to gardeners and there exists in cultivation various forms – those with scapose or racemose flowers and petal colours from the purest blues to purple, mauve or lilac. It has to be said that the most beautiful forms of all come from high elevations in Nepal, with purple-blotched, thickly spiny, leaves and glorious mid-blue flowers with translucent petals, but these are by no means easy in cultivation. Most of the strains in cultivation hail from early collections from China and Tibet – the species has been in cultivation from about 1904.

In cultivation the leaf-rosettes die down to a resting bud in the autumn, this terminating a solitary taproot. Plants normally flower in their second or third season from seed. Plants are easily raised from seed, indeed this is a species that will self-sow in favoured gardens and some even find it a pest, seeding around too freely – I am not among those fortunate few. Seedlings are rather few-leaved and untidy with floppy leaves that are easily damaged by strong winds. However, this is essentially a robust species that tolerates pricking out and planting out without too many problems. In the racemose forms it is the uppermost flowers that open first and, by the time the lower have come into bloom, those at the top are well into fruit.

In cultivation pure strains of *M. horridula* do exist, though most seed will produce a range of colours. If saving ones own seed it is wise to ruthlessly rogue out poor colour forms, especially those with pale pinky or mauve hues. The white form sometimes seen is of little consequence, indeed it is a rather dull little plant. There is no doubt that the blue forms have the greatest appeal. Plants can be grown in semi-shaded or sunny positions in open woodland or amongst low shrubs such as rhododendrons, or alternatively in the rock or scree garden. As with most meconopsis, plants respond to a rich, moist, humusy soil and a group planting is a far more satisfactory way of seeing this plant in the garden.

A yellow-flowered form was found by Ludlow, Sherriff and Taylor in Bhutan in 1938, however this is not in cultivation, but would be an interesting novelty if it were to be refound one day.

Other names sometimes found in association with *M. horridula* include *M. racemosa*, occasionally seen in horticultural literature. The name was based on specimens collected by Przewalski in Kansu in the 1870s and described by Maximowicz. The plant is typical of many Chinese forms of *M. horridula* in having a well developed, rather narrow racemose inflorescence. There are five to eight petals per flower but such numbers can be found virtually throughout the range of the species. *M. prattii* was based on specimens collected by Pratt near Tatsien-lu (now Kangding), Sichuan (originally described by Prain, in fact, as a variety of *M. sinuata*). Various features of the leaves, the amount of spines and the colour of the flower parts were used to separate this plant, but later research (by Taylor) showed that none of these characters would stand up when the full range of available herbarium material was studied. Likewise *M. rudis*, originally collected by Père Delavay in the Lijiang mountains of north-west Yunnan. In isolation these seem distinct enough but not when viewed overall.

M. horridula can be grown in virtually any garden, provided it is given enough moisture during the growing season. Winter protection is unnecessary and plants can generally be relied upon to produce a good crop of seed. Soil alkalinity does not appear to affect flower colour and good blues can be seen growing on alkaline soils. In my own garden, because it is generally a very dry garden during the summer months, it grows best in a semi-shaded peat border where it can be more carefully attended to. Care has to be taken to give plants enough space for crowding together with other plants can spoil the look and symmetry of the plants when they come into flower.

Meconopsis integrifolia (Maxim.) Franch. [Pl. 53]

(Syn. *Cathcartia integrifolia* Maxim.; *Meconopsis pseudointegrifolia* Prain;
M. souliei (Fedde) Farrer; *M. brevistyla* Hort. ex Prain)
FARRER'S LAMPSHADE POPPY, YELLOW POPPYWORT

This is a very variable monocarpic species forming a solitary leaf-rossette
which produces a stout flowering stem up to 90 cm (36 in) tall, though often
far less. The whole plant is covered in pale straw-coloured or golden hairs.
The leaves are narrow and untoothed, elliptical, tapered at the base into the
long petiole, pointed or rounded at the apex, up to 37 cm (15 in) in length
overall; although hairy when young, by maturity the leaves have sometimes
lost most of their hairs. From two to ten, erect to nodding, flowers are borne
on rather erect branches from the upper leaves, or solitary from basal scapes;
they are large, to 22 cm (9 in) across, ranging in colour from pale yellow to
rich lemon. The overlapping rounded or oval petals number from six to eight
in most flowers. There is a huge central boss of orange or yellow stamens.
The oblong fruit-capsule is covered in dense golden hairs and splits by four
to nine valves in the upper third.

M. integrifolia was first discovered by Przewalski in Kansu in 1872 and has
subsequently been collected on numerous occasions. Its known distribution
extends from north-eastern Tibet (Xizang) to western Kansu and Sichuan
south into north-western Yunnan. In these remote regions it inhabits moist
grassy meadows and screes, often steeply sloping, as well as open scrub of
rhododendron or willow, at altitudes from 2,800 to 5,300 m (9,200–17,400 ft).

This is the largest flowered species of meconopsis which, in its best forms,
is a very beautiful plant. It is very variable in stature, flower shape and size
in the wild. Early authors attempted to split off a number of variants as
separate species or varieties but none proved particularly satisfactory. George
Taylor in his monograph of 1934 acknowledges this variability but includes
all of them under a single species – others have tended to accept this view.

I have twice seen it in the wild, both times in Yunnan. The first time in
the heart of George Forrest country on the steep grassy slopes of the eastern
side of the Lijiang (Lichiang) mountains where it grew in scattered colonies.
The plants were moderately tall, to 60 cm (24 in), with rather small globular,
pale yellow flowers, erect or semi-erect, a form very similar to some of those
in cultivation. On the second occasion, in the company of Tony Schilling,
Ron McBeath and David Chamberlain, we ventured to the west onto high
marshy meadows surrounded by rhododendron woodland on the Mekong-
Yangtse Divide, close to Li-ti-ping. Beneath some spindly willows grew a
simply breathtaking colony of *M. integrifolia*, robust plants 1 m (3 ft) tall,
perhaps taller, with huge deep lemon-yellow flowers, exquisite in their
nodding poise and in their spreading oval petals. This was a plant to cherish
and one of those moments 'in the field' that long lingers in the memory. I
have to say that this magnificent plant, the like of which I have never seen
in cultivation, is very difficult to equate with the smaller, globular flowers
generally encountered. However, species can be remarkably variable and
without a good deal of research into distribution and variability one must be
content to accept a single species view for the time being.

M. integrifolia is not particularly difficult in cultivation and generally sets copious seed, which is easy to germinate, indeed it has been known to self-sow in favoured gardens. It responds to a rich diet and a deep humusy soil and will succumb to summer drought if not carefully attended. The symmetrical rosettes have a charm of their own and in the second year appear as an expanding tuft flushed with pink and yellow or bluish-grey. Plants generally bloom in their second season but may linger on to the following year. The form most widely available is of moderate size with globular, erect, good yellow flowers, which may open fairly close to the ground, but in the best specimens up to ten are borne on a plant 40–60 cm (16–24 in) tall. More recent introductions, especially those of Cox and Hutchinson in 1986, offer a more spectacular form with a taller habit and larger more spreading flowers, which open after the danger of frost has past, a problem that can afflict some forms in cultivation, leading to distorted buds and foliage.

Seedlings grow on fast and, if well fed, will be large enough to plant out by mid-summer, allowing them to become well established before winter.

White-flowered forms have been reported from the wild but these are not in cultivation.

M. × beamishii (*M. integrifolia* × *M. grandis*) [**Pl. 36**] is a hybrid similar to *M. × sarsonii* (p. 97) but with leaves like *M. grandis* tapered below into the stalk. The large, rather elegant flowers are cream, sometimes flushed or streaked with purple in the centre – these make it an easy plant to identify in the garden. The hybrid is fertile and resultant seedlings may be perennial or monocarpic. Good forms of the former can be increased by vegetative division of the parent plant. This is a hybrid which well deserves a large following in gardens – the colour and size of the flowers make it an interesting addition to any collection.

M. × finlayorum (*M. intregrifolia* × *M. quintuplinervia*) is a rather improbable cross that has produced a plant of great charm, with neat fresh-green leaf-rosettes and nodding bell-shaped flowers of ivory, sometimes with a greenish-yellow tinge towards the base. This was a deliberate hybrid raised by Mike and Polly Stone of Fort Augustus and given the name 'Askival Ivory'. The finest forms are dwarf and fully perennial.

Meconopsis latifolia (Prain) Prain   [Pl. 54]
(Syn. *M. sinuata* var. *latifolia* Prain)

This species is regarded by some as the most beautiful in the group characterised by *M. horridula* and *M. aculeata*. It is perhaps most closely allied to the latter, being distinguished by having less cut leaves and softer spines on the leaves and stems. Flowering plants may reach 1 m (3 ft) or slightly more in height, being leafy in the lower half, but with a pyramidal raceme of flowers above. The leaves, up to 20 cm (8 in) long, are oblong in outline with regular rounded teeth along the margin, or pinnately lobed, sparsely covered on both surfaces by rather soft, straw-coloured spines; the lower leaves are stalked, the upper ones unstalked. The flowers, which are often described as being duck-egg blue to mid-blue, are 4.5–6 cm (2–2½ in) across and cup-shaped, with orange-yellow anthers and a purple stigma. There are four, almost rounded petals, which have a satiny appearance, being slightly wavy along the margin. The oblong fruit-capsule is covered with dense spreading spines and splits by the four to seven valves close to the styled apex.

M. *latifolia* is endemic to northern Kashmir in the western Himalaya, where it reportedly inhabits rock crevices and screes at 3,125–4,060 m (10,500–13,300 ft) altitude.

It is perhaps surprising that this species is not more common in gardens. The exquisite flowers, which are longer lasting than its brethren, would excite any gardener. Plants are quite easy to raise from seed and providing plants are not allowed to dry out during summer or winter, kept free from waterlogging in winter and given the usual rich humusy, moisture-retentive soil in sun or partial shade there should be no real problem. Plants normally flower in their second season, emerging after the winter as an expanding silvery rosette, flushed with pink. At this time they may be prone to both severe frost and marauding slugs so some protection may be required. It is certainly wise to put some form of slug bait down before growth begins as plants can be ruined before any damage is noticed.

M. *latifolia* has been in cultivation since 1908, having been introduced by Appleton from Kashmir. Appleton stated that it 'is always found growing in the crevices of rocks or among loose piles of stone debris on stone slides and below cliffs. It likes the full sun, and springs to full growth after the snow melts off, while the ground is still damp!' White-flowered forms have been seen in the wild but are not in cultivation.

A beautiful poppy well deserving a greater audience and worth every bit of attention that can be lavished on it.

Putative hybrids with M. *aculeata* [**Pl. 35**] have been reported from gardens. These are often fine plants distinguished by the greater degree of dissection of the leaves and in the stigmas that may often be green or whitish, rather than purple. Another reported hybrid is M. *grandis* × M. *latifolia* (Farrer, *The English Rock Garden*) which seems rather improbable and cannot be proved as the plant in question is no longer in cultivation.

Meconopsis napaulensis DC   [**Pl. 55–57**]
(Syn. *Papaver paniculatum* D. Don, in part; *Stylophorum nepalense* (DC.) Spreng., in part)
SATIN POPPY

One of the most robust species, which is widely grown in gardens. Plants are monocarpic forming a large leaf-rosette 60 cm (24 in) across, sometimes larger, in the first two or three years. The solitary stiff, erect, leafy stem rises to 2.5 m (8 ft) tall in vigorous specimens and is covered like the leaves in dense rather bristly hairs. The leaves may be as much as 50 cm (20 in) long, oval to elliptical and pinnately lobed, less deeply so in the upper half, below tapering into the petiole. The bowl-shaped flowers are pendent or semi-pendent, red or purple, occasionally white, 60–80 mm (2½–3 in) across, borne in a narrow panicle with the lower branches with several (up

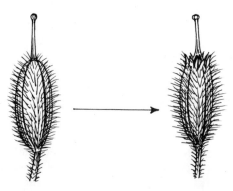

Fruit capsule of *Meconopsis napaulensis*, before and after dehiscence

to 17) flowers, the upper often with a solitary flower. The broad-oval, almost rounded petals are usually four in number. The stamens bear orange or yellowish anthers. Stigma greenish. The oblong capsules are covered in dense adpressed or slightly spreading bristles and dehisce by five to eight short valves close to the apex.

M. napaulensis is distributed from the central Nepalese Himalaya eastwards into south-eastern Tibet and western China, north as far as western Sichuan, where it inhabits woodland margins, scrub, stream banks and alpine meadows between 2,800 and 5,300 m (9,200–17,400 ft), altitude.

Although plants are widely available under this name few can be said to be the pure species. The very ease of cultivating *M. napaulensis* and its close cousins *M. paniculata* and *M. regia* has rather led to their downfall for they hybridise readily with one another. The result is a hybrid mixture, often of uncertain parentage [**Pl. 58**]. Admittedly many of these plants are very handsome and exciting to look at and indeed are fine and easy garden plants well worth growing. To find the species proper one must look to recent introductions, particularly from Nepal. To keep these 'pure' in the garden they must be isolated from their promiscuous cousins.

M. regia can be distinguished by its unlobed, finely toothed leaves and yellow flowers with a noticeable purplish-black stigma. *M. paniculata* also bears yellow flowers, which have a 'give away' soft-purple (not greenish) stigma amongst the boss of yellow anthers. The leaves are similar to those of *M. napaulensis* but have a rather hoary appearance, rather than the more rusty hairs characteristic of the latter.

The winter rosettes of these three species are quite magnificent and when interplanted can produce a most striking effect. Those of *M. napaulensis* often take on a golden hue during the winter as do the larger, silkier leaf-rosettes of *M. regia*. Those of *M. paniculata* are, on the other hand, greyer or greener. These rosettes can be so striking when well grown that it can be a disappointment to loose them to flowers in due course. Only then do the rosette leaves begin to die away.

Producing robust plants requires a moist, well-manured place and regular feeds during the growing season. In flower poor forms should be ruthlessly discarded; select only the best coloured and most floriferous. In any event it is more than likely that plants will not be pure species but hybrids between those already referred to and will produce a range of flower colours from yellow through to orange, apricot and various shades of pink and red, some even being bicoloured. A few of the red and yellow forms appear to breed true to form, but most do not. Many are first rate garden plants to arrest the sight and astound the neighbours. Evidence of parental genes often reveal themselves over several generations. Thus large yellow flowers and undissected leaves reveal *M. regia*, hoary dissected leaves and smaller yellow flower *M. paniculata* and pink and red flowers and dissected, rusty-haired leaves *M. napaulensis*. Purists will, however, want to seek out the genuine *M. napaulensis*. Unfortunately for them, hybrids are fully fertile and set copious seed and, in favoured gardens, will sow themselves around.

Whether true *M. napaulensis* or hybrid, the evergreen rosettes may take as many as six years to reach flowering size – three to four is a good average.

As with *M. paniculata*, *M. regia* and their allies, some winter protection – cloches or frame-lights placed overhead – will prevent crown-rot in some plants, but care must be taken that the rosettes do not desiccate beneath their protective cover, especially during dry but windy winter weather.

Readers will have perhaps noticed a complete lack of any mention of blue-flowers in relation to *M. napaulensis*. Such colour turns up in *M. wallichii*. George Taylor lumped this plant into *M. napaulensis* in his monograph, but there is no doubt in my mind that it is a distinct species native to central and east Nepal and Sikkim (p. 124) where I have been lucky enough to observe it on a number of occasions.

Besides the hybrid complex between *M. napaulensis*, *M. paniculata* and *M. regia*, *M. napaulensis*, or what often purports to be that species, also hybridises with *M. dhwojii*, but the offspring are disappointing in most respects and fortunately sterile.

Meconopsis paniculata (D. Don) Prain   [Pl. 59]
(Syn. *Papaver paniculatum* D. Don, in part; *Meconopsis himalayansis* Hort. ex Hay)

This robust monocarpic species is generally likened to a yellow-flowered *M. napaulensis* and, indeed, the two species have much in common. In cultivation much confusion as to the true identity of these species and *M. regia* has resulted from their habit of freely hybridising with one another (p. 112). To gardeners what matters most is not species purity but a good growable and attractive plant – the hybrids certainly conform to these criteria well. Most plants sold as *M. paniculata* are in fact of hybrid origin. These are likely to have yellow flowers and dissected leaves, but not necessarily so.

True *M. paniculata* is common in the eastern Himalaya from eastern Nepal through to Assam, inhabiting open pine and fir forest, shrub, stream banks and, at higher altitudes, sloping grassy meadows, often below ridge tops. The altitudinal range is 3,125–4,500 m (11,900–14,800 ft).

In leaf plants form handsome spreading rosettes, the individual leaves oval to elliptical, pinnately lobed in the lower half, less so above, the surface

Fruit capsule of *Meconopsis paniculata*, before and after dehiscence

covered in dense hoary hairs giving them a somewhat greyish appearance. The stems rise to 2 m (7 ft), more in particularly strong specimens. The yellow flowers, 50–70 mm (2–3 in) across, are similarly shaped to both *M. napaulensis* and *M. regia* but rather smaller, the petals always rather pale yellow and, if anything, more spreading. The anthers are yellow or orange-yellow and the stigma is characteristically pale purple – an extremely useful diagnostic character lost in yellow-flowered hybrids with *M. napaulensis*.

Much has been made of the differences in the hairs of *M. napaulensis* and *M. paniculata*; those of the later being apparently more branched, especially near the leaf-surface. However, this character is difficult to observe and in all probability quite variable and, for most purposes, it is better to concentrate on better visual characters such as dissected leaves, smaller yellow flowers and purple stigma.

M. paniculata, like *M. napaulensis* and their hybrids, is easy from seed and worth growing as much for its winter rosettes as for its towering inflorescences. A sheltered site is advisable as a strong wind at peak flowering can bruise plants or, worse still, knock them over. Gaps in shrubs borders or a woodland setting are ideal. A slope or hollow where one can look down upon them, or view them from below, can be most effective.

Meconopsis punicea Maxim.   [Pl. 60]
(Syn. *Cathcartia punicea* Maxim.)
RED POPPYWORT

One of the more astonishing species in the genus. It is a perennial, occasionally monocarpic, with a solitary taproot crowded by one or several leaf tufts. The leaves, up to 35 cm (14 in) long, are loosely tufted, oval to elliptical and untoothed, tapering below into the petiole and clothed all over in long, rather soft hairs giving the tufts an overall greyish or somewhat ginger colouration. The solitary nodding flowers arise on slender elegant scapes to 60 cm (24 in) long, sometimes longer, and are a vivid crimson and

Meconopsis punicea

shaped like a flaired skirt. The satiny petals, generally four (five to six in cultivated plants), are large, to 10 cm (4 in) long, and elliptical in outline. There are numerous stamens hidden within the 'skirt' which bear dull purplish-brown pollen. The fruits are held on erect stalks, the oblong capsules bristly, although sometimes almost smooth.

M. *punicea* is unique in the brilliant red of its flowers and its streamer like petals. Reginald Farrer in *The English Rock Garden* (1918) raves about it: '*M. punicea* is well known by now with its thick tufts of loose long oval-pointed hairy green leaves, and its abundant uprising single stems, at the top of each of which comes a single large flower of a royal crimson, so floppy and tired in texture that each blossom hangs on its stem like a blood-stained flag hoisted to its pole on a windless dull day in late autumn?'

Farrer gives the impression that this breathtaking species is easy and common in cultivation. However, this has never been so and early introductions all died out. In 1986 the species was reintroduced by Peter Cox and Peter Hutchinson from Sichuan in China but unfortunately, despite growing and flowering well since, it gives every impression of eventually going the same way as the earlier introductions.

M. punicea first came into cultivation as the result of a special six week journey undertaken in 1903 by Ernest Henry Wilson (Chinese Wilson) in north-western Sichuan (Szechwan) especially to gather seed. Although plants successfully flowered the following year in Britain the plant soon died out. It was reintroduced subsequently by Joseph Rock from south-western Kansu and others and remained in cultivation until the 1960s. The most recent Cox and Hutchinson collections have been more widely distributed.

The species was discovered by Przewalski in north-eastern Tibet in 1884. Since then its known distribution has extended to cover north-western Sichuan and southern Kansu, where it inhabits damp grassy meadows and slopes and bushy places often dominated by rhododendrons, generally in partial shade and at altitudes of 2,960–4,500 m (9,700–14,800 ft).

There is no doubt that this is a sensational species worth every effort to maintain in cultivation. Like the best of the blue poppies it is a real 'eye-catcher' in the garden. A strong plant will carry a close cluster of leaf-tufts up to 30 cm (12 in) across and as many as 20 flowers at a time. The leaves wither away in the late autumn and unfortunately the crowded shoots borne on the end of a solitary taproot make it an impossible plant to divide, even if one had the courage to do so. If the taproot dies then the whole plant perishes.

M. punicea is not particularly difficult to grow. Its decline in cultivation is due more to the apparent low fertility of plants and to the fact that home-produced seed is often difficult to germinate. However, like many a fine but 'difficult' plant there are always those who will succeed wonderfully well with it and their dedication is to our benefit.

James Cobb (*Meconopsis*, 1989) points out that it is essential to sow fresh seed of this species in the autumn. It will then overwinter to germinate the following spring. Spring-sown seed will skip a year to germinate a year after sowing. Seedlings grown on and fed regularly will soon form substantial plants that will mostly flower the following year – a few may even put up a flower or two in their first season.

Plants are fully hardy and will thrive equally well in the usual moist rich loamy soils that meconopsis appear to demand, whether it be in sun or partial shade. I have not tried it in my own dry garden but at the Royal Botanic Gardens, Kew, which is scarcely less dry, it thrived recently for two or three years in a semi-woodland setting. However, even there plants were hardly as vigorous and impressive as those shown off to perfection in more northerly gardens.

Plants come into flower in late June and will often continue to produce a flower or two well into the autumn. Some plants will behave monocarpically, others will hopefully survive for several years, though it is doubtful whether plants are ever very long-lived, at least in cultivation. A group grown close together should ensure some seed set, unless the summer is exceptionally dry. Although hardy, during very severe winter weather a protective covering of straw or bracken may be advisable.

One glance of the red petals bursting from the flower buds makes this species worth every effort. It can be guaranteed to create the deepest envy amongst gardening friends.

Recent reports from friends suggest that this glorious species can be found in the wild in a rare white-flowered form, but such a plant has never cropped up in cultivation.

Meconopsis quintuplinervia Regel
(Syn. *M. punicea* var. *limprichtii* Fedde)
HAREBELL POPPY

Reginald Farrer (*The English Rock Garden*) held this very pretty little plant in high esteem: '. . . it is certain that despite its place in the group, *M. quintuplinervia* is going to prove the sounder perennial of the family; and so beautiful that the senses ache at the multitudinous loveliness of its myriad dancing lavender butterflies over the rolling Alps of the Da-Tung chain (Northern Kansu – Tibet). In fact, in well-bred exquisiteness of charm, it stands, in my eyes, supreme over its race'.

M. *quintuplinervia* is a hardy deciduous perennial that forms a slow-creeping low mat by means of a fibrous root-system and branching underground stems. The lax leaf-rosettes, like exotic plantains, appear in the spring from below-ground resting buds. The simple leaves are up to 25 cm (10 in) in length, oval to lanceolate with an untoothed margin and covered above and beneath with straw- or rust-coloured bristles. The slender flower scapes, which are also bristly, rise to 60 cm (24 in) tall, though as little as 15-20 cm (6–8 in) in some forms and carry a solitary nodding bell. The flowers are a delicate shade of pale lavender, each four-petalled, occasionally five or six, and slightly more than 3 cm (1⅕ in) long in the finest forms. The stamens have pale lavender or whitish filaments and usually pale yellow anthers. The fruit-capsule is more or less elliptical in outline, bristly and splitting by three to six valves towards the top.

M. *quintuplinervia* was first discovered by Przewalski in Kansu, China, in 1880 and described from cultivated plants (sent as seed by him) at St. Petersburg. Introduction to British gardens came through seed sent home in 1914 and 1915 by Reginald Farrer. Since then it has proved to be a fine and rather amenable garden plant, particularly in cooler and damper regions. The perennial creeping habit makes it an easy plant to propagate and most plants are reproduced by division. In fact seed is rarely produced in any quantity and, even then, it is not very easy to germinate.

M. *quintuplinervia* thrives in any good garden soil, providing it is moist and a generous helping of compost or leaf-mould has been added. Since it is perennial an annual dressing of fresh compost, applied before growth commences, should suffice to keep plants vigorous. Even then, it pays to remove clumps and split them up every three or four years, taking the opportunity at the same time to reinvigorate the soil in the bed. It is a super plant for the peat bed or rock garden, given a sheltered site and a sunny or semi-shaded (but not too shaded) aspect. Plants commence flowering in May and will continue on and off all summer provided that dead flowers are removed. Of the forms in cultivation the more compact one, known as 'Kaye's Compact Form', is the finest and easiest. It forms compact, close, leaf-rosettes and is not too tall in flower.

Although generally hardy, some protection during the winter may be necessary, if only to keep cats, birds and squirrels from disturbing the bed and uncovering vulnerable resting buds.

In the wild *M. quintuplinervia* is found from north-eastern Tibet (Xizang) to southern Kansu, north-western Sichuan, eastwards to Shensi, at an altitudinal range of 2,340–4,375 m (7,700–14,350 ft). It is primarily a plant of alpine meadows and open rhododendron scrub. According to Farrer it is abundant in some areas and forms a 'shimmering surf'.

Despite being considered an easy species to cultivate, this charming little species can prove temperamental in some gardens. In my experience it dislikes too much disturbance and being 'bullied' by coarser more robust plants in the border. This is a species well worth nurturing and its dainty harebell flowers will delight all who see it.

M. quintuplinervia finds its closest ally in the red-flowered *M. punicea* which, apart from flower colour and size, can be distinguished by its monocarpic non-spreading habit.

The species hybridises with *M. punicea* (*M.* × *cookei*), a rare plant of little merit, with muddy purple flowers borne on lanky scapes.

The hybrid with *M. integrifolia* is described on p. 110.

Hybrids with *M. cambrica* and *M. betonicifolia* have also been recorded.

M. quintuplinervia is clearly of great potential in breeding programmes – especially in helping to establish a great range of fully perennial forms for gardens. The charm of the species though would be difficult to match, indeed it would be sad to see the species swamped by coarser and easier hybrids as has happened in so many other genera in cultivation.

Meconopsis regia G. Taylor

This grand species is one of the most handsome and stately in the genus. Its bold leaf-rosettes and towering panicles of yellow-flowers are as eye-catching as any. *M. regia* comes in that close group of similar species exemplified by *M. napaulensis*, *M. paniculata* and *M. wallichii*. It can be distinguished from these species at once by its unlobed, finely toothed, leaf-margins.

M. regia, like its allies, is a monocarpic species. The leaf-rosettes, which may last for up to four years before flowering, are extremely attractive and can (in vigorous specimens) reach more than 1 m (3 ft) across, the whole being covered in soft gold hairs. The leaves, up to 60 cm (24 in) in length, are elliptical, narrowed at the base into a short broad petiole, the margin finely and evenly serrated; the upper stem leaves are similar but smaller and unstalked. The stout flowering stems often reaches 2 m (6½ ft) in height, the upper flowers solitary on long stalks, the lower several (up to 10 in a good specimen) on a common stalk from the upper leaf-axils. The flowers are a soft pure yellow, deeply cupped, 9–13 cm (3½–5 in) across, and with four

Leaves of *Meconopsis regia* (left), *M. paniculata* (centre) and *M. napaulensis* (right)

(occasionally six) overlapping petals. The boss of stamens are yellow with orange-yellow anthers and the style and stigma are a characteristic purple-black. The fruit-capsule is more or less oblong in outline and densely covered by closely packed, non-spreading, bristles, and splitting by 7–12 valves close to the apex.

This exciting species is confined to the central Nepalese Himalaya at an altitude of 3,750–4,680 m (12,300–15,400 ft), where it is a plant of open scrub, meadows and stream banks.

M. regia was described by George Taylor in 1929 and first flowered in cultivation in 1931. Since then it has been reintroduced as seed on a number of occasions. The collections of Stainton, Sykes and Williams from Nepal in the 1950s introduced red-flowered forms that possessed the leaf-characters and dark style colour of the type. There were said to be two forms of the yellow type in cultivation at that time that differed in vigour and rosette colouration. In the more vigorous the leaf-rosettes were golden with hairs, in the less vigorous form the hairs gave the rosettes a silkier more silvery appearance.

Today it is a shame that *M. regia* is so rare in our gardens, indeed the true species may not be with us any longer. The problem is not to do with difficulty in cultivation but rather the reverse for it hybridises all too readily with its brethren, particularly *M. napaulensis* and *M. paniculata* – the result a hybrid swarm in which the parental characteristics have been swamped by their hybrid offspring. Many of these hybrids are very attractive and set abundant fertile seed so they thrive in cultivation. Genuine *M. regia* must be sought anew – its presence in gardens, if it still exists untainted, would be revealed by the uncut leaves and the relatively large flowers with a purple-black stigma.

There is some evidence that *M. regia* and *M. napaulensis* hybridise in the wild where the two species grow in close proximity to one another, but such revelations needs careful analysis in the field.

In the meantime we must enjoy the multitude of hybrids and await fresh introductions of seed from the wild.

Like other large-rosetted and monocarpic *Meconopsis* species, *M. regia* requires a rich humusy soil, plenty of moisture during the growing season and regular feeding. These are all greedy and require every encouragement to produce their large handsome rosettes and bold flowering panicles. Where plants have flourished for a number of years in the garden they often greatly impoverish the soil and it is then wise to move new plants onto a fresh site. These are plants for a sheltered site in sun or partial shade; a woodland setting is admirable, though so to is a wide space amongst tall shrubs.

Meconopsis sherriffii G. Taylor

This rare and little-known species was discovered by Frank Ludlow and George Sherriff in Bhutan in 1936. It is generally likened to a pink-flowered *M. integrifolia* and the two species are undoubtedly very closely related.

Plants differ often in that they may become properly perennial and multi-crowned, but the single taproot makes it very difficult to divide and, as little seed is ever produced, this has remained a rare species in cultivation and is rarely offered in catalogues or seed lists.

Seedlings need to be handled with great care but are scarcely as robust as those of *M. integrifolia*. Plants are best protected by a cloche or similar during the winter, and may flower in their second season. Flowers are solitary, borne on a long stem that is leafy in the lower half.

Young shoots and buds are susceptible to frost damage and care must be made to protect them as growth commences in the spring. Mature leaf-rosettes generally have a collar of persistent leaf-bases below the live leaves.

The discovery of this species is related by Harold Fletcher in *A Quest of Flowers* (1975): '. . . on this pass he [Ludlow] discovered a new poppy which

Ludlow thought was the gem of the whole 1936 collection – "rose pink like the first flush of dawn on the snows". Sherriff was rather more restrained in his enthusiasm; "came across a nice meconopsis which I do not know, and cannot make out from Taylor's book. The flowers are a pretty pinkish wine-red, one on a scape and I don't think more than two to a plant. Leaves basal and cauline, all very thickly covered with bristle". Dr George Taylor (now Sir George) appropriately named this beautiful poppy which grows no more than 8 inches high and carried 4 inch flowers with up to 8 petals'.

In the wild *M. sherriffii* inhabits screes and cliffs as well as alpine scrub, especially of dwarf rhododendrons, at altitudes of 4,200–4,600 m (13,800–15,100 ft). It flowers during June and July.

Meconopsis simplicifolia (D. Don) Walp.

(Syn. *Papaver simplicifolium* D. Don; *P.s.* var. *baileyi* Kingdon-Ward; *M. uniflora* Gumbleton; *Stylophorum simplicifolium* (D. Don) Spreng.)

Farrer (*The English Rock Garden*, 1928) regards this species as 'quite the most gorgeous of the single-bloomed Meconopsids, with big flowers of dazzling hue'. Certainly in its best forms this is a blue poppy that is a must in any collection.

M. simplicifolia finds its closest ally in *M. grandis*. The most obvious difference is in the scapose flowers of *M. simplicifolia* where all the leaves are confined to a basal tuft. However, there are other differences: the flowers have five to eight petals, instead of the usual four in most *M. grandis*, and the filaments are the same blue as the petals and not whitish.

M. simplicifolia is perennial, though sometimes monocarpic, and forms a rather dense rosette of leaves or, indeed, a number of close rosettes on top of the slender taproot. The leaves, which vary a great deal in size from plant to plant, are simple and undivided, lanceolate, up to 30 cm (12 in) in length, covered on both surfaces with golden or rather rusty-coloured bristly hairs; the leaf-stalk can be as long as the leaf-blade, the one tapering into the other. The solitary flowers, 6–10 cm (2½–4 in) across, arise on bristly scapes up to 60 cm (24 in) tall, though 30–45 cm (12–18 in) is more normal; they are semi-pendulous and vary in colour from pure pale blue to deep blue or purple. The five to eight petals are broadly oval. The fruit-capsule is narrow-oblong, smooth or with reflexed bristles, and splits by four to nine valves in the upper third.

This highly desirable species is found in the wild from central Nepal to south-eastern Tibet (Xizang) at high altitudes of 3,450–5,450 m (11,300–17,900 ft). In these regions it inhabits alpine meadows, rhododendron scrub, rocky places and screes.

In its best forms this is a highly desirable species. That it is not as common in cultivation as it should be is perhaps a result of the fact that it sets little seed, what is produced germinates poorly and the best forms tend towards being monocarpic. It is a point of irritation to gardeners that the easier perennial forms of this species are usually those with the poorest flowers, especially as regards shape and colour. The best forms are very fine with flowers of clear sky blue. However, there are others almost as desirable with good deeper blue flowers or purple, though be warned, some of the purple forms are very poor and a nasty muddy purple that even the compost heap might object to.

Seed should be treated in the same way as for *M. punicea*. Plants require a rich soil, full sun or half-sun, and are fine plants for the rock garden or scree, or alternatively a peat border providing it is not too moist during the winter months. Winter protection (a cloche or frame light) is necessary; unless one is particularly lucky some plants will rot off during the winter months.

Until recently there have been two forms in cultivation: a vigorous form with deep purplish-blue flowers that is properly perennial and a finer form with sky blue flowers that is, unfortunately, usually monocarpic. The latter form was introduced from south-eastern Tibet in 1913 by Col. Bailey and is generally referred to as 'Bailey's Form' (not to be confused with Bailey's Blue Poppy, *M. baileyi*, see *M. betonicifolia*, p. 94). However, the species in the more usual perennial, purple-flowered form was introduced considerably earlier, having been collected in 1848 in Sikkim during Joseph Dalton Hooker's famous journey in that region and written up so methodically in his *Himalayan Journals* of 1869. More recent collections of seed especially from Sikkim and Bhutan, have introduced other good forms into our gardens:

M. simplicifolia has been crossed with several other species.

M. × *hybrida* (*M. simplicifolia* × *M. grandis*) – perennial with flowers on basal scapes. First raised by F.C. Puddle at Bodnant in North Wales.

M. × *harleyana* (*M. simplicifolia* × *M. integrifolia* (syn. *M. simplicifolia* var. *eburnea*)) – a striking perennial hybrid with basal scapes and large cream-coloured flowers. It occurred by chance in the garden of Andrew Harley in Devonhall, Scotland. Probably no longer in cultivation. It was given the cultivar name 'Ivory Poppy'.

M. sherriffii × *M. simplicifolia* – a spontaneous hybrid between two fairly closely related species. The hybrid, which is perennial and certainly less temperamental than its parents, produces rather small flowers best described as muddy-pink. As it is a fertile hybrid it may have value in a breeding programme.

Meconopsis sinuata Prain

A poor relation of *M. latifolia* with few, rather small, blue to purple or violet flowers that reportedly open only one at a time. The leaves grow up to 17 cm (7 in) long and are oblong in outline, with an irregularly lobed margin and adorned by sparse bristly spines on both sides. The distinctive fruit pod is slender-oblong, with three or four valves in the top one third.

M. sinuata has been in cultivation but is no longer so. In gardens it appears to have no particular merits, being inferior in most respects to its brethren. However, new material and better forms may eventually be introduced to prove these statements wrong.

It is a native of the Himalaya, from central Nepal to eastern Bhutan, where it is stated to be a plant of alpine meadows at 3,750–4,400 m (12,300–14,400 ft).

Meconopsis superba King ex Prain   [Pl. 63]

This is another beautiful monocarpic species often likened to a white-flowered *M. regia*. In fact the two species are particularly closely related. The handsome leaf-rosettes may reach up to 90 cm (36 in) across in time and the leaves, like those of *M. regia*, are unlobed, but with a toothed margin. The evergreen rosettes have a silky and silvery appearance due to the presence of numerous closely appressed hairs. The leafy flowering stems rise to 2 m (7 ft) tall in the strongest specimens, with the upper flowers solitary but the lower with three to five flowers on short lateral branches, the whole forming a large panicle. The individual flowers are cup-shaped and nodding, 7–9 cm (3–4 in) across, pure white; petals four, occasionally six, rounded; stamens with white filaments and yellow anthers; stigma purple-black and very distinctive. The fruit-capsule is 4–6 cm (1⅗–2⅖ in) long, oblong in outline and covered in appressed hairs, opening eventually by 7–11 short valves close to the apex.

M. *superba* is restricted in the wild to western Bhutan, where it inhabits screes and dwarf scub at 4,100–4,250 m (13,450–13,900 ft) altitude, flowering from June to August.

Although originally recorded from Chumbi Region, Tibet, Grierson and Long (*Flora of Bhutan* 1(2), 1984) point out that *M. superba* appears to be endemic to western Bhutan and that the original locality was almost certainly in Bhutan and not Tibet.

In the wild plants appear to have simple racemose inflorescences, but in cultivation they are decidedly more paniculate.

The original plants first flowered in cultivation in Britain in 1927, although the origin of the introduction remains a mystery. Ludlow and Sherriff introduced further seed in 1933. *M. superba* can be cultivated in much the same way as *M. regia*. Plants usually take three to five years to come to maturity, although some may flower in their second season. Leaf-rosettes are prone to rotting in the winter and some losses must be expected, so it may be wise to cover them with large frame lights or cloches. Beware, however, that the protected plants do not become too dry during the winter otherwise they may well perish. Seedlings are very prone to damping off (like those of *M. betonicifolia*) and thin sowing and the use of fungicides may help prevent the loss of too many at this vulnerable stage in their life. Seeds are slow to germinate and young plants may not be large enough to plant out during their first season and may have to wait until the following year. Like the other evergreen rosette species, plants require ample moisture and generous mulches throughout the growing season. In addition the inflorescences, when they finally appear, emerge early and may be frosted unless they are protected in some way. This may be one reason why this extremely handsome species is not seen more often in our gardens. This is a pity for it is a very fine species and worth every effort that can be lavished upon it. There is no doubt that it responds best to cooler, more northerly gardens where the spring arrives late and there is at least some chance of a protective layer of snow during the winter months.

Meconopsis wallichii Hook. [Pl. 64]
(formerly included under *M. napaulensis*)

This is an evergreen, monocarpic species of the *M. napaulensis* persuasion. It differs primarily in its narrower, more dissected, yellowish-green leaves with remoter lobes, which are generally more bristly, by having rather smaller pale blue or purplish-blue flowers and by the small fruit-capsules that are adorned with spreading stiff bristles.

M. wallichii is a splendid plant. In cultivation and in the wild it flowers several weeks later than *M. napaulensis*, *M. paniculata* or *M. regia*. Indeed I have seen it still in flower in eastern Nepal as late as early September. In cultivation this is to its advantage as only the first (uppermost) flowers are likely to open whilst those of the other species (referred to above) are still in bloom and little hybridisation is likely to result. This can be circumvented easily by ignoring the upper fruits and collecting seed from the fruits of the later flowers, located on the lower lateral branches of the plant. Any hybrids generally produce unsatisfactory muddy blue and purples and are frequently sterile according to James Cobb (*Meconopsis*, 1989). The true species is a charmer and needs every encouragement.

In cultivation it is generally sold under the name *M. napaulensis* blue form or simply, 'Wallich's Form'. The blueness of its sky blue flowers is not affected by soil alkalinity.

In the wild this species inhabits open forest, scrubby slopes and stream margins at about 2,850–3,400 m (9,350–11,150 ft) altitude. I have seen it on several occasions on the high forested ridges overlooking the Tamur Valley in east Nepal. It has always struck me as a very elegant species with its arching stems, often fully 2 m (7 ft) tall, and in the purity of its transparent pale blue flowers and charming bristly fruit capsules. It grows in lush dank places where leeches abound during the monsoon but is always a total delight to come upon on those distant misty ridges.

INTERESTING SPECIES NO LONGER IN CULTIVATION
[not in the key]

Meconopsis forrestii Prain

Another species related to *M. horridula*. It can be easily identified by its racemose inflorescence (never with accompanying basal scapes) and the pale blue flowers concentrated on the upper half of the stem. In addition, the fruit-capsules are narrower, almost cylindrical and with scarcely any style. The flowers are rather small, being rarely more than 4 cm (2 in) across. The long narrow fruits are perhaps the most useful diagnostic feature of this species.

M. forrestii has been introduced into cultivation on a number of occasions. Seed was certainly collected by Forrest, Rock and more recently by the Sino-British Lijiang Expedition (SBLE). Plants are said to inhabit alpine meadow-land, but in the only situation that I have seen it in the wild (in the Lijiang Mountains of north-western Yunnan) it inhabited a coarse, rather moist scree. The altitudinal range of the species is 3,050–4,400 m (10,000–14,400 ft). Besides north-western Yunnan, *M. forrestii* also occurs in south-western Sichuan.

Early introductions failed to produce flowering plants and it is to be hoped that more recent seed collections will prove more successful.

Meconopsis henrici Bur. & Franch.

An interesting but little-known species of the *M. horridula* persuasion from China (south-western Sichuan to south-western Gansu) where it is a plant of high alpine pastures and dwarf scub at 3,600–4,500 m (11,800–14,800 ft) altitude. It can be distinguished by the stamen filaments, which are distinctly expanded towards the base. The flowers, which are described as deep violet or purple, are borne on basal scapes as in some forms of the variable *M. horridula* and both leaves and stems are covered in reddish-brown bristles.

Seed was introduced by E.H. Wilson in 1906 and later by both Reginald Farrer and Frank Kingdon-Ward. However, although flowering plants resulted the species failed to persist in cultivation.

The species is named in honour of Prince Henri d'Orleans who journeyed through China with Bonvalot in the 1880s. They discovered it growing in the region of Tatsien-lu (now Kangding), Sichuan (Szechwan) Province.

Meconopsis impedita Prain

Yet another species related to *M. horridula* and distinguished by its sparsely bristly leaves and narrower fruit-capsules. The flowers are all borne on basal scapes. The striking flowers have four to ten petals and are dark, being described as 'reddish-purple or dark-violet to almost black' and the anthers 'cream, orange, golden, or yellow'.

M. impedita has a range from Upper Burma northwards to north-western Yunnan and south-eastern Tibet (Xizang) where it is a plant of alpine meadows, screes and rocky slopes at 2,850–4,575 m (9,350–15,000 ft) altitude.

This desirable little species has been introduced a number of times but has never persisted in cultivation for long. Forrest, Kingdon-Ward and Rock all collected seed early in the century but to no avail and we must await new introductions. Like others of this *M. horridula* persuasion, seedlings appear to be difficult to over-winter and bring successfully to maturity. Most are plants of rather drier mountains but with most of the rainfall in the summer and with a protective layer of snow during the winter months. The leaves die down to a resting bud during the winter.

Meconopsis lancifolia (Franch.) Franch. ex Prain.

An extremely variable species, again of the *M. horridula* type which, despite a number of seed introductions earlier in the century (primarily by George Forrest), has never succeeded in cultivation. In the best forms this is a plant with deep rich purple flowers. The flowers can be scapose or borne in a distinct raceme in which the flowers are bractless or the lower have leaf-like bracts (in *M. horridula* the lower flowers are borne in the axils of leaves or minute, scale-like bracts). In some forms of *M. lancifolia* the leaves may be pinnately lobed, although most have entire or undulate leaves.

M. lancifolia has a wide range from Upper Burma to Yunnan, south-eastern Tibet (Xizang) and south-western Gansu. It is a plant primarily of limestone formations, inhabiting screes and rocky meadows and cliffs, often in rather shady places and at 3,350–4,880 m (11,000–16,000 ft) altitude.

George Taylor in *An Account of the Genus Meconopsis* (1934) discusses the variability of this interesting little species, stressing the fact that although some elements have one distinguishing feature or other, they are joined together by such a network or variability that separation into distinct species is practically impossible. Such minutiae need not concern us here. Suffice it to say that among the best forms of this species there are some highly desirable little alpine poppies.

Meconopsis longipetiolata G. Taylor ex Hay

A rare and little known relative of *M. paniculata* not apparently in cultivation at the present time, although seed sometimes circulates under this name. However, it has been in cultivation in the past as the original description of the species (1932) was based on a live plant from seed of Nepalese origin.

M. longipetiolata is a slighter plant than *M. paniculata* and besides differing in fine details of the leaf pubescence has, as the specific name implies, long leaf-stalks (petioles). The pale yellow flowers are relatively small, being 3–5 cm (1⅕–2 in) across. The stigma is green.

Although certainly a native to the Nepalese Himalaya little is known of its exact distribution and habitat.

Meconopsis robusta Hook. f & Th.

A close relation of *M. paniculata*, but a slighter plant scarcely as good in cultivation. It is distinguished by its rather small pale yellow flowers, not more than 4 cm (2½ in) across, and mostly borne on solitary stalks along the inflorescence. Plants may reach 1.5 m (5 ft) in height in flower.

M. robusta is a native of the Indian Himalaya (Kumaon Province) and inhabits wooded slopes and ravines at relatively low altitudes from 2,400–3,000 m (7,900–9,850 ft). In cultivation it can be treated as the other evergreen rosette species such as *M. napaulensis* and *M. paniculata*. James Cobb (*Meconopsis* 1989) suggests that it may tolerate drier conditions than its allies in the garden, coming as it does from the drier end of the Himalaya. Seed is sometimes available.

Meconopsis taylori L.H.J. Williams

An interesting plant that can be likened to a pink-flowered *M. regia*, but also differing in difficult-to-observe details such as leaf pubescence and, worse still, chromosome characteristics. This need not concern the reader and in any case this plant is no longer in cultivation, having made a brief appearance shortly after its discovery. *M. taylori*, which is named in honour of Sir George Taylor, was found in the Nepalese Himalaya (Annapurna Himal) in 1954 by the prolific Stainton, Sykes and Williams expedition of that year.

Meconopsis torquata Prain.
(See also *M. discigera*, p. 101)

A species of the Tibetan High Plateau in an area to the south of Lhasa. Seed was introduced from the region by Ludlow and Sherriff but the plant failed to stay in cultivation for long. It is certainly never likely to linger long in our gardens and like many similar Himalayan/Tibetan species their survival in cultivation depends on the skills of a few dedicated growers. Monocarpic species add a further degree of difficulty for a dry period or frost whilst they are in flower may prevent any seed set – with obvious results.

Meconopsis violacea Kindon-Ward

Another close relation of *M. napaulensis* and *M. wallichii*, distinguished primarily by its neat, finely dissected foliage and simple racemose, rather than paniculate infloresence. In cultivation the lower flowers may sometimes be borne two to three together on short lateral branches. The pendulous flowers, 4–5 cm (1⅗–2 in) across, are a silky bluish-violet and the plant may reach up to 1.5 m (5 ft) in flower.

M. violacea was first discovered in the Burmese Himalaya in 1926 by Frank Kingdon-Ward, who stated that 'in its first year it produces an enormous crown of pale sea-green leaves encased in golden hairs of silken texture'. It was subsequently found close by in adjacent Tibet. Although formerly in cultivation, it is no longer and is unlikely to be so until those remote regions become more accessible and safe to travel in. Coming from the wetter eastern end of the Himalaya this is undoubtedly a plant for cool, moist gardens and a humid atmosphere, but it must be shielded from too much winter wetness.

The True Poppies
Papaver

The various poppies of the genus *Papaver* have long been favourite plants in our gardens. Their simple yet bold flowers with their satiny petals make them eye-catching features in borders. At the same time, their diversity of form from small annuals to robust perennials and their enormous range of flower colours from whites and yellows to oranges, pinks, mauves, purples and reds to almost black make them suitable subjects for various different aspects in the garden.

The word *Papaver* itself comes from the Latin for the poppy and is said to have been derived from the sound that is made when chewing poppy seeds. Others, however, would claim that the word has the same origin as the Celtic word *papa* (pap) because juice of the poppy (probably *Papaver somniferum*) was given to fractious children to make them sleep – indeed the soporific nature of the poppy was well known to early civilisations.

The genus *Papaver*, the largest in the poppy family, contains some 70 species scattered primarily across the northern hemisphere from sea level to the high mountains. A number of species, such as the annual *P. rhoeas* and *P. dubium*, are almost exclusively associated with arable and cultivated land, others with northern Arctic regions (e.g. *P. radicatum*) or high mountain habitats (e.g. *PP. burseri, rhaeticum*).

The species can be annuals, biennials or perennials with leafy stems or, alternatively, all the leaves may be basal (in which case the flowers are borne on leafless scapes). When cut the stems generally ooze a white, yellow or orange juice or latex. The leaves vary greatly from one species to another from simple and toothed to variously pinnately lobed, with broad or slender segments; like the stems or scapes they may be smooth (glabrous), hairy or beset with spreading or appressed bristles. The flowers are usually nodding in bud, becoming erect as the flowers open, this being caused by asymmetric growth of the pedicel, which rectifies itself as the buds mature. Flowers are often solitary but can also be borne in racemes or panicles. There are two sepals, which fall away quickly as the flowers open and usually four petals (more in some cultivated forms). Numerous stamens surround the ovary. The ovary has no style but is capped by a stigmatic disk with between four and ten (occasionally more) stigmatic rays. The characteristic fruit-capsule is a 'pepper pot', rounded to oblong or club-shaped, which opens by a ring of pores just below the stigmatic disk; the fine seeds are shaken through the pores by the slightest breeze and scattered over the ground; the number of pores per capsule is the same as the number of stigmatic rays.

Only a handful of poppies are widely grown in gardens. These include the various forms of the opium poppy, *P. somniferum*, some with large double or peony-flowered blooms, the brightly coloured 'Iceland Poppy', *P. nudicaule*, the various races of the common poppy, *P. rhoeas*, including the popular Shirley Poppies, and the large-flowered herbaceous oriental poppies, which have been derived primarily from two Asiatic species, *P. bracteatum* and *P. orientale*. Of the small perennial species the most commonly seen in our gardens are the rock garden forms of '*P alpinum*' (a complex of various alpine poppy species), *P. rupifragum* and *P. lateritium*. However, there are a host of other annual and perennial species well worth seeking out, some being first rate garden plants, which are unaccountably scarce in gardens.

Cultivation

The annual species are readily grown from seed, in fact many are the simplest plants to raise in this way. Being far easier than their *Meconopsis* cousins (with the exception of *M. cambrica*) the majority can be sown in the spring where they are to flower. In fact most resent disturbance and do not take kindly to being transplanted. In order to get good robust plants thin sowing is essential, otherwise much laborious thinning will have to take place at the seedling stage.

The taller growing annual types can be supported by suitable 'peasticks', or similar, placed around the groups while they are still young so that the sticks are hidden by the time the plants come into bloom. Most require a well-drained open sunny aspect, although any soil, providing it is neither waterlogged or too acid, will suffice. Few will succeed in dense shade. Most will produce copious seed, which can be collected and stored in a dry container for the following year. Some will self-sow freely, although not all can be relied upon to do so. Named cultivars of *P. somniferum* will undoubtedly hybridise if planted close together so that they must be isolated from one another if 'pure' seed is required. Many of the strains of *P. rhoeas* and *P. radicatum* produce a range of colours and it is rather pot luck which will appear from a sowing.

The perennial species can also be grown from seed, which can be sown in pots or direct sown in the border. However, few bother to sow seed of the robust oriental poppies. These can be readily divided or, alternatively, may be propagated from root cuttings (p. 21). Others such as *P. rupifragum* and *P. spicatum* are short-lived perennials with a solitary undividable taproot and these must be propagated from seed. In some gardens they may self-sow and young plants can be moved providing they are dug up with a good rootball attached – they will generally sulk for a while but, if carefully nurtured, will generally grow well after a few weeks. Spring and early summer are the best time to attempt such moves.

The small perennials of the '*P. alpinum*' complex, as well as the Japanese *P. miyabeanum*, make charming subjects for the alpine or scree garden. Although short-lived they are very floriferous and can generally be relied upon to self-sow. In any event seed can be easily collected and resown.

The annual poppies like *P. commutatum*, *P. radicatum* and *P. rhoeas* make striking fillers for gaps in flower borders or indeed for a border devoted to colourful annuals. If space permits, a drift of poppies can be a breathtaking sight that will provide interest over many weeks during the summer. *P. rhoeas*, in its normal red–flower mixtures, is ideal for wild flower meadows or for sowing along road verges or motorways.

The bold forms of oriental poppies with their brazen colours can be eye-catching subjects in the herbaceous border but they need to be placed with care as their colours can clash with those of neighbouring plants. I once saw an entire border devoted to various oriental poppies – a bold piece of planning to excite the eye and attract the neighbours!

Classification

The species of *Papaver* divide conveniently into a number of sections of which the bare outlines are presented here, together with typical examples for each.

Section Argemonorhoeades Fedde. Annual herbs, generally hairy or bristly, with the stem leaves not clasping (amplexicaule). Flowers often red, pink or purplish, with the filaments dilated towards the top. Fruit-capsule bristly, at least near the stigmatic disk, which is generally somewhat narrower than the capsule. e.g. *PP. argemone, hybridum, pavoninum*.

Section Carinatae Fedde. Annual herbs, hairy, without clasping stem leaves. Fruit capsules with a disk as wide as the capsule, generally with five to ten keeled rays, which have a deep sinuse between each. e.g. *P. macrostomum*.

Section Macrantha Elk (= Oxytona Bernh.). A group of robust, bristly perennials with large flowers, the petals generally red (in the wild species) and 30–90 mm (1⅕–3⅗ in) long, four or occasionally six in number; filaments dilated. Fruit capsule often egg-shaped, smooth with the disk as broad as the capsule and with 7–20 rays. e.g. *PP. bracteatum, orientale, paucifoliatum*.

Section Mecones Bernh. Annual herbs, glaucous and generally hairless, occasionally somewhat bristly, the stem leaves usually clasping and unstalked. Fruit-capsule oblong to rounded, smooth, with a flattish disk as wide as the capsule and 5–18 rays. e.g. *PP. glaucum, somniferum*.

Section Miltantha Bernh. Biennial herbs with bristly stems and leaves and red to orange flowers. Fruit-capsule elliptical to club-shaped with a narrow, pyramidal disk, which has four to seven rays usually. e.g. *PP. armeniacum, caucasicum, triniifolium*.

Section Papaver (= Orthorhoeades Fedde). Annual herbs, occasionally biennials or perennials, generally hairy or bristly, the stem leaves not clasping. Flowers pink, red, orange or purple usually, with linear filaments. Fruit-capsule smooth, with a disk as wide as the capsule, with 4–18 rays; sinuses small. e.g. *PP. commutatum, hybridum, rhoeas*.

Section Pilosa Prantl. (= Pseudo-pilosa M. Pop.). Perennial herbs, usually hairy, with orange flowers which have linear filaments. Fruit capsule oblong to club-shaped with a disk as broad as the capsule and six to seven rays. e.g. *PP. oreophilum, pilosum, spicatum*.

Section Scapiflora Rchb. Plants with basal leaf-tufts, often caespitose, and with solitary scapose flowers. Flowers white, yellow, pink, orange or red, more rarely pink. Fruit-capsule often oblong, sometimes rounded, beset with stiff hairs or bristles, with a disk about as wide as the capsule, mostly with four to eight rays. e.g. *PP. burseri, miyabeanum, nudicaule, radicatum, rhaeticum*.

Key to Species

1. Plants with leafy stems, annuals, biennials or perennials (except
   P. monanthum which has white-bristly sepals and glabrous
   fruit-capsules) 2
   Plants scapose perennials – all leaves basal; fruit-capsules always hairy .37

2. Perennials, monocarpic or polycarpic 3
   Annuals, occasionally over-wintering 17

3. Monocarpic plants (dying after flowering in the second or third
   year); inflorescence paniculate 4
   Polycarpic plants (perennials); flowers solitary or in spike-like racemes .7

4. Leaves 1-pinnate; fruit-capsule 10–15 mm (⅖–⅗ in) long; petals
   20–30 mm (⅘–1⅕ in) long 5
   Leaves 2–3-pinnate; fruit-capsule up to 10 mm (⅖ in) long; petals
   10–15 mm (⅖–⅗ in) long 6

5. Fruit-capsule hairy: **P. persicum**
   Fruit-capsule glabrous: **P. fugar**

6. Leaf-margins revolute; fruit-capsule somewhat beaded (torulose):
                                                       P. armeniacum
   Leaf-margin flat; fruit-capsule smooth: **P. triniifolium**

7. Flowers relatively small, not more than 6 cm (2½ in) across 8
   Flowers large, 6–14 cm (2½–6 in) across, sometimes larger 12

8. Flowers borne in spike-like racemes 9
   Flowers solitary, not in spike-like racemes 10

9. Fruit-capsules with a rounded base; petals pale brick-red: **P. spicatum**
   Fruit-capsule with a narrowed (attenuate) base; petals orange-red to
   deep orange, often with a pale base: **P. pilosum**

10. Stems unbranched: **P. lateritium**
    Stems branched close to the base 11

11. Leaves and stems silky-hairy; sepals hairy: **P. atlanticum**
    Leaves and stems subglabrous; sepals glabrous: **P. rupifragum**

12. Petals generally pink or orange-red, unblotched; filaments filiform,
    pale yellow; stigmatic disk with five to nine rays 13
    Petals red, deep orange or pinkish-red (sometimes also pink or
    white in cultivars) often blotched; filaments dilated distally; stigmatic
    disk with 11–18 rays 14

13. Flowers scapose; sepals covered by whitish hairs; fruit-capsule
    12–15 mm (½–⅗ in) long: **P. monanthum**
    Flowers borne on leafy stems; sepals covered by reddish-brown
    hairs; fruit-capsule 15–17 mm (⅗–¾ in) long: **P. oreophilum**

14. Bracts present immediately beneath the flower .15
    Bracts absent 16

15. Bracts three to five, at least 2 cm (⅘ in) long: **P. bracteatum**
    Bracts two, not more than 1 cm (⅖ in) long: **P. intermedium**

16. Pedicels with appressed hairs; petals four to six: **P. orientale**
    Pedicels with spreading (patent) hairs; petals six: **P. lasiothrix**

17. Fruit-capsules hairy or bristly, usually densely so but occasionally
    with just a few bristles at the top 18
    Fruit-capsules glabrous 24

18. Flower buds glabrous: ***P. apulum***
    Flower buds hairy or bristly 19

19. Flower buds with two large hollow-horns: ***P. pavoninum***
    Flower buds without horns 20

20. Fruit-capsules subglobose 21
    Fruit-capsules oblong to elliptical or clavate (club-shaped) 22

21. Petals 2–4 cm (⅖–1⅗ in) long, bright red with a basal black blotch
    edge in white; flowerbuds globose: ***P. ocellatum***
    Petals 1.5–2 cm (⅗–⅘ in) long, wine-red or pinkish-red with
    a violet-black basal blotch; flowerbuds oblong: ***P. hybridum***

22. Plants decumbent, not more than 15 cm (6 in) tall; petals 10–15 mm
    (⅖–⅗ in) long: ***P. minus***
    Plants erect, 20 cm (8 in) or more tall; petals 20–30 mm (⅘–1⅕ in) long . 23

23. Fruit-capsule 10–15 mm (⅖–1⅕ in) long; petals with a large
    dark basal blotch: ***P. nigrotinctum***
    Fruit-capsule 15–20 mm (⅗–⅘ in) long; petals unblotched or
    with a small basal blotch: ***P. argemone***

24. Fruit-capsule subglobose, with a rounded base 25
    Fruit-capsule oblong to clavate (club-shaped), attenuate at the base ... 30

25. Plants glaucous, usually glabrous, sometimes slightly bristly; upper
    leaves amplexicaule 26
    Plants not glaucous, pubescent to bristly; upper leaves rarely
    amplexicaule 27

26. Leaves entire to markedly toothed; fruit-capsule 3 cm (1⅕ in)
    long or more: ***P. somniferum***
    Leaves pinnately-lobed; fruit-capsule to 2 cm (⅘ in) long: ***P. glaucum***

27. Leaves pinnate with rounded lobes: ***P. chelidoniifolium***
    Leaves pinnately-lobed, with narrow, pointed segments 28

28. Petals with a dark blotch above the base (almost in the middle
    of the petals); pedicels with appressed hairs: ***P. commutatum***
    Petals with a dark or pale blotch or zone at the base; pedicels with
    spreading (patent) hairs 29

29. Flowers 5–9 cm (2–4 in) across; petals red often with a dark blotch
    at the base, sometimes edged in white: ***P. rhoeas***
    Flowers 1.5–3 cm (⅗–1⅕ in) across; petals red with a greenish
    zone at the base: ***P. californicum***

30. Stigmatic disk deciduous, falling away in one piece when the
    fruit-capsule is ripe, the rays distinctly keeled: **P. macrostomum**
    Stigmatic disk persistent on ripe fruit-capsule, the rays not keeled 31

31. Fruit-capsule stipitate (i.e. stalked between the capsule and
    the point of attachment of sepals and petals); petals
    unblotched: **P. stipitatum**
    Fruit-capsule sessile; petals sometimes with a dark basal blotch 32

32. Flowerbuds with two short, nipple-like horns; leaves all
    bipinnately-lobed: **P. arenarium**
    Flowerbuds without horns; leaves simple pinnately-lobed 33

33. Plants practically glabrous; stem leaves amplexicaule: **P. decaisnei**
    Plants bristly or hairy; stem leaves not amplexicaule 34

34. Anthers violet: **P. dubium**
    Anthers yellowish or brownish 35

35. Stems appressed-hairy throughout: **P. lecoqii**
    Stems with spreading (patent) hairs below 36

36. Stems and leaves hairy: **P. pinnatifidum**
    Stems and leaves beset with stout, sharp spines and
    bristles: **P. aculeatum**

37. Flowers large, 4–6 cm (1⅗–2½ in) across; plants 20 cm (8 in) tall
    or more in flower: **P. nudicaule**
    Flowers smaller, 4 cm (1⅗ in) or less across, plants rarely more
    than 15 cm (6 in) tall in flower, often less 38

38. Fruit-capsule sub-globose, broader than long: **P. miyabeanum**
    Fruit-capsule elliptical, oblong or clavate, clearly longer than broad ...39

39. Flowers small, the petals less than 15 mm (⅗ in) long, yellow,
    orange or red 40
    Flowers larger, the petals at least 15 mm (⅗ in) long, white, yellow,
    pink, rarely orange or red 41

40. Pedicels 4 × the length of the leaves; flowers 1–2 cm (⅖–⅘ in)
    across, with persistent petals: **P. involucratum**
    Pedicels 1–2 × the length of the leaves; flowers 2–3 cm (⅘–1⅕ in)
    across, without persistent petals: **P. suaveolens**

41. Leaf-bases forming a close tunic around neck of plant; lower
    leaf-segments, alternate.......................................42
    Leaf-base not forming a tunic or only a loose one; lower
    leaf-segments opposite 43

42. Flowers white; leaf-segments pointed: **P. sendtneri**
    Flowers yellow rarely orange or red; leaf-segments
    blunt: **P. rhaeticum★**

43. Flowers yellow or orange, rarely red 44
    Flowers white or pink 48

44. Leaves two- to three-pinnate: ***P. kerneri*** ★ **& *P. nivale***
    Leaves simple-pinnate, rarely two-pinnate 45

45. Leaves glabrous; petals not becoming blue-green
    on drying: ***P. corona-sancti-stephani***
    Leaves bristly; petals becoming blue-green on drying 46

46. Fruit-capsule widest about the middle, the stigmatic disk usually
    flat or somewhat concave, often with five rays: ***P. radicatum***
    Fruit-capsule widest near the top, the stimatic disk convex, with
    five to eight rays usually 47

47. Stems with white latex when cut, pedicels curved: ***P. dahlianum***
    Stems with yellow latex when cut; pedicels straight
    and erect: ***P. lapponicum***

48. Scapes decumbent; petals white or pink, often yellowish
    at the base: ***P. alboroseum***
    Scapes erect; petals usually white, occasionally pink or red, with a
    yellowish base 49

49. Leaves two- to three-pinnate; petals not drying blue-green: ***P. burseri*** ★
    Leaves simple pinnate; petals becoming blue-green on drying 50

50. Fruit-capsule widest above the middle, the stigmatic disk usually
    flat or somewhat concave, often with five rays: ***P. radicatum***
    Fruit-capsule widest near the top, the stigmatic disk convex, with
    five to eight rays usually: ***P. dahlianum***

Papaver aculeatum Thunb.
(Syn. *P. gariepinum* Buch. ex DC.)
SOUTH AFRICAN POPPY

This poppy has the distinction of being the only species native to Africa south
of the equator. It is an annual species in the same group as *P. rhoeas* and
P. dubium, and may reach 30–60 cm (12–24 in) tall, with most of the leaves
crowded towards the base of the plant. The whole plant, except for the fruit-
capsule, is markedly bristly. The leaves are pinnately-lobed and toothed. The
solitary flowers are plain orange with yellow stamens and the smooth fruit-
capsule, 18–22 mm (⅔–⅞ in) long, is roughly oval in outline, somewhat
narrowed at the base and with a small stigmatic disk with six to eight rays.

  P. aculeatum is confined primarily to the Drakensberg Mountains of the
Transvaal, South Africa and to neighbouring areas of Botswana, up to
altitudes of 1,850 m (6,100 ft). It is rare in cultivation today, although it has
been cultivated since about 1825.

★ *P. alpinum* of cultivation

Papaver alboroseum Hultén

An interesting little poppy related to *P. radicatum* and differing primarily in its dwarf stature, being rarely more than 10 cm (4 in) tall in flower, with thin, flexuous scapes that are clearly decumbent at the base. The small flowers, only 10–20 mm (²/₅–⁴/₅ in) across are white or very pale pink, each petal often with a yellowish basal blotch. The fruit-capsule, 10–15 mm (²/₅–³/₅ in) long is covered in yellowish or brownish hairs.

P. alboroseum is confined to the eastern CIS, Kamschatka region, and Alaska as well as northern British Columbia, where it is to be found growing on gravelly soils and rock outcrops. It is a dainty Iceland-type poppy ideal for screes and raised beds in the garden, where its delicate habit can be best appreciated. It is offered by a number of seed merchants and nurseries and is a real gem to acquire.

The decumbent bases to the flowering scapes and the pale colour of the flowers set this species apart from the other members of the *P. nudicaule* complex.

Papaver alpinum L., nomen ambig.

This much confused name has been widely applied to a number of small alpine poppy species native to the Pyrenees, Alps and the Carpathian Mountains. They are small tufted plants with all the leaves basal and finely dissected. The solitary flowers, often 2–5 cm (⁴/₅–2 in) across, are borne on slender bristly scapes and range in colour from white to yellow, more rarely in shades of orange or red. The fruit-capsules are small, oblong or elliptic in outline and with appressed or spreading bristles.

In the garden they are delightful plants for pockets in the rock garden, raised bed or scree, revelling in gritty, well-drained soils. Although perennial, they are not long-lived but can generally be relied upon to seed around and excess seedlings can be easily removed. If several of the species are grown in close proximity they will undoubtedly hybridise, producing a charming range of hybrids often in pastel shades of pink, yellow or orange or pure white. Regular removal of dead flowers will generally ensure a supply of blooms throughout the late spring and summer. Seedlings flower within a few months of germination.

For details of the species involved see *P. burseri*, *P. kerneri*, *P. rhaeticum*, *P. suaveolens* and *P. sendtneri*. These are generally listed by seed merchants and nurseries as '*P. alpinum*'. Related species from Arctic regions and central Asia include *P. lapponicum*, *P. nudicaule*, *P. radicatum*, *P. miyabeanum* and *P. nivale*.

'Summer Breeze' [**Pl. 65**] is a particularly fine selection of floriferous F1 hybrids with bright flowers in shades of red, orange, yellow and white, above mounds of ferny foliage. A white selection is sometimes offered as *P. alpinum* 'Alba', a plant almost indistinguishable from *P. burseri*. They can be grown as half-hardy annuals or direct sown in the spring, where they are to flower.

Papaver apulum Ten.   [Pl. 66]

A Mediterranean poppy very similar to the more widespread *P. argemone*. It can at once be separated by its oval, smooth flower buds and bright scarlet flowers, each petal with a prominent, basal, black blotch. Although the flowers are a similar size and shape to those of *P. argemone* the fruit-capsule is noticeably smaller, being rarely more than 10 mm (⅖ in) in length and scarcely ribbed.

    P. apulum is distributed from southern Italy and Sicily to the Balkan Peninsula, east as far as the Turkish Aegean islands of Ikaria and Ag. Nickolaos, where it grows in grassy and stony places, orchards, olive groves and along roadsides at low altitudes – to 500 m (1,650 ft) at the most. It is one of a number of colourful annuals that help to make a tapestry of colour in these Mediterranean regions during the spring – late March to May.

    P. apulum is another neglected annual poppy in our gardens. It is quite one of the prettiest and well deserves a little more attention, although one is unlikely to come across it in seed catalogues at the present time.

Papaver arenarium M.–B.
(Syn. *P. dubium* var. *arenarium* Elk.; *P. rhoeas* var. *arenarium*)

The affinities of this species can be readily judged from its synonymy. It can at once be distinguished from *P. rhoes*, *P. dubium* and their allies by the pair of short horns (about 1–2 mm (¹⁄₁₂ in) long) terminating the flowerbuds; these are most easily observed in the young bud stage. As in *P. dubium* the flower stalks (peduncles) are appressed–hairy and the fruit-capsule oblong in outline, smooth and generally with seven to nine stigmatic rays. The flowers approach the size of those of *P. rhoeas*, being mostly 5–7 cm (1–2 in) across but are a purple-red rather than scarlet; each petal has a large basal, black blotch.

    The mammil-like apex to the flower buds are a useful diagnostic feature. Similar nipple-like horns occur in *P. pavoninium* except that in that species they are much larger and more pronounced. In addition, the fruit-capsules of *P. pavoninium* are distinctly bristly, rather than smooth.

    P. arenarium is a delightful, though unaccountably neglected, garden annual, easy to grow and as charming as any annual poppy. A sunny position and a light sandy soil are its chief requirements. It is occasionally offered in seed catalogues.

Fruit of *Papaver arenarium*

Like its cousins *P. arenarium* is a plant of stony steppes and hillslopes, often at low altitudes but up to 1,900 m (6,200 ft) in the mountains of northern Iran, but it is rarely associated with cultivation. Its main area of distribution is from southern Russia and the Caucasus to Iraq and Iran; it is apparently absent from central Asia.

Papaver argemone L.
PRICKLY POPPY

This charming little poppy is one of the commoner poppies seen in Western Europe, being closely related to the rough poppy, *P. hybridum*. It differs primarily in its paler, scarlet or brick-red flowers, the petals widely spreading, rather narrow, rarely overlapping, and with or without a dark basal blotch, and by the oblong fruit-capsule with a few erect bristles; in *P. hybridum* the fruit-capsules are globose and densely beset with curved, straw-coloured bristles.

P. *argemone* has a wide distribution from Western Europe and North Africa eastwards to Iran, although it is rather rare in old Soviet Central Asia where *P. hybridum* is far commoner and more widespread. Like *P. hybridum* it is a plant of cultivated land, fallow fields and stony places, generally at rather low altitudes but up to 2,000 m (6,500 ft) in the mountains of western Iran.

It is rarely cultivated on purpose in gardens, being less spectacular than some of its showier cousins. However, the more muted, less startling flower colour may be more to some 'tastes'. In some gardens it turns up as a weed and is worth tolerating for its pretty effect amongst other annuals.

Papaver atlanticum (Ball) Cosson [Pl. 67]
(Syn. *P. rupifragum* subsp. *atlanticum* Ball)
MOROCCAN POPPY

An attractive poppy that is very similar to *P. rupifragum*, indeed it was at one time placed under that species. It can be distinguished on three counts: the leaves and stems are silky with hairs, the flowers, somewhat larger at 5–6.5 cm (2–2⅗ in) across, are dull orange and the fruit-capsules are narrowly club-shaped.

Despite these obvious differences these two pretty little poppies have been much confused in gardens. Of the two, *P. atlanticum* is the commonest, indeed it is sometimes offered for sale as *P. rupifragum*. The soft orange, tissue-paper blooms are a great delight and, although never produced in great quantity, appear throughout the summer until the first frosts of autumn. Removing the seedheads will promote more flowers and prevent too many unwanted seedlings appearing. There is a semi-double form 'Flore Pleno', perhaps more often seen in gardens than the single form. A very similar strain named 'Double Orange' is offered; this has flowers ranging in colour from brick red to tangerine. These semi-double strains of *P. atlanticum* generally produce some ordinary single-flowered seedlings in their midst and these are best weeded out, saving seed only from the best 'doubles'. *P. atlanticum* is confined in the wild to rock crevices in the mountains of Morocco.

Papaver bracteatum Lindl.
(Syn. *P. orientale* var. *bracteatum* Ledeb.)
'ORIENTAL POPPY'

Few plants in the garden are as spectacular in the vividness of their blooms or indeed for sheer size as the various races of oriental poppy. As explained under *P. orientale* (p. 154) the oriental poppies of gardens have been derived from both that species and *P. bracteatum* and it is often difficult to assign a particular cultivar to one or the other. The differences between these two closely allied species are outlined under *P. orientale* and to avoid confusion all the oriental cultivars are listed and described under that species.

In the wild *P. bracteatum* is a more robust species than *P. orientale*, making substantial clumps with thick erect, rough bristly stems to 1.2 m (4 ft), occasionally taller; the lower stem has spreading bristles whilst on the upper stem they are clearly appressed. The large leaves, to 45 cm (18 in) long, sometimes larger, are primarily basal, pinnately-lobed, the segments rough, bristly and deeply toothed; the stems are leafy to the top, generally with five or six leaves per stem, the upper two leaves small and pressed close to the base of the flower bud where there are also, in addition, three to five oval sepal-like bracts. The flowers are very large, cup or bowl-shaped, 10–18 cm (4–7 in) across (but to 28 cm (11 in) in cultivated forms), blood red to purple-crimson, each of the four to six petals with a prominent, oblong, black basal blotch (longer than broad; the reverse situation is found in *P. orientale*); the stamens have dark filaments and violet or blackish anthers. The large, smooth fruit-capsule, 3–4 cm (1⅕–1⅗ in) long, has a flat stigmatic disk often with 14–20 stigmatic rays.

P. bracteatum is endemic to the Caucasus, eastern Turkey (Anatolia) and northern and western Iran, where it is to be found on rocky and scrubby slopes as well as on the neighbouring plains, 1,750–2,800 m (5,750–9,200 ft) altitude; flowering in the wild from June to July.

The species was described by John Lindley in 1821 from a specimen growing in Chelsea, London. The seed had been sent to Fischer from the Mineralnye Vody region of the Caucasus and specimens in the Fischer Herbarium, under the name *P. orientale*, clearly belong to *P. bracteatum*.

The *Flora of the USSR* (vol. 7) considers *P. bracteatum* to be a relict species isolated geographically from the related *P. intermedium*, which differs in its small, paired, flower bracts. However, other authorities (especially James Cullen in *Flora Iranica*) consider the species to embrace a large range of variability and to encompass a greater area in the wild from the Caucasus and eastern Anatolia (Turkey) to northern Iran.

P. intermedium DC. (= *P. pseudo-orientale* Medw.) almost certainly represents a hybrid of ancient origin between *P. bracteatum* and *P. orientale* and the presence of this species has certainly caused some of the confusion in the orientalis-type poppies. However, there is a good deal of evidence that, despite their origins, *P. bracteatum* and *P. intermedium* form a more or less continuous range of variability, one to the other. In such an event it is probably best to consider them to be a single species. Certainly as far as the garden is concerned the oriental poppies have complex origins that may well encompass all these various elements originally.

P. *orientale* and P. *bracteatum* (including P. *intermedium*) have flower colours in the orange and red range of the spectrum. However, many garden forms have flowers of pink or white. Such colours may have originated from other species introduced into cultivation under the P. *orientale* 'blanket' but no longer in cultivation, indeed superseded by more robust cultivars. For instance the Caucasian P. *paucifoliatum* (Trautb.) Fedde, which is closely allied to P. *orientalis* itself, has almost leafless stems and medium-sized flowers of pinkish-red or brick-red, with unblotched petals; native of the extreme north-eastern Turkey and the Caucasus, to an altitude of 2,700 m (8,850 ft). Some of the almost scapose double oriental poppies are probably derived from this species rather than P. *bracteatum* or P. *orientale*. Another allied species, P. *monanthum* Trautb. (also a Caucasian endemic), has leafless stems and orange-pink flowers, 5–8 cm (2–3 in) across. What is quite certain is that the origins of the oriental poppies is clearly complex and confused through time and initially, at least, a lack of understanding of the wild species involved.

P. *monanthum*, which is not at present in cultivation, is placed in a separate section (the Pilosa) to P. *orientale* and its allies. This section is distinguished on account of its paler flowers (generally in the pink to pale orange or pinkish-red range), unblotched petals and the slender yellow stamen filaments. Despite this, there are clear transitions between P. *monanthum* and P. *orientale* and the sectional boundaries would not stand up to close scrutiny. Incidentally P. *monanthum* also shows close affinities with another group of poppies well represented in gardens but restricted to the western Mediterranean region – namely P. *atlanticum* and P. *rupifragum*.

Papaver burseri Crantz [Pl. 68]
(Syn. P. *alpinum* subsp. *alpinum* sensu Markgraf, non L.)
ALPINE POPPY

A small tufted alpine poppy, almost hairless, with the leaf-bases forming a loose tunic around the base of the plant. The symmetrical leaves are two- to three-pinnately lobed with narrow, lanceolate or linear, pointed segments; the lower leaf-segments are opposite, in contrast to those of the closely related P. *sendtneri*, which are alternate. The single-flowered scapes rise to 20 cm (8 in), though often less, and are appressed-bristly. The cupped flowers, 3–4 cm (1–2 in) across, are pure white with a generous boss of yellow anthers. The club-shaped, bristly capsule usually has only four stigmatic rays.

This species is a true delight – one of the whitest of poppies. It is the most widely grown of the alpine poppies, though generally hiding under the umbrella of 'P. *alpinum*' in gardens, which is unfortunate as it is well worth seeking out and by no means difficult to grow. P. *alpinum* 'Alba' is almost certainly a form of P. *burseri* (p. 135).

P. *burseri* is a native of the northern Alps and the Carpathian Mountains, inhabiting high limestone rocks, screes and moraines between 1,200–2,000 m (3,900–6,650 ft).

See also *P. kerneri* (p. 145) and *P. corona-sancti-stephani* (p. 141).

Papaver californicum Gray   [Pl. 69]
WESTERN POPPY

A little-cultivated Californian poppy in the same general section as familiar European species like *P. rhoeas* and *P. dubium. P. californicum* inhabits the Coast Ranges where it grows on disturbed soils or areas that have been burnt, flowering in the spring during April and May.

Plants are annual with rather erect, smooth or hairy, stems 30–60 cm (12–24 in) tall. The pinnately-divided leaves, to 8 cm (3 in) long, have narrow, lobed or sharply toothed segments, the lower leaves stalked but the upper sessile. The flowers are small, 1.5–3 cm (⅗–1⅕ in) across, brick-red with a distinctive greenish zone at the base of each petal, borne on appressed-hairy stalks. The smooth capsule is more or less club-shaped, 12–18 mm (½–⅔ in) long, the stigmatic disk with 6–10 rays.

An interesting little poppy occasionally grown in botanic gardens but seldom seen outside their domain. It is interesting in being one of the few true poppies, *Papaver*, native to North America, indeed it is the only *Papaver* native to the western states where other genera in the family have proliferated – *Eschscholzia* and *Argemone* for instance. The green base to the petals is a useful feature for distinguishing this rather isolated species from its cousins.

Papaver commutatum Fischer & Meyer   [Pl. 70]
(Syn. *P. rhoeas* var. *commutatum* Elk.; *P. strigosum* var. *commutata* Fedde ex Busch)

This handsome species is very closely related to *P. rhoeas*, being a bristly annual, often branched from close to the base, though rarely more than 50 cm (20 in) tall; the stems are soft with greyish hairs in the lower part, which is especially apparent in young plants. If anything, the flowers are an even more intense vivid scarlet but rather smaller, deeply bowl-shaped, mostly 5–6 cm (2–2½ in) across. The main differences are to be found in the petals, which are broadly oval, rather longer than broad (they are broader than long in *P. rhoeas*) and with a large black blotch (often square) located not at the base of the petal but almost in the middle. The blotch varies from rounded to square, occasionally waisted in the middle or running almost to the edge of the petal. The stamens have black filaments and the fruit-capsule is also quite smooth, with five to ten stigmatic rays, and has a distinct, though short, stalk.

P. commutatum is native primarily from Turkey eastwards to north-western Iran, the Caucasus and the surrounding regions, as well as isolated localities in Crete. It is essentially a plant of arid steppes, rocky mountain slopes and roadsides, but also invading cultivated land, particularly arable fields; mainly 800–1,800 m (2,600–5,900 ft) altitude; flowering during May and June. In the wild it is said to hybridise on occasions with *P. dubium* where the two species grow in close proximity to one another.

This attractive species is easily distinguished from other similar red poppies by its distinctive petal blotch. Even in fruit, the capsules can be readily differentiated by their short stalk (between the capsule and the point where petals and stamens join the pedicel).

P. commutatum is a fine garden plant generally seen in a form given the name 'Ladybird', which is closely similar to the wild type, though selected for the intensity of its flowers and the especially bold black blotches, which dominate the centres of the petals. In some gardens it will self-sow but, to be sure, it is wise to save some seed each year. It is that startling red that must be placed with care in the garden to avoid clashes with gaudy neighbours. A patch well placed is a certain winner near the front of any border.

P. commutatum finds its closest ally in *P. lacerum* Popov. which hails from Turkey and Armenia. It can be distinguished by its stiffer habit and red or pink petals, which have a basal black blotch. Both also clearly come close to the common poppy, *P. rhoeas*, in which the petals are, however, broader than long and the terminal segments of the leaf-lobes are noticeably longer.

Papaver corona-sancti-stephani Zapal.
(Syn. *P. alpinum* L. subsp. *corona-sancti-stephani* (Zapal.) Borza)

This alpine poppy, with its tongue-twisting name, is not in cultivation as far as I am aware, although it is listed by Llanbrook Alpine Nursery near Clinton, Shropshire. However, it is another delight in the '*P. alpinum*' complex, coming closest to *P. burseri* and *P. kerneri*; being distinguished by its less divided hairless leaves, only one- or two-pinnate, and more rounded fruit-capsules, only 7–10 mm ($\frac{2}{7}$–$\frac{2}{5}$ in) long. The small flowers are yellow, 18–26 mm ($\frac{2}{3}$–1 in) across.

A native of the eastern and southern Carpathian Mountains of Romania.

P. pyrenaicum subsp. *degenii* Urum. from south-western Bulgaria, with rather smaller flowers in yellow or orange, is probably only a variant of *P. corona-sancti-stephani* and is sometimes listed by nurseries as *P. degenii*. I have grown plants of the latter for a number of years on a raised scree bed, where they seed around with abundant regularity. The small flowers with rather narrow petals vary in colour from pale yellow to orange, salmon and white. They are probably better referred to the '*P. alpinum*' complex as I am very doubtful whether they are the true *degenii*. Despite this, they are a joy to have about and always attract the attention of visitors to the garden, who often carry away a seedpod to try for themselves.

Papaver dahlianum Nordh.
(Syn. *P. radicatum* subsp. *brachyphyllum* Tolm. & subsp. *polare* Tolm.)

A little-known species most closely related to *P. lapponicum* but with white latex when the stems are cut and more dissected leaves. The scapes are often decumbent and the yellow or white flowers relatively small, 3–4.5 cm (1⅕–4⅘ in) across.

P. dahlianum is restricted to Arctic Norway and the neighbouring part of Russia. Seed is rarely offered.

Papaver dubium L.
(Syn. *P. modestum* Jordan; *P. obtusifolium* Desf.)
LONG-HEADED POPPY

A poppy of the *P. rhoeas* persuasion but in every way more modest. The pinnately dissected leaves often have a somewhat greyish-green appearance and when cut, like the stem, exude a prominent white latex. The pedicels have distinctly appressed rather than spreading bristles. The flowers are paler and smaller, generally being pale scarlet or pinkish-red, 2.5–5 cm (1–2 in) across. The petals are often wider than long, with or without a basal dark blotch. The smooth fruit-capsule is decidedly oblong to club-shaped in outline and up to 2 cm (1 in) long, with generally five to nine stigmatic rays.

P. dubium is equally widely distributed as *P. rhoeas*, occurring from Europe and north Africa, eastwards well into western Asia to Iran and the Caucasus, and southwards to Ethiopia, where it is a plant of cultivated and waste land, rather bare stony slopes and roadsides.

It is rarely grown in gardens, though often turning up in some as a weed. However, it is worth growing if only for the more subtle hue of its flowers, less brazen than many red poppies and perhaps more easy to place in the border. It is an example of a common plant being ignored through familiarity.

In Cyprus, parts of Turkey and Syria a similar, though more prostrate plant, with rather smaller, pale scarlet or orange-red flowers is distinguished as *P. postii* Fedde. The fruit-capsule is only 6–8 mm (¼–⅓ in) long when mature and bears only five or six stigmatic rays. *P. postii* is primarily a plant of rocky places and screes in the mountains, above 450 m (1,500 ft).

Papaver fauriei Fedde.

See *P. miyabeanum* (p. 149).

Papaver fugax Poir.
(Syn. *P. caucasicum* M.–B.; *P. floribundum* Desf.)

An interesting western Asian species related to *P. triniifolium* and, like that species, a biennial. It differs primarily in its angled lower stems, simply dissected (one-pinnately lobed) leaves, one pyramidal, paniculate inflorescences and rather larger pink or pale red flowers, each petal with a pale yellow base. The stamens are yellow and the grey-green fruit-capsules smooth, oblong-club-shaped, 10–15 mm (⅖–⅗ in) long, the stigmatic disk usually with only four to six rays.

P. fugax is a plant of dry rocky slopes and screes, 1,700–3,100 m (5,600–

10,200 ft) altitude, in eastern Turkey (Anatolia), the Caucasus, northern and north-western Iran, as well as northern Iraq.

This is another species apparently lost to cultivation. It is very variable and authorities are not generally agreed on the circumscription of the species or indeed its relationship to its allies. For instance, intermediates between it and *P. persicum* occur in the wild, particularly in Iraq. These are generally given the name *P. partuschianum*, although it is not clear whether this represents a hybrid between two distinct species or indeed intermediates linking two extremes of a single variable species. Such problems are scarcely likely to hinder the horticulturist and gardener as none of these plants are in cultivation at the present time. *P. persicum* in fact represents an altogether more bristly version of *P. fugax*, the leaves, flowerbuds and fruit-capsules being furnished with yellowish or brownish bristles.

All these 'species' are well worth growing and should seed become available they should certainly be given a try. All will undoubtedly require a hot sunny site and an acutely drained light soil. Plants under the names of *P. caucasicum* and *P. persicum* have certainly been cultivated in the past and there was then no question as to their hardiness.

It seems a pity that such plants should be lost to cultivation purely from neglect or from not being more widely distributed in the first instance. Today, when such efforts are still being made to bring new species into cultivation and to reintroduce those lost, it seems extremely important that a real effort must be made to maintain those species already in cultivation, otherwise the whole exercise becomes rather pointless, especially as so many desirable plants are becoming increasingly rarer in the wild. Annuals and biennials have always presented a challenge to the cultivator. Many are not too difficult to grow, but because they are transitory, seed needs to be collected on a regular basis to ensure that they remain in cultivation. Changes in fashion in recent years, especially in the growing of such subjects, has unfortunately relegated many to the scarce or rare category in our gardens.

Papaver glaucum Boiss. & Hausskn.   [Pl. 71]
TULIP POPPY

This charming, but little grown, species is closely related to the opium poppy, *P. somniferum*, but it is a slighter plant not more than 45 cm (18 in) tall and with distinctly more deeply lobed leaves. The flowers, 6–10 cm (2½–4 in) across, are borne on bristly stalks and are deep scarlet, each petal with a black blotch at its base. The small fruit-capsule is globose and quite smooth, not more than 2 cm (⅘ in) long.

P. glaucum is native to Anatolian Turkey, Iraq, Syria and Iran, where it inhabits rocky and waste land, olive groves and vineyards, mountain slopes and sandy places, generally between 700–1,800 m (2,300–5,900 ft) altitude, flowering in May and June.

A neglected annual in gardens, well worth acquiring if it can be found. It tends not to self-sow with any vigour so that it is wise to collect some seed each year for sowing the following spring.

Papaver hybridum L.
ROUGH POPPY

This widespread European and Asian Poppy is one of the common 'red poppies' of the region, although it is in fact rather rare in Britain, being confined to scattered localities in the south and east of the country.

The species is an annual to 30 cm (12 in) tall, occasionally taller, the bristle-haired stems generally branched from the base, ascending to erect. The bristly leaves are bipinnately lobed, the lanceolate to oval segments toothed or further lobed, the lower leaves stalked, the upper sessile, smaller and less lobed. The solitary flowers are borne on slender, appressed-hairy, rather flexuous stalks, the somewhat bristly flower buds without apical horns. The flowers, 20–30 mm (⅘–1⅕ in) across, are crimson or rose-red, the petals with a conspicuous black or violet basal blotch; stamens relatively few in number with black or violet filaments and blue pollen. The globose to broadly oblong fruit-capsule, 10–14 mm (⅖–⅗ in) long is ribbed and covered with rows of spreading to recurved, straw-coloured bristles; the stigmatic disk has four to nine rays.

P. hybridum occurs from western Europe eastwards to Pakistan and central Asia, where it is a plant of cultivated, fallow and waste ground, stony and sandy steppes, generally at low altitudes, occasionally to 800 m (2,600 ft) in the lower mountains.

The broad, short fruit-capsules and the lack of horns on the flower buds serve to distinguish this species from its closest allies *P. pavoninum* and *P. argemone*. In addition the flowers are generally rather smaller.

P. hybridum is seldom cultivated in gardens, although sometimes occurring there as a weed. Its prickly fruits are useful for small dried arrangements in the house.

Fruits of *Papaver hybridum* (left) and *P. argemone* (right)

Papaver involucratum M. Pop.

Another little poppy of the *P. radicatum* persuasion but scarcely known in cultivation. In general stature it is about the height of *P. radicatum* but is at once distinguished by its very small flowers, only 15–20 mm (⅗–⅘ in) across, which are orange-red, each petal with a yellow basal zone. These are borne on long slender, hairy scapes held well above the leaf tuft. As in *P. radicatum*, the dried petals persist around the developing fruit-capsule.

   P. involucratum has a very restricted distribution, being endemic to the western Pamir Alai in the southern CIS (Tadzikistan), where it is apparently confined to indurated moraines at 2,800–3,300 m (9,200–10,800 ft). It may also possibly be found across the border in the Afghan Pamir, in the mountains of the Wakhan Corridor.

Papaver kerneri Hayek

A small alpine poppy of the *P. burseri* persuasion but readily distinguished on account of its yellow, rather than white, flowers. The fruit-capsule usually has five stigmatic rays.

   A native of the south-eastern Alps of Austria, Italy and the neighbouring regions of Yugoslavia where it inhabits high mountain rocks, screes and moraines.

   Occasionally offered in seed lists but by no means common in cultivation.

Papaver kluanense D. Löve

A delightful little sulphur-yellow poppy of the *P. radicatum* complex endemic to the Canadian rockies where it inhabits rocky places, particularly screes. In the wild it is seldom more than 9 cm (4 in) tall, though in cultivation it can be rather taller. I am not sure how it differs from *P. radicatum* and its brethren, so have not included it in the key to species. That as it may be, this is a charming little plant which, like its cousins, tends to be short-lived in cultivation and seed needs to be resown at regular intervals. A well-drained scree or sheltered raised bed suit it best. Seed is sometimes offered by specialist alpine societies.

Papaver lapponicum (A. Tolm.) Nordh.
(Syn. *P. radicatum* subsp. *lapponicum* A. Tolm.)

A tufted perennial closely related to *P. radicatum* but stems and flowerbuds grey-brown rather than blackish- or reddish-brown hairy; this gives them an overall grey appearance. Plants are densely tufted and produce yellow latex. The leaves, 5–12 cm (2–5 in) long, are covered in whitish hairs. The flowers are relatively small, 25–35 mm (1–1⅖ in) across, the petals generally falling off as the fruits develop. The fruit-capsule is usually more slender than those of *P. radicatum*, being only 4-7 mm (⅙–²⁄₇ in) wide (not 7–10 mm (²⁄₇–⅖ in)) and widest in the upper part, the stigmatic disc has five to eight rays.

P. lapponicum is restricted to Arctic Norway and western Siberia where it is a plant of stony tundra, screes and moraines. It is occasionally offered in seed lists but scarcely as good a plant in gardens as '*P. alpinum*'. However, *P. lapponicum* has probably been used in the breeding of the modern Iceland poppy strains, together with *P. nudicaule* and *P. radicatum*.

In Arctic Siberia similar but stockier plants, seldom more than 15 cm (6 in) tall are distinguished as *P. pulvinatum*. In addition, plants with very narrow, linear, leaf-segments and elegant, tapered fruit-capsules, also from Arctic Siberia (Yenisei region), are called *P. angustifolium*.

Papaver lasiothrix Fedde

This little-known species is probably not in cultivation at the present time or vary rare. It is closely related to *P. orientale* from which it differs in having blood-red flowers with consistently six petals, only 4–5 cm (1⅗–2 in) long (not 4.5–9 cm (1⅘–3½ in) in the wild form). In addition, the bristles on the flower stems (peduncles) are spreading rather than appressed. The flower may occasionally have two small bracts immediately beneath.

P. lasiothrix is found in the wild up to 1,450 m (4,750 ft) on meadows and woodland margins, occasionally on rocky slopes, in Turkey (Lazistan to Cappodocia), the Caucasus and northern and north-western Iran.

Papaver lateritium C. Koch   [Pl. 72]
ARMENIAN POPPY

A tufted perennial with mostly basal leaves and many slender, hairy stems reaching up to 50 cm (20 in) tall, though often less. The leaves are lanceolate, coarsely toothed to pinnately-lobed, stalked, hairy like the stems. The solitary flowers are a bright brick-red, sometimes apricot, 4.5–6 cm (1⅘–2⅖ in) across, with orange-yellow anthers; the sepals are covered in long yellowish hairs. The smooth fruit-capsule is club-shaped, the broadest part below the stigmatic disk.

P. lateritium is a native of the mountains of Turkish Armenia (Lazistan) where it inhabits rocky places, cliff crevices and screes at 1,200–3,000 m (3,900–9,850 ft) altitude; flowering in July and August.

This is another good garden poppy fairly closely related to the western Mediterranean *P. atlanticum* and *P. rupifragum*. Like those species it is a short-lived perennial, readily raised from seed and, in favoured gardens at least, sowing itself around once established. Unlike its cousins, *P. lateritium* is more seasonal in flowering with most blooms appearing during May and June. It is perfectly hardy – to at least −15°C (5°F).

The relationship of these poppies to *P. orientalis* and its allies is not properly understood and it is not clear whether or not these species all hybridise readily in cultivation. *P. lateritium* is very close to the Caucasian *P. oreophilum* and *P. monanthum*. This latter species does (as explained on p. 139) form an interconnecting series with *P. orientale* and its allies despite the fact that some botanists place them in different sections of the genus.

Papaver lateritium

P. lateritium has become naturalised in several localities in Britain, perhaps elsewhere in southern Europe.

The exact status of 'Fireball' [**Pl. 73**] (= ×*hybridum* 'Flore Pleno', 'Nanum Flore Pleno', 'Nana Plena'), a charming little poppy, is unclear although current thinking would have it as a form of *P. lateritium*, or at least to have that species in its parentage. In literature it is often classed as a form of *P. orientale*, although that is clearly wrong. This is a small plant with mostly basal, bristly leaves and slender bristly stems 20–30 cm (8–12 in) tall, carrying double, orange-scarlet flowers, each 3–4 cm (1⅕–1⅗ in) across and with numerous rather narrow uneven petals. This dainty poppy is perfectly hardy; a nomadic plant that seldom stays where planted for long but soon pops up elsewhere.

Because of its stature this is a plant for the front of the border but its bright colour is not always easy to place sympathetically – perhaps it should be isolated amongst grey- or silvery-leaved plants in the herbaceous border. Unfortunately it does not stay in bloom for very long and does not repeat flower in my experience. In cultivation there is at least two forms of 'Fireball' available, one more robust and almost twice the height of the other and with rather larger flowers, but both the same fiery colour. Like *P. lateritium* it is a long-lived perennial in the garden.

Papaver lecoqii Lamotte
BABINGTON'S POPPY

Very similar to *P. dubium*, but flowers more orange-yellow and with yellow anthers. In addition the leaves are more deeply dissected and less glaucous-looking. An interesting feature of this plant is that the latex produced from a cut surface quickly turns yellow on exposure to air; in *P. dubium* it remains white.

A native of western and south-western Europe from Britain and Belgium southwards to Spain, Portugal and Corsica. It is also found in a few localities in Greece. *P. lecoqii* is a plant of cultivated, fallow and wasteland like its close cousins, being sometimes found along roadsides where it flowers from May to July, occasionally later. Rarely cultivated.

Papaver macrostomum Boiss. et Huet
(Syn. *P. dalechianum* Fedde; *P. divergens* Fedde; *P. floribundum* Ledeb.; *P. kurdistanicum* Fedde)

A spectacular Asian poppy with large flowers of deep purple or red. *P. macrostomum* is a softly bristly annual 20–60 cm (8–24 in) tall, generally branching close to the base. The leaves are pinnately lobed, or at least deeply incised with long, lanceolate, sharply toothed, pointed segments, each terminating in a bristle, otherwise virtually hairless. The solitary flowers are borne on long and flexuous, appressed-bristly stems, the hairy, oval buds relatively large, to 20 mm (⅘ in) long. The flowers, 4–5 cm (1⅗–2 in) across, occasionally larger, are purple or deep rose-red, each of the wide overlapping petals with a black oblong, squarrish or kidney-shaped, basal black blotch; stamens with slender black filaments and black anthers. The fruit-capsule is very distinctive, smooth and bluish-green, oblong-club-shaped, 10–20 mm (⅖–⅘ in) long, with the stigmatic disk falling away to open the capsule when it is ripe; the disk has five to ten distinctly keeled rays with wide sinuses between the lobes.

This striking and distinctive poppy is native from Anatolian Turkey eastwards to the Caucasus, Syria, Iran and Afghanistan, as well as occurring in southern Russia. Like so many annual poppies *P. macrostomum* inhabits cultivated and fallow land, roadsides and wasteland, but it can also be found

Fruit capsule of *Papaver macrostomum*

on stony steppes and hillslopes, at 1,300–2,000 m (4,250–6,550 ft) altitude; flowering from late May until July.

The distinctive feature of the ripe fruit-capsule serves to distinguish it from the other annual red poppies. It is primarily for this feature that *P. macrostomum* occupies its own section, the Carinatae, within the genus.

P. macrostomum is occasionally seen in cultivation, primarily in botanic gardens, however, it is a very fine and colourful annual and certainly deserves to be more widely known. Like its cousins it requires an open sunny site, thriving best in light, well-drained, soils.

P. piptostigma Biernert ex Fedde and *P. tubuliferum* Fedde, both endemic to Kurdistan (north-eastern Iraq and north-western Iran), are probably only forms of *P. macrostomum* and little known.

Papaver minus (Boiv.) Meikle
(Syn. *Closterandra minor* Boiv.; *Papaver belangeri* Boiss.)

A small poppy very closely related to *P. argemone* with which it is frequently confused. It differs primarily in its decumbent habit, crimson or purplish, funnel-shaped flowers with erect petals, each 10–25 mm (⅖–1 in) long and with a dark blotch at the base. The oval fruit-capsule has generally a few erect bristles close to the top.

P. minus, which is more widely known than *P. belangeri*, is native to the eastern Mediterranean region and western Asia eastwards to Iran and the Caucasus. It is a plant primarily of cultivated and fallow fields to 1,500 m (4,900 ft) altitude. It is probably not in cultivation.

Papaver miyabeanum Tatew. [Pl. 74]
JAPANESE POPPY

Another delightful little poppy in the *P. nudicaule* – *P. radicatum* association. *P. miyabeanum* is seldom more than 8–10 cm (3–4 in) tall and forms quite dense tufts of rough greyish, pinnately-lobed leaves. The bristly scapes bear solitary pale yellow poppies, 3–4 cm (1⅕–1⅗ in) across with similarly coloured or somewhat darker stamens. The fruit-capsule is almost globose, with appressed bristles and a broad stigmatic disk with six to nine rays.

This dainty poppy has only been in cultivation for a few years, yet it is quite widely available. It is without doubt one of the finest poppies for the scree or rock garden. Plants are short-lived and resent winter moisture, often rotting off at ground level. However, it is easy to collect some seed each year and sow afresh in the spring. I find that, although the parent plants invariably succumb to the vagaries of the winter, seedlings often appear spontaneously the following year so that I have never needed to sow fresh seed to maintain stock.

P. miyabeanum comes from the Kurile Islands, to the north of Japan. The name has been much abused in literature, appearing variously as *P. moyabeanum, P. myabeanum, P. myerbeanum, P. moyabenum* var. *tokwokri, P. takedaki* var. *myerbeanum* . . . I could go on. The plant was in fact named by Dr Misao Tatewaki in honour of Dr Kingo Miyabe (1860–1951) a well-known Japanese botanist and author of the *Flora of the Kurile Islands*, so the correct name and spelling of the plant is *Papaver miyabeanum* Tatewaki.

P. fauriei Fedde, a rare species described from the island of Rishiri off the north-west coast of Hokkaido is very similar to *P. miyabeanum* and the two may be conspecific. However, I have not had the opportunity to study relevent material of these two entities and literature scarcely helps to clarify the differences. If they should prove to be the same species then *P. fauriei* would be the prior and correct name to use.

Papaver nigrotinctum Fedde

A little-known Greek species closely related to *P. argemone* but a smaller plant not more than 20 cm (8 in) tall with numerous ascending stems and bipinnately dissected leaves, and broad, scarcely overlapping red petals with

Papaver nigrotinctum

a large basal, black blotch. The fruit-capsule is narrower than that of *P. argemone*, not more than 15 mm (⅗ in) long.

This interesting species is restricted to the Aegean region, to Korinthos and the Cyclades where it grows on stony ground and in sandy or waste places at low altitudes, flowering there during April and May.

P. nigrotinctum is generally believed to be of hybrid origin between *P. argemone* and *P. apulum* and reveals more or less intermediate characters between these two species. It differs from *P. apulum* primarily by its hairy rounded, rather than smooth and oval, flowerbuds. Although it has been in cultivation from time to time it does not appear to be so at the present time, although it may be present in collections at botanic gardens.

Papaver nivale A. Tolm.

A small poppy restricted to eastern Siberia at relatively low altitudes of 914–977 m (3,000–3,200 ft). Unlike the other scapose poppies of the CIS, *P. nivale* has two-pinnately divided, rather than simple pinnate, leaves. This and its other characteristics put it closer to the European '*P. alpinum*' complex, being perhaps closest to *P. rhaeticum* in its bright yellow flowers, 3–4 cm (1⅕–1⅗ in) across. The darkly bristly fruit-capsule are smaller, not more than 10 mm (⅖ in) long.

A little-known species but clearly with the charm and elegance of its '*P. alpinum*' cousins. It has not, to my knowledge, been recorded in cultivation but should present few problems should seed ever become available.

Papaver nudicaule L. [Pl. 75]
'ICELAND POPPY'

This name conjures up as much confusion in horticulture as does the related *P. alpinum*. *P. nudicaule* is commonly called the Iceland poppy, however, it does not come from Iceland, indeed it is restricted to Asia. But, this species is related to a whole group of closely allied species that form a complicated network of variability, which can leave the poor gardener wholly distracted. The species concerned have a wide distribution across many of the cold regions of the northern hemisphere, stretching southwards into Asia, Afghanistan and the western Himalaya. Of these a number of elements can be clearly recognised amongst wild populations including *P. nudicaule* itself, *P. alboroseum*, which is restricted to the Kamschatka region, *P. involucratum* centred on the mountains of southern central Asia, particularly the Pamir Alai, *P. lapponicum*, which is to be found in Arctic Europe and the neighbouring parts of Russia, and *P. radicatum*, which perhaps has the widest distribution of all, encompassing as it does much of Arctic Europe and North America, Greenland, Iceland and western Russia and Siberia.

This latter species is almost certainly the true Iceland poppy. In cultivation *P. nudicaule* has been crossed with its cousins and selected to produce a sturdy race of rather gaudy poppies commonly called Iceland poppies and generally found in catalogues and lists under the name *Papaver nudicaule*.

True *P. nudicaule* is a relatively tall plant with solitary-flowered, rather bristly, scapes up to 50 cm (20 in) tall, though often 30–40 cm (12–16 in). The basal leaf-tufts are covered with greyish hairs, the leaves pinnate with oblong or lanceolate segments. The flower buds are quite large being 1–2 cm (⅖–⅘ in) in diameter, the sepals with greyish or brownish hairs. The flowers are yellow, broadly cup-shaped and mostly 4–6 cm (2–3 in) across. The fruit-capsules are narrowly club-shaped to oblong and covered in appressed whitish or reddish-brown bristles.

P. nudicaule is distributed in Asia from Siberia to Mongolia southwards into the mountains of central Asia as far as Afghanistan. In these remote regions it is primarily a plant of mountain screes and moraines, steppes and river gravels, at altitudes up to 4,600 m (15,100 ft).

Although it has been noted that *P. nudicaule* is commonly listed in catalogues and plant lists, the wild species is seldom seen in cultivation, but rather a complex derived from various species which hybridise readily – for more details see under *P. radicatum* (p. 163).

The following are sometimes listed as varieties of *P. nudicaule* but are considered by some to be distinct species in their own right, often with a very limited distribution (see, for instance, *Flora of the USSR* Vol. 7: 456–494).

var. *croeceum* (Syn. *P. alpinum* var. *croeceum* Ledeb.; *P. croeceum* Ledeb.; *P. nudicaule* subsp. *commune* var. *rubro-aurantiacum* N. Busch)

Differs in having bright orange or red flowers, the buds with rusty-brown hairs and the leaf segments often toothed.

Native to scattered localities in Siberia, the mountains of central Asia, the western Himalaya and Mongolia.

var. *microcarpum* (Syn. *P. alpinum* var. *microcarpum* Ledeb.; *P. microcarpum* DC.)

A small plant to 20 cm (8 in) tall, though often less. Flowers small, 20–30 mm (⅘–1⅕ in) across, orange to orange-red, the petals falling off as the fruit develops.

Restricted to Kamchatka where it may intergrade with *P. alboroseum*.

var. *rubro-aurantiacum* Fisch. ex DC. (Syn. *P. rubro-aurantiacum* Fisch. ex Steud.)

Distinct on account of its grey leaves and the flower buds which are silky with whitish hairs. Flowers orange or orange-red, 35–40 mm (1⅖–1⅗ in).

Restricted to eastern Siberia (Dauria) and Mongolia.

The Iceland poppies, as known today in gardens, have strong scapes up to 60 cm (24 in) tall and carry large flowers, to 18 cm (7 in) across, in a range of brash colours – orange, red, yellow, apricot, pink, salmon, cream and white shades predominating. They often have more than the normal ration of four petals and semi-double forms are not uncommon. The first flowers to open on each plant are the largest.

These bright poppies are good garden plants, excellent in summer bedding displays and will flower over a long season. They can be raised from seed in much the same way as many hardy and half-hardy bedding plants. Sow thinly in pots to avoid the problem of damping off and prick out seedlings when they have developed one good leaf. Alternatively direct sow where the plants are to flower, thinning seedlings out to 15–20 cm (6–8 in) in order to get good strong plants. They are often sold in pots at garden centres where individual colours can be selected but it is far better to buy seed if more than just a few plants are wanted. Although perennial, these tufted plants often rot off during wet winters so that annual sowings are perhaps the best way of maintaining it in the garden.

The Iceland poppies also make excellent cut flowers and these are commonly seen for sale in bunches in both Holland and Germany. Commercially they are grown in light airy glasshouses or polythene tunnels. They are normally sown successively from early spring until the summer in rows some 25–30 cm (10–12 in) apart for summer and autumn harvesting. Alternatively, mid-summer sowing will produce a saleable crop of flowers early the following year, though modest heat is required during the winter for such production or indeed for producing pot-grown plants early in the season. The wide range of bright colours and the 'crepe de chine' petals make them popular cut flowers in some countries. For cutting they are best gathered whilst the sepals are still attached but after the buds have taken on an unright position – just before the petals burst out. The cut stems ends should be sealed in hot water or burnt to improve the lasting quality of the blooms.

Various strains of Iceland poppy are sold by seed merchants; they are invariably listed under *P. nudicaule*. They include:

'Aurora Borealis' – a fine strain with exceptionally large flowers in the full range of colours.

'Champagne Bubbles' – to 40 cm (16 in) tall; large flowers in various shades.

'Garden Gnome' ('Gartenzwerg') – a dwarf strain only 30 cm (12 in) tall, neat and compact, with flowers in a range of reds, pinks, yellow, orange and white.

'Hamlet' – another large-flowered race, in shades of orange and red mainly.

'Kelmscott Giant' – to 80 cm (32 in) tall with flowers in pastel shades.

'Matador' – large flowers 10–12 cm (4–5 in) across of the deepest, brightest scarlet.

'Oregon Rainbows' – a strain developed for the cut-flower market in the USA with sturdy stems with blooms often 18 cm (7 in) across, single or semi-double, in the full range of colours, including also bicoloured forms and picotées with pale or darker margins.

'Pacino' – dwarf form with pale yellow flowers.

'San Remo' – another large flowered mixture with mostly single flowers in a wide range of the usual colours.

'Unwins Giant Coonara' – bright flowers in yellow, orange and red, 50 cm (20 in).

'Wonder Hybrids' – another good colourful dwarf mixture, sometimes available, and includes whites.

In addition several companies offer a general or special mixture of Iceland poppies, both single- and double-flowered.

Papaver occelatum Woron.

This poppy is sometimes regarded as a synonym of *P. pavoninum*, but differs primarily in its hornless sepals and in the stamen filaments, which are clearly thickened towards the anther end. The flowers are very pretty, being a pure red, the petals with a basal black arch often with a red area or ocellus inside, like a large bright eye. The fruit-capsule is adorned with thin spreading bristles.

P. ocellatum is native to Central Asia from the Caucasus to the Tien Shan, including northern Iran, where it inhabits sandy and clayey steppes, fields and roadsides, flowering from April to July. It is probably not in cultivation at the present time, but confusion with *P. pavoninum* may mean that it is still being grown somewhere but under the wrong name.

Papaver oreophilum Rupr.
(Syn. *P. lateritium* var. *minus* Boiss.)

This interesting Caucasian poppy looks like a dwarf *P. orientale*, being generally only 10–20 cm (4–8 in) tall. The leaves are mostly basal, narrow lanceolate and pinnately lobed into sharply toothed segments, often terminating in a weak bristle; most of the leaves, except for the uppermost, are stalked. The solitary flowers, 6–10 cm (2⅖–4 in) across, are borne on long peduncles, the oval flower buds covered in soft reddish-brown hairs; the four petals are bright orange-red without a dark basal blotch; stamens with yellow filaments and anthers. The smooth fruit-capsule is 15–17 mm (⅗ in) long, greyish-green, the stigmatic disk usually with five to seven rays.

P. oreophilum is endemic to the Caucasus where it inhabits alpine meadow, rocks and stony slopes at 1,700–2,500 m (5,600–8,200 ft) altitude.

This interesting species is occasionally cultivated in gardens although it is not generally available in trade. In many ways it is a half-way species between *P. orientale* and *P. lateritium*, being clearly more closely associated with the latter from which it differs in its larger flowers and broader fruit-capsule.

Papaver orientale L.   [Pl. 76]
(Syn. *P. pollakii* A. Kerner)
ORIENTAL POPPY

Much confusion has surrounded this name both in botanical as well as horticultural circles. In gardens, the oriental poppies are in fact primarily a mixture of two distinct, though closely allied species, *P. orientale* and *P. bracteatum*. If this is not confusing enough, most plant catalogues fail to

Fruit of *Papaver orientale*

distinguish between the two, grouping all the cultivars under *P. orientalis* or under a general heading of oriental poppies. Perhaps this is of little concern to the gardener but, from a botanical perspective at least, it is necessary to distinguish these entities most clearly.

The main confusion stems from the fact that not only do these two species look alike but they inhabit the same geographical region in the wild – broadly, western Asia from Anatolian Turkey to Iran and the Caucasus; although they grow in the same general region they appear to be mostly isolated from one another.

P. orientale differs from *P. bracteatum* in being a slighter plant, rarely more than 90 cm (36 in) tall, often less, with slender stems 2–3 mm (⅛ in) in diameter. The flowers, somewhat smaller, are without bracts immediately below (at the top of the pedicels and pressed close to the base of the calyx) and the petals have a rounded or squarrish black blotch just above their base, or no blotch at all. In contrast, *P. bracteatum* is a more robust plant, to 1.2 m (4 ft) tall, sometimes taller, the stem stouter, 3–5 mm (⅛–⅕ in) diameter. The large flowers have three to five oval, sepal-like bracts immediately below the sepals; in addition there may also be one or two small leaves. The petals have a prominent oblong, basal, black blotch.

The oriental poppy (in its widest sense) was certainly known to John Miller and in his *Gardener's Dictionary* he recorded '*Papaver Orientale hirsutissimum, flore magno* – Very Rough Oriental Poppy with large flower' and stated: 'The Oriental Poppy is an abiding Plant, which produces a large single flower in May, which make a beautiful appearance. This may be propagated from Seeds, or by parting their roots. The best time to transplant them is at the beginning of March; this must have a light soil and a warm situation.'

P. orientale is a tough, tufted perennial with the new leaves appearing in the autumn and generally with a stoloniferous habit. The bristly stems rise to 50–90 cm (20–36 in) and are generally unbranched, leafy in the lower two-thirds – usually with three to six leaves per stem. The large bristly leaves, to 30 cm (12 in) long, are oblong to lanceolate in outline, but deeply pinnately-lobed, each lobe toothed and terminating in a large bristle; the basal and lower leaves are clearly stalked, while the upper are smaller and unstalked. The large showy flowers are bright orange or orange-red, broadly cup-shaped, 10–16 cm (4–6 in) across (rather larger in cultivated specimens), the four to six petals with a violet-black blotch just above the base, or sometimes unblotched; the numerous stamens have dark filaments, which are dilated towards the top, and violet anthers. The smooth, globose fruit-capsule, 2–3 cm (⅘–1⅕ in) long, has a flat stigmatic disk with 10–16 rays, occasionally fewer.

P. orientale is native to the Anatolian region of Turkey, the Caucasus and northern and north-western Iran, where it is primarily a plant of meadows, stony slopes, open forest glades, especially in the subalpine zone at altitudes of 1,950–2,800 m (6,400–9,200 ft) where it flowers during May–July.

P. orientale was first described by Linnaeus who cited it as 'in oriente'. It was subsequently discovered by the seventeenth-century French botanist J.P. de Tournefort near Erzurum in eastern Anatolia and described in his Relation d'un voyage au Levant. It was first grown in Britain early in the eighteenth century by the royal gardener and nurseryman George London.

It is undoubtedly a very fine garden plant and for those who desire a less brash and more delicate oriental poppy then this is the one to select, rather than the robuster more overbearing races of P. bracteatum. Some may find its stoloniferous and invading habit (at least in some forms) annoying, though it does afford a ready and time-saving means of propagation. In my experience these stolons are best removed and replanted in the autumn as the new leaves begin to emerge, for this allows the new plants time to build up sufficiently for a good display of flowers the following summer.

The oriental poppies are the most accommodating garden plants, vigorous and free-flowering and succeeding on light or heavy garden soils, indeed virtually any soil providing it is not waterlogged. Their boldness and brashness of colour make them often difficult to place satisfactorily in the garden but, when well placed they will make a spectacular feature. They are so bold that they will often swamp associated plants in the herbaceous border by sheer size and colour, so it is perhaps best to plant later flowering perennials in their immediate vicinity – michaelmass daisies, red hot pokers (Kniphofia) or rudbeckias for instance. If the oriental poppies have an irritating habit then it is that once having flowered the plants immediately begin to die down and turn brown. This ugly mass of stems and leaves can soon be cleared away but it does leave a nasty void in the border so that planting later flowering subjects close by is a good means of filling such gaps.

Propagation is simple. For most gardeners, who just need one or two extra plants, lifting and dividing the clumps in the late summer is probably the best method. The various cultivars grow in rather different ways; some sucker freely whilst others remain as a discreet dense clump. The former can be propagated simply by carefully digging up suckers while leaving the parent clump intact. With the latter, the whole clump needs to be lifted and prized apart with a couple of forks placed back to back. In effect a careful slicing up with a spade does not, in my experience, cause significant damage and mutilated pieces will soon sprout anew. Most oriental poppies start into growth again in the early autumn, the leaves remaining small until the following spring when they rapidly grow away.

Commercially, the oriental poppies are propagated by root cuttings. The thick fleshy roots are ideal for this purpose. Healthy roots can be chopped into 3–4 cm (1⅕–1⅗ in) long pieces and placed upright in a peat/sharp-sand mixture in pots or a gently heated propagating frame. The cuttings should be placed topside up and just covered. They will soon sprout new leaves. This habit of growing from pieces of root can be irritating in the border, for the slightest piece left in when clearing a piece of ground will sprout anew. Despite this, these flamboyant plants, so characteristic of the cottage garden, deserve a place in every garden.

Oriental poppies can be grown from seed and some seed merchants offer several varieties or a mixture. Many of the resultant seedlings are fine plants but can be expected to vary in colour from plant to plant and this offers great scope for further selection and hybridisation. Indeed new colours are constantly coming onto the market. Seed can be sown in pots or sown directly into the soil where they are to flower, either in drills or scattered – spring is the best time. Young plants should be finally set apart at about 40–50 cm (16–20 in) and will flower in the second or third year from seed. Plants are best moved or divided in the autumn.

Many of the strong-stemmed oriental poppies make spectacular cut flowers and are quite commonly sold in the summer flower markets of Holland, Germany and elsewhere. They are best cut just before the sepals split apart to reveal the petals. The cut ends of the stems should be sealed by burning them or placing them for a short while in boiling water; this prevents them wilting.

Although many 'oriental poppy' cultivars are available today this was not always so. At the turn of the century only the wild red form existed in gardens. Their development is due primarily to the nurseryman Amos Perry, of Enfield near London. In 1906 he discovered a pink-flowered one amongst a batch of red-flowered seedlings and named it after his wife; 'Mrs Perry' is a fine cultivar still much grown today. In 1913 he received an irate letter from a customer complaining that his pink and red border had been ruined by a single white poppy – another chance seedling that Amos Perry had sent out unflowered. Perry managed to exchange this non-conformist poppy for a few Montbretia corms and named it 'Perry's White', which is still the finest white 'oriental poppy' today. Perry's Hardy Plant Farm began to select and specialise in this 'gorgeous group of plants'. Among the finest selected were 'E.A. Bowles', 'Mary Queen', 'Indian Chief', 'Mrs Stobart' and 'Peter Pan', besides the two already mentioned.

The cultivars of *P. orientale*, though far fewer in number than those of *P. bracteatum*, are in every way as fine and spectacular garden plants. What is unclear is the part played by *P. orientalis* in the breeding of *P. bracteatum* hybrids because few have been produced by a deliberate and systematic programme of hybridisation. To avoid confusion all the oriental poppy cultivars are listed here whether or not they have bracts below the flower buds. All flower in the period from mid-May to early July.

'Allegro' – 60–75 cm (24–30 in) tall bearing large papery bright scarlet flowers, the petals with a bold black blotch at the base.

'Beauty of Livermere' – a fine old variety formerly very popular in the garden. Strong stems, to 1.2 m (4 ft), carry large crimson-scarlet, single flowers, each petal with a large basal black blotch.

'Beauty Queen' – a rather tall variety to 1 m (3 ft), with single flowers of brown flushed with apricot.

'Black and White' – a striking plant with single white flowers with a dark centre, each petal with a black blotch just above the base. Only 70–80 cm (28–32 in) tall.

'Blue Moon' – a 1 m (3 ft) tall plant produces giant flowers, 20–25 cm (8–10 in) across, of a mauve-pink marked with black in the throat and with contrasting maroon veins on the reverse of the petals. The heavy flowers usually require some support.

'Cedric's Pink' (= 'Cedric Morris') – 80–90 cm (32–36 in) tall with soft pink flowers with a contrasting black blotch at the base of each petal; tends to fade in strong sun. [**Pl. 77–79**]

'Curlilocks' – 70–75 cm (28–30 in) tall, with large orange-red flowers with distinctive lacerated petals with a large basal black blotch.

'Darkness'* – an old cultivar no longer available; flowers deep maroon.

'Doubloon'* – 90 cm (35 in) tall with double orange-red flowers; rarely offered.

'Double Flame'* – 50–70 cm (19–28 in) tall with huge double or semi-double flame flowers.

'Dwarf Allegro' – not more than 50 cm (20 in) tall, this variety makes compact clumps with 15 cm (6 in) blooms of vivid scarlet.

'Fatima' – a compact variety to 50 cm (20 in) with white flowers edged with pink; petals with a dark basal blotch.

'Flore Pleno' – See *P. lateritium* 'Fireball' (p. 147).

'Glowing Embers' – a vigorous variety to 110 cm (44 in) tall with glowing orange-red flowers, with somewhat ruffled petals.

'Goliath' – (probably the same as 'Beauty of Livermere') perhaps the most common oriental poppy in gardens. A big bold plant with huge scarlet flowers with a large basal black blotch to each petal. [**Pl. 80–81**]

'Harvest Moon' – a startling variety, 110 cm (44 in) tall with semi-double, deep orange flowers; one of the boldest of all oriental poppies.

'Helen Elizabeth'* – a dwarf type, seldom exceeding 70 cm (28 in) tall, with attractive rich pink flowers.

'Indian Chief' – has large deep mahogany-red flowers of great substance and certainly one of the most spectacular cultivars.

'Ladybird' – a dwarf type, to only 60 cm (24 in) tall, but with substantial vermillion-red blooms, each petal with a basal black blotch.

'Lord Lambourne'★ – 70–90 cm (28–36 in) with large orange-scarlet flowers.

'Mahony'★ – an old cultivar no longer available; flowers deep maroon.

'Marcus Perry' – 75 cm (30 in) tall with strong erect stems and orange-scarlet flowers.

'May Queen'★ – a vigorous plant with double orange-scarlet flowers.

'Midnight' – a leafy variety to 75 cm (30 in) with large orange-pink flowers, each up to 15 cm (6 in) across.

'Mrs Perry' – a fine old variety with rich salmon-pink flowers, each petal with a basal black blotch. [**Pl. 79**]

'Mrs Stobart' (= 'Mrs George Stobart') – a large flowered plant with cerise flowers flushed with rose and with black blotches at the base of the petals.

'Nanum Flore Pleno' – See *P. lateritium* 'Fireball' (p. 147).

'Olympia'★ – a *P. orientalis* type with semi-double red flowers, the petals with a dark basal blotch.

'Olympic Flame' – 90 cm (36 in) tall with medium-sized orange-scarlet blooms; one of the earliest to flower.

'Oriana'★ – 70 cm (28 in) tall with ruffled orange flowers with a black centre.

'Pale Face' – a bractless variety with pale pink, white-centred, blooms; to 90 cm (36 in).

'Peter Pan'★ – a dwarf variety with numerous large bright crimson blooms.

'Perry's White' – 90 cm (36 in) tall with pure white flowers with a dark 'eye' but the petals with scarcely any sign of a dark blotch.

'Picotée' – a delightful picotée with pure white petals with a contrasting broad orange frilled edge; 60–70 cm (24–28 in) tall; very distinct.

'Prinzessin (Princess) Victoria Louise' – a 75 cm (30 in) tall with strong stems and significant salmon-rose flowers, each petal with a conspicuous basal black blotch.

'Redizelle'★ – 90 cm (36 in) tall with deep scarlet flowers, each petal with a bold black blotch at the base.

'Suleika'★ – 90 cm (36 in), with deep red flowers with a bluish gloss; petals fringed and with a basal black blotch.

'Sultana' – a popular variety with large deep rose flowers, the petals slightly darker at the base; 80–90 cm (32–35 in) tall.

'Tulip'★ – an old cultivar no longer available, which had distinctive long-tapered flowerbuds and deep red flowers.

'Türkenlouis' ('Turkish Delight') – 60–80 cm (24–32 in) tall, without bracts; flowers soft pink without the usual dark centre.

'Waterloo'★ – woolly leaves and dark crimson flowers suffused with purple – an old cultivar no longer available.

★ not available in trade.

In addition selections are offered as seed and called 'Border Vars. Mixed'. 'New Hybrids' is a fine large-flowered mixture with blooms in shades of white, pink, salmon, orange, scarlet, crimson and mahogany tinted with gold or violet, mostly with dark centres and some with picotée edges. A delightful mixture but it is potluck which colours will appear.

Papaver paucifoliatum (Trautv.) Fedde.
(See also general remarks under *P. bracteatum*, p. 139)

This species, which looks like a small and daintier version of *P. orientale*, has practically leafless stems and smaller flowers. In gardens it tends to make a spreading patch and is ideal where the robuster 'oriental' types would be out of place.

This species is restricted to subalpine meadows in the Caucasus Mountains. It is sometimes listed as *P. orientale* var. *paucifoliatum* Trautv. and indeed it was first described as such. In gardens it is perhaps best considered a variety of that species.

Papaver pavoninum Schrenk   [Pl. 82]
PEACOCK POPPY

This is another of those exciting scarlet poppies that can cause a mass display of colour in the early summer. In the steppes and hill country of Uzbekistan and Kazakhstan where I have seen it, blankets and ribbons of scarlet stretch across the landscape, a gaudy profusion reminiscent of the poppy fields of western Europe. In the wild *P. pavoninum* often grows in association with

Papaver pavoninum flowerbud and fruit

Roemeria refracta and at a glance the two can readily be confused. However, examination of the fruits soon reveals the difference, those of the latter long and linear, of the former broad and bristly.

P. pavoninum is an annual, generally 20–30 cm (8–12 in) tall, though occasionally taller in deep and moister soils. The erect stems are generally branched close to the ground and are beset with stiff bristles. The basal leaves are long-stalked and bipinnately lobed, with oblong to oval, sharply toothed, segments, each lobe ending in a short bristle; the stem leaves are similar although often less dissected and short-stalked or sessile. The flower buds are oval in outline, bristly and terminating in a characteristic pair of hollow horns. The flowers, 3.5–5.5 cm (1⅖–2⅕ in) across are scarlet, each petal with a basal black blotch, which is sometimes outlined by a thin white line; the black or dark violet anthers produce blue pollen. The fruit-capsule is oval in outline, 5–10 mm (⅕–⅖ in) long, ribbed and with semi-spreading pale bristles, the stigmatic disk with four to eight (occasionally up to 11) rays.

P. pavoninum has a wide distribution in central Asia from northern Iran to Pakistan and northwards through the Tienshan and Altai from Turkmenistan to Kazakhstan. In these regions it is a plant of cultivated land, stony steppes, foothills and dry mountain slopes at altitudes of 500–2,600 m (1,650–8,500 ft), though mostly at the lower altitudinal range.

This species is closely related to *P. hybridum* and *P. argemone*; they all belong to section Argemonorhoedes, which is characterised by fruit-capsules that are covered in stiff bristles and capped by a narrow stigmatic disk. Within this section *P. pavoninum* is at once distinguished by the two conspicuous hollow horns which terminate the sepals and by the uniformly linear stamen filaments; in the other related species the filaments are distinctly thickened towards the top.

P. ocellatum is sometimes regarded as a variant of *P. pavoninum* in which the sepal horns are virtually obsolete.

In gardens *P. pavoninum* is sometimes confused with *P. commutatum*. They look superficially alike in flower but the hornless flower buds and smooth fruit-capsules of the latter are 'give away' identification features.

P. pavoninum is an easy and floriferous garden plant, best sown in the early spring where it is to flower. It will sometimes self-sow in the garden but cannot always be relied upon to do so, therefore it is wise to collect some seed each summer for the following year. Some forms in cultivation have a violet, or violet and black, basal blotch to each petal, rather than plain black.

Papaver pilosum Sibth. & Sm.

This Turkish poppy is very closely related to *P. spicatum*, differing primarily in its fruit-capsules, which are broader and with a rounded rather than tapered base and capped by a more or less flat (not pyramidal) stigmatic disk. The flowers range in colour from orange-red to deep orange or lurid scarlet, the petals often with a pale, whitish, basal blotch. The flower buds are almost spherical rather than oval as in *P. spicatum*.

Fruit of *Papaver pilosum*

P. pilosum is restricted to the provinces of Bithynia and Galatia where it is a plant of rocky mountain habitats; flowering in July and August. The related *P. apokrinomenon* Fedde, from Phrygia in Turkey, is generally regarded to be rather intermediate between *P. spicatum* and *P. pilosum* and may show that these elements are in fact extremes of a single variable species – this requires further investigation.

Occasionally seen in cultivation but by no means common. Treat as for *P. spicatum*.

Papaver pinnatifidum Moris.
MEDITERRANEAN POPPY

Very similar to *P. dubium*, but differing mainly in the stems, which have spreading hairs in the lower part of the plant and also in the yellow rather than violet anthers. In addition, the fruit-capsule is more club-shaped and has a somewhat tapered base and a slightly convex rather than flat stigmatic disk, with six to eight rays.

P. pinnatifidum is a native of the Mediterranean region from Spain and north-west Africa, eastwards to Greece, as well as Portugal. It is also found in the Canary Islands and the Azores, where it may also be native rather than introduced. It flowers from April to June. It is not in cultivation at the present time.

Papaver postii Fedde

A small spreading to decumbent, slighly bristly annual, not more than 20 cm (8 in) tall, often only 6-10 cm (2½–4 in). The leaves are deeply pinnately-lobed, 2–8 cm (⅘–3 in) long, with narrow, pointed segments, sometimes slightly toothed, mostly in a basal rosette. Flowers solitary on slender stalks (pedicels), orange-red to pale scarlet, 2–3.5 cm (⅘–1⅖ in) across, the petals without a dark basal blotch; stamens with yellow or brownish anthers and violet-purple filaments. The fruit-capsule is smooth or somewhat ribbed, top-shaped or broadly club-shaped, 6–8 mm (⅓ in) long, with a flat disk with five to seven stigmatic rays.

This small poppy inhabits rocky places, hill and mountain slopes, screes, up to 800 m (2,600 ft) altitude, sometimes being found along roadsides, where it flowers from April to June. *P. postii* is native to Turkey, Cyprus and Syria.

P. postii is related to *P. rhoeas* and *P. dubium*, being readily distinguished by its spreading to decumbent habit and small flowers, the petals never more than 2 cm (⅘ in) long. As far as I am aware it is not in cultivation.

Papaver radicatum Rōttb.
ARCTIC POPPY

This widespread Arctic species is closely related to *P. nudicaule*, being a tufted perennial, but it is a small plant, seldom over 25 cm (10 in) tall in flower. The stems and leaves, like those of *P. nudicaule*, exude a yellow, occasionally white, latex when cut. The leaves, 3–6 cm (1⅕–2⅖ in) long usually, are pinnately-lobed with small oblong to lanceolate, pointed segments and are clothed with darkish hairs. The slender scapes and sepals are covered in distinctive dark brown or blackish hairs. The flowers are usually dark yellow, 2.5–4 cm (1–1⅗ in) across, more rarely pinkish or white, the petals often withering and persisting around the developing fruit. The fruit-capsule is oval to rounded in outline, 10–17 mm (⅖–⅗ in) long and covered in dense, appressed or spreading, reddish-brown bristles; there are generally five stigmatic rays.

P. radicatum is a plant of moraines and screes, river gravels and stony steppes from North America to Greenland, Iceland, Arctic Europe and Arctic Russia, where it sometimes forms large scattered colonies from near sea level to 1,850 m (6,050 ft) in the mountains of Scandinavia.

This is undoubtedly a very variable species with many local forms and races – no less than 14 subspecies have been described from Europe alone, mostly restricted to small areas in the mountains of Scandinavia.

Seed of the wild type is sometimes available in cultivation. However, it is as a contributor to the garden forms of the Iceland poppy that it is perhaps best known. These vigorous, often gaudy, large-flowered poppies have an obscure origin that involves a number of closely related species which, though often isolated from one another in the wild, freely hybridise with one another in cultivation.

Other names in the 'P. radicatum complex' that occasionally turn up in seed lists include *P. alaskanum* Hultén, *P. macounii* Greene, *P. nigro-flavum* Hultén and *P. walpolei* Porsikil. However, it must be emphasised that although many of these entities can be separated geographically, their overall characters show considerable overlap and a wide-based research programme in both the Old and the New World is needed to ascertain whether or not any of these 'minor species' can be properly maintained. In cultivation they are often very difficult to separate, generally hybridise freely and tend to be short-lived. All are colourful and pretty little poppies well worth growing.

Fruit of *Papaver rhaeticum*

Papaver rhaeticum Leresche   [Pl. 83–84]
(Syn. *P. alpinum* subsp. *rhaeticum* (Leresche) Hayek; *P. pyrenaicum* subsp. *rhaeticum* (Leresche) Fedde)
RHAETIAN POPPY

A charming little alpine poppy confined to high mountain rocks, moraines and screes in the Pyrenees, south-western and eastern Alps as far as Yugoslavia, at altitudes of 1,500–3,050 m (4,900–10,000 ft); a plant generally found on limestone.

P. rhaeticum is a small tufted, bristly perennial with the leaf bases forming a compact tunic around the base of the plant. The leaves are one- or two-pinnately divided into short blunt lobes; the lower leaf-segments are alternate. The scapes, up to 20 cm (8 in) tall, have appressed bristles and bear solitary yellow (rarely red) flowers, 4–5 cm (1⅗–2 in) across. The oblong fruit-capsule, to 14 mm (⅗ in) long, has five to seven stigmatic rays.

One of the finest members of the '*P. alpina*' group sometimes offered in seed exchanges and catalogues. Not difficult to grow but short-lived in gardens.

See also the closely related *P. sendtneri* (p. 169). Both species were formerly grown in gardens as *P. pyrenaicum* and occasionally still occur under that name.

Papaver rhoeas L.   [Pl. 85–87]
COMMON POPPY, CORN POPPY, FLANDER'S POPPY

This is undoubtedly the most familiar of the poppies and probably the 'flowers of the field' mentioned in the Bible. It is the red that stains the arable lands of Europe and western Asia, reddens the motorway verges and roadside embankments. It is the poppy of Flanders fields and its blooms have come to symbolise the dead of the two World Wars – the crimson petals drops of precious blood spilt in battle. In Britain Poppy Day, when artificial red poppies are sold by the millions, symbolises the dead of the World Wars and the wars that have occurred subsequently. Yet this so familiar plant has become drastically reduced in many areas in recent years due to modern farming practises, particularly the widespread use of herbicides.

P. rhoeas, like a number of related species, is almost exclusively associated with cultivated habitats, particularly where land has been recently disturbed; seeds can persist in the soil for many years without germinating and it is often quite remarkable how huge colonies of *P. rhoeas* spring up on land shortly after it has been ploughed or otherwise disturbed. This effect will last as long as regular annual disturbance is repeated.

It is wrong to think that all the red poppies seen in 'the wild' are *P. rhoeas*, for there are a number of similar looking species that are generally readily distinguished in fruit. In Europe *P. argemone*, *P. dubium* and *P. hybridum* are also widespread red poppies of cultivated, especially arable, land and in addition, in parts of the Mediterranean region *P. apulum* and *P. nigrotinctum* add to the confusion. In western Asia *P. arenarium*, *P. commutatum* and *P. pavoninum* are equally widespread. In parts of central Asia, especially the southern CIS (Tadjikistan to Kazakstan and Uzbekistan), Iran and Afghanistan *Roemeria refracta* can be easily mistaken for *P. rhoeas*, however, its tell-tale linear pods, quite unlike those of any true *Papaver*, make it easy to distinguish.

Papaver rhoeas

Comparison of the fruits of *Papaver rhoeas* (left), *P. dubium* (right) and *P. commutatum* (below)

P. rhoeas is a very variable annual, 25-90 cm (10-36 in) tall, with bristly stems and leaves. The stem is usually branched and leafy, but in depauperate specimens growing on poor thin soil, they may be unbranched. The leaves are once or twice pinnately-lobed into narrow, toothed segments, the lower leaves stalked but the upper generally sessile. The buds are bristly, nodding at first but becoming erect as the petals emerge. The solitary, erect flowers open to a broad bowl shape, 6-9 cm (2½-3½ in) across and are usually rich scarlet, although paler shades often occur amongst large populations. The broad rounded, overlapping petals often, though not always, have a basal black blotch, which is sometimes edged with white. The stamens bear purplish filaments and characteristically blue anthers. The fruit-capsule is quite distinct in being almost rounded, smooth and capped by 8–12 stigmatic rays, occasionally more.

P. rhoeas is widespread in Europe and North Africa eastwards into western and central Asia, where it is primarily a plant of cultivated and disturbed land from sea level to the hills and lower mountains, rarely above 1,800 m (5,900 ft) altitude.

This splendid plant, often considered a weed in gardens, has been cultivated for many centuries and presents no problem to the cultivator, indeed once sown germinates readily and sets abundant seed, which will appear year after year without fail.

The common scarlet forms are as delightful as any, but in the wild occasional colour variants can be found – those with pale red or orange flowers, or red edged with white, or purely pink petals are not infrequent, as are others with fully or semi-double flowers [**Pl. 88–89**]. A particularly fine strain in gardens are the famous single-flowered Shirley Poppies [**Pl. 90**], developed from a wild selection by the Rev. W. Wilkes, vicar of Shirley near Croydon in Surrey. He told how 'in the summer of (I think) 1879 or 1880 I noticed in a wilderness corner of my garden, among a patch of field poppies, one bloom with a narrow white edge'. After he had subsequently carefully selected from this, eliminating those with black blotches on the petals, he raised a race with a 'wonderfully light, bright, tissue paper-like appearance'. These varied in colour from palest pinks to deep reds, lilacs and mauves with varying degrees of white around the edge of the petals and became known as Shirley Poppies.

The true Shirley Poppy has single flowers in a number of colours from white to pink, orange to red, with no hint of a black blotch at the base of the petals, and with pale stamens. The finest Shirley Poppies are perhaps the picotée types, the petals edged with a paler or darker colour. Modern strains of Shirley Poppies often contain double and semi-doubles, but these scarcely have the elegance and charm of the singles. The mixture of doubles and singles once found favour as the 'Reverend Wilkes Strain' though these poppies are not nearly so popular as they once were, due in large measure to the decline of the annual border in our gardens. However, one does not need an annual border to enjoy these delights but simply scatter the seed about in the early spring in any vacant patch in a border; thin sowing and ample thinning produce the best results. Some strains of Shirley Poppy have too many plain red forms. Rogueing out these the moment they come into bloom will tilt the balance in favour of the paler shades for future generations of poppies and ensure a pleasant balance of colours. Today most seed merchants supply selected mixtures of single- or double-flowered Shirley Poppies.

Today the loveliest strain of *P. rhoeas* is 'Mother of Pearl' (sometimes called 'Fairy Wings'), a pastel mix of whites, pinks, greys and delicate lilacs of subtle beauty, some with paler borders. These were originally developed by Sir Cedric Morris at his wonderful garden in Hadleigh, Suffolk. Here he ruthlessly selected for the paler shades, relentlessly removing any that were brash or gaudy in any way – his ambition to achieve a mother of pearl effect. Whatever the name, seed eventually found its way into the trade. In gardens, vigorous rogueing, as with the Shirley strains, will ensure perpetuation. Plants will self-sow with ease and seed bought from reputable seedsmen of any of these strains (except the Shirley Poppies) should not contain reds. 'Valerie Finnis' is similar to 'Mother of Pearl' and possibly of the same origin.

Searching back through old seed catalogues from the turn of the century one will see other forms of *P. rhoeas*, including a dwarf form with double flowers in a variety of colours and so-called 'Japanese Pompon' varieties. Sadly these are no longer with us today. Forms with lacerated petals are sometimes seen, though these are rather rare today.

Although these various strains of the corn poppy are considered to be of relatively recent origin, similar plants were certainly known to John Miller and are graphically described in the third edition of his *Gardener's Dictionary* of 1768. Miller describes *Papaver erraticum majus* as the red poppy or corn rose and states: 'The Red Poppy, or Corn Rose, is never propagate in the garden, but is very common upon chalky dry soils in almost every part of England, where the Plants come up amongst the Corn, and are very troublesome. The Flowers of this kind are brought into Markets for Medicinal use. There are many varieties of this Plant with double Flowers, which are cultivated in the Flower Garden, but especially the Dwarf Sort, of which there are some with very double Flowers, which are beautifully edged with white.' Miller goes on to list the various sorts:

'Great Wild Poppy, whose flowers-leaves are variegated'
'Double Wild Poppy, commonly called the Dwarf Poppy'
'Wild Poppy, with a double Vermilion-colour'd flower'
'Wild Poppy, with a double fiery Flower'
'Wild Poppy with a double purple Flower and white Bottom'
'Lesser Wild Poppy or Dwarf Poppy' (this may refer in fact to *P. dubium*)

Seed of all the types available today can be sown in the autumn or spring and seedlings should not be closer than 15–20 cm (6–8 in) if good strong plants are desired.

Apart from its horticultural merits *P. rhoeas* has a number of economic uses. The dried flowers ('*Flores rhoeades*') were formerly used in medicine; they contain rhoeadine and tiny quantities of morphine, often used as a soporific drug. The petal pigment, anthocyanidin, is sometimes used as a colour dye in some medicines, syrups and wines.

Ancient preserved flowers of this species found in tombs dating back to 1100 B.C. are housed in the famous Cairo Museum and shows that, even in former times, this poppy was held in high esteem by man.

Papaver rupifragum Boiss. & Reut.   [Pl. 91]
SPANISH POPPY

This perennial species and the closely related *P. atlanticum*, which comes from Morocco, are delightful and accommodating garden poppies, long-lived and often seeding around freely once established.

P. rupifragum has a slender branched taproot and a basal tuft of sparsely bristly leaves; these are oblong to elliptical in outline, pinnately-lobed and with toothed segments and a slender stalk. Many sparsely branched stems (to 50 cm (20 in) tall) arise from the leaf-rosettes and are sparsely leafy below, the slender stalks hairless or somewhat bristly carrying solitary flowers, 35–45 mm (1⅖–1⅘ in) across, the crimped petals a clear brick-red. The sepals are smooth and the stamens have orange-yellow anthers. The fruit-capsule is smooth, oblong-club-shaped, to 2.5 cm (1 in) long and slightly ribbed.

This dainty perennial poppy inhabits limestone cliff crevices and mountain rocks in southern Spain (Andalucia) in the region of Serrania de Ronda. Despite its very restricted distribution in the wild it has proved an easy garden plant. Semi-double flowered forms 'Flore Pleno' are equally common in gardens as are those with the normal 4-petalled flowers.

The closely allied *P. atlanticum* can be distinguished by somewhat larger dull orange flowers and hairier leaves and stems. Both species are readily raised from seed. Young plants can be moved without ill effect but I have found that mature plants resent disturbance and, although they don't die, they sulk without properly flowering and never ever regaining their full vigour.

P. rupifragum is a plant for the front of the border where it will flower throughout the summer. Although sometimes recommended for the rock garden and scree, its invasive seeding habit really does preclude it from such a position unless one enjoys weeding amongst the gravel.

Papaver sendtneri Kerner ex Hayek
(Syn. *P. alpinum* subsp. *sendtneri* (Kerner ex Hayek) Schinz & Keller;
P. pyrenaicum subsp. *sendtneri (Kerner & Hayek) Fedde)*

This species is very closely related to *P. rhaeticum* and is generally separated by its more pointed (acute) leaf-segments and somewhat smaller white flowers. The fruit-capsule usually has only five stigmatic rays.

P. sendtneri is a plant of moraines and screes, 2,000–2,700 m (6,550–8,850 ft), in the central and eastern Alps.

It is rarely offered in seed catalogues or, if it is, it is generally masked under the '*P. alpinum*' aggregate. All the members of this complex are well worth cultivating – jolly little poppies ideal for the small garden and with a long flowering season.

Papaver somniferum L. [Pl. 92–94]
OPIUM POPPY

This widely cultivated plant is familiar in many gardens where, once sown, it often comes up without fail year after year, never failing to surprise and delight in its subtle variations of flower shape and colour.

It is almost certain that the opium poppy was first cultivated for seed in Neolithic times and that it was gradually spread by humans throughout western and northern Europe from the eastern Mediterranean Basin. At the same time it spread eastwards to India. The oldest known reference to this poppy is to be found in Mesopotania in the *Assyrian Herbal* of 2000 BC, although its use almost certainly goes back as far as the Sumerians, 5000 BC. In ancient Egypt the narcotic properties of the opium poppy were well known and it was employed as a sleep-inducing medicine.

In ancient Greece various gods were directly associated with the sleep-inducing properties of opium – the god of dreams, the god of death for instance; indeed the word *opium* is of Greek origin. The Greeks prepared extracts from the stems, leaves and fruit-capsules called *meconium*, drunk as a pain killer and thought to have first originated in the town of Mekon, near modern-day Corinth, round about 800 BC. Hippocrates, the Greek physician (460–370 BC), referred to this drink as 'poppy-wine' and noted carefully its effect. The Greeks also learnt how to extract opium resin from the unripe fruit by making incisions along the capsule, a method well known to Theophrastus (300 BC). The Roman physician Galen was also enthusiastic about the use of opium.

Although the Greeks are generally credited with discovering how to extract opium by incision of the capsule and the medicinal uses of opium, it is the Arabs who appear to have disseminated this knowledge to various parts of the world. Certainly by the seventh century AD the cultivation of opium was common throughout the Arab empire and its narcotic and medicinal uses well established. The Arabs referred to the opium poppy as *Abou-el-noum* 'father of sleep'.

By about 1000 AD the growing of opium was widespread in Europe and Asia. The earliest record of it in India dates from about this period.

In China at this time *P. somniferum* was regarded more as a food and ornamental plant. By the fifteenth century it was widely grown in most provinces of China. However, opium was primarily imported into the country from India during the eighteenth century, where its widespread use as a narcotic drug had long been established. Britain found a highly lucrative trade in opium, which was grown in British India and exported to China in exchange for gold and silver. This in turn was used to buy tea and silks for import into Europe. This dangerous trade was controlled by the British East India Company who employed local traders (called country traders) licensed by the Company to smuggle opium along the Chinese coast, passing the proceeds in turn to the East India Company.

By the middle of the following century opium addiction had become rife in China and the Chinese government banned the use and import of opium. This, in turn, led to dire conflict within China culminating in the Opium Wars fought against the British, the first of which lasted from 1839 to 1842. In 1860 China was forced to finally agree to the import of the drug, but in turn charged a tax on it. In 1917 voluntary restrictions finally finished off this heinous trade.

The fact is that for many centuries opium was the only effective painkiller and its dangers as an addictive drug were not generally realised in the West until the beginning of the present century.

Today opium, the source of heroine, is still a major narcotic drug widely grown in the Third World and smuggled into many of the better-off countries. Much comes from the area of northern Burma, Thailand and south-western China known as the Golden Triangle. In this region the opium poppy is grown as a cash crop after the main crop of maize. The collection and refinement of opium takes places in numerous small factories along the Burma–Thai border and the revenue is used by local insurgents to fight their wars. The resultant heroine finds its way to Europe and America and today it is one of the major sources of drug abuse and addiction. Yet the opium poppy is, at the same time, of immense use in medicine, especially for its sleep-inducing and pain-killing properties.

In fact, opium resin contains a complex mixture of alkaloids (over 20 have been isolated) that include codeine, morphine, narceine, narcotine, papaverine and thebaine, all of which are of significant use in the pharmaceutical industry. These are extracted from the latex present primarily in the fruit-capsule and in the upper stem. Many different varieties of opium poppy are grown for medicine and differ primarily in the ratio and quantities of different alkaloids. Medinical drugs based on opium are analgesic, sedative, anti-spasmodic as well as soporific and are also used in the treatment of various stomach disorders.

Crude opium is gathered for the narcotic trade by lancing the semi-mature capsule with a series of longitudinal grooves using a special implement for the purpose. Latex, which is contained in specialised tissue (articulate lactiferous vessels) close to the surface, exudes along these grooves to accumulate at the base of the capsule. Within twenty-four hours it solidifies and can then be collected. This brown gum is rolled into balls and stored –

it will keep for a long time – and is converted to heroine by a process of 'cooking' and the addition of various chemical catalysts.

P. somniferum is also widely grown for its seeds (which contain no appreciable levels of harmful alkaloids) which are edible and can be used as a condiment on breads, salads and so on. They also have importance as a source of oil used for a variety of purposes – cooking oil, paint, soap and illumination. It is also used to make an important oil cake, (prepared as a mash from the whole plant) that forms a wholesome food for cattle, etc.

Other species of *Papaver* also contain appreciable quantities of useful pharmaceutical alkaloids – *P. bracteatum* and *P. orientale* for instance, are sometimes grown on a commercial scale for such purposes.

Despite its sinister attributes, the opium poppy is a delightful garden plant, existing in a range of different and exciting forms. The plant was well known to Gerard (1597) who states: 'The leaves of White Poppie are long, broad, smooth, longer than the leaves of Lettuce . . . There are divers varieties of Double Poppies of both these kindes, and their colours are commonly either white, red, dark purple, scarlet, or mixt of some of these. They differ from the former only in the doubleness of their flowers.' Gerard also records the use of this poppy: 'The oile which is pressed out of it is pleasant and dilightfull to be eaten, and is taken with bread or any other waies in meat, without a sense of cooling . . . A greater force is in the knobs or heads, which doe specially prevaile to moove sleepe, and to stay and represse distillations or rheums, and come neere in force to opium, but more gentle. Opium, or the condensed juice of Poppie heads is strongest of all: Meconium (which is the juice of the heads and leaves) is weaker. Both of them any waies taken either inwardly, or outwardly applied to the head, provoke sleepe. Opium somewhat plentifully taken does also bring death, as Pliny truely writeth.'

John Miller (1768) refers to the opium poppy as *Papaver hortence, semine nigro* – garden poppy, with black seeds. Of it he states: 'The Black Poppy grows wild in divers Parts of England: The Seeds of this kind are sold to feed birds, by the name of Maw Seed. Of this sort there are a vast Numbers of Varieties, some of which produce exceedingly large Double Flowers of various colours, and beautifully strip'd: but there are apt to vary from seed; therefore you should never save the Seed of any but such as are very double, and well colour'd, from which you may always expect to have good sorte produced.'

P. somniferum is an erect, generally unbranched, hairless, leafy annual, up to 1 m (3 ft) tall, sometimes more. The bluish- or greyish-green leaves are rather fleshy, oblong in outline but pinnately lobed and rather undulate along the margin, the lower short-stalked but the upper unstalked and clasping the stem with broad bases. The large cup-shaped, erect flowers are 5–12 cm (2–5 in) across in wild forms (up to 18 cm (7 in) in cultivated forms), white to pink or purple, often with a dark blotch at the base of each petal; the flowers are borne on long stalks, drooping at the tip in bud. The petals are broad, rounded and partly overlapping and the yellow or cream anthers are borne on pale filaments. The smooth fruit-capsule, up to 9 cm (4 in) long, is globose or egg-shaped with a deeply lobed stigmatic disk with 5–12 rays, sometimes more.

P. somniferum is probably native to the Mediterranean Basin but it is widely naturalised in many temperate regions of the world so that its precise natural distribution is uncertain. Plants are usually found growing on cultivated or wasteland, orchards, olive groves, disturbed places or on rocky hillslopes, generally at low altitudes.

This species is extremely variable and a number of subspecies have been described in the past. Of these the most important is subsp. *setigerum* (DC.) Corb. (syn. *P. setigerum* DC.) which is a sligher plant, rarely more than 60 cm (24 in) tall, the leaves with bristly midribs and veins, with each lobe terminating in a characteristic bristle. The flowers are pale purple and the fruit-capsule not more than 6 cm (2⅖ in) long, often less. Taxonomists often believe this to be the wild ancestor of the opium poppy and native to the west and central Mediterranean region, but widely naturalised further east.

In gardens the opium poppy presents few problems, except that it will often seed around in profusion. Seedlings should be ruthlessly thinned if they are to produce good strong plants. The ordinary single-flowered forms grown in gardens have a range of colours though pinks, purple and reds predominate, the petals sometimes with a delightful gradation of colour reminiscent of shot-silk. Poor-coloured forms should be rogued out the moment they come into flower, otherwise after only a few years poor pinks and dirty purple will begin to dominate.

It is, however, the double-flowered [**Pl. 99**] or peony-flowered types [**Pl. 95–96**] that have found greatest favour in gardens; so named because of their resemblance to the double flowers of the peony. In these some, or indeed most, of the stamens are replaced by a close mass of petals filling the entire centre of the flower and obscuring the ovary. A wide range of colours are available from white and cream, to pink, purple, red, lilac and almost black. These are listed by seed merchants variously as peony (paeonia)-flowered, peony series or 'paeoni-florum' and are sold most often as a mixture of different colours or as 'Black Peony', 'Golden Peony', 'Pink Peony', 'Purple Peony', 'Red Peony', 'Salmon Peony' [**Pl. 97**], 'Scarlet Peony' or 'White Peony'. Forms with double flowers with fringed petals are included in the 'Carnation-flowered series'. Other named cultivars include 'Pink Beauty' with flowers of delicate salmon pink, 'Pink Chiffon' with delicate pink blooms, 'White Cloud' [**Pl. 98**] with large double white flowers. Others with cut or lacerated petals are also seen from time to time.

All these plants are vigorous, sometimes reaching 1.5 m (5 ft) tall so they require plenty of space to develop. They are certainly an arresting sight in full flower – dare one say that some are almost too gaudy for the average garden? The doubles have a distinct advantage over the single-flowered forms in that their blooms last far longer, although heavy rain can bow their voluminous heads. All of them have a pleasing, though somewhat heady fragrance, much loved by bees.

The stiff-stemmed seed heads are a joy for dried decorations and are best gathered when matured but before they become too discoloured. They can be hung in bunches, upside down in a warm airy room to dry. The seeds can be collected for use on breads, buns and so on. A large-fruited form sold in the trade as 'Giganteum' or 'Gigantic Podded Mixed' has the largest fruits and is ideal for drying and painting.

Another, rather eccentric form is 'Hen and Chickens' in which the main fruit-capsule is surrounded by a halo of small pods; a novelty much enjoyed by some flower arrangers and a real curiosity in the mixed flower border.

Most of the double-flowered forms are good as a cut flower – bruising or burning the cut end of the stems will generally prevent them wilting in water; choose recently opened blooms for the best effect. Successive sowings from March to June will ensure a supply of blooms throughout the summer. Like all the annual poppies, sow them where they are to flower as they hate disturbance and will sulk or die if moved.

Papaver spicatum Boiss. [Pl. 100]
(Syn. *P. heldreichii* Boiss.; *P. pannosum* Schwarz)
SPICATE POPPY

This fine Turkish species is one of the most handsome and distinctive poppies grown in our gardens. Its specific name aptly describes its slender spike-like racemes of flowers held close to the main axis of the inflorescence.

Plants are perennial with a long thick, generally forked taproot that produces a large tuft of leaves at the top that more or less dies away each autumn. The leaves are pale green and softly white-hairy, oblong to elliptical, to 20 cm (8 in) long and coarsely toothed; the basal and lower leaves are stalked, the upper stem leaves smaller and generally sessile. The erect branched inflorescence rises to 60 cm (24 in), although often less; each branch has a slender raceme carrying a succession of pale brick-red flowers, each 3–4.5 cm (1⅕–1⅘ in) across and held close to the stem, often facing sidewards. The uppermost flowers are usually sessile. The stamens have pale filaments and pale orange-yellow anthers. The smooth fruit-capsule is small, 10–15 mm (⅖–⅗ in) long, narrowly oblong (tapered below) and smooth, the stigmatic disk pyramidal with four to six rays.

Fruit of *Papaver spicatum*

P. spicatum is native to the Taurus Mountains in western and southern Turkey where it is endemic to limestone mountain screes and rocks of Lydia and Lycia as well as adjacent Iscaurian and Pisidian, usually at altitudes of 600–1,400 m (1,950–4,600 ft); flowering during June and July.

This distinctive poppy makes a fine addition to the front of the herbaceous border where its rather pale flowers are a relief from the brilliant blooms of so many other poppies. This is certainly one of my favourite poppies, a dignified plant whose erect habit can provide interesting contrast in the border. Although never a profuse bloomer, the flowers are borne over quite a long season, each branch with one or two blooms open at a time. In gardens it is not always easy to please, sulking in some and prone to rotting off during the winter months in others. However, when properly established it is certainly long-lived and there are even gardens where it will, on occasions, self-sow.

P. spicatum needs a light, well-drained soil in the full sun. Plants greatly resent disturbance and once planted should be left well alone. In fact they normally set copious seed and it is little effort to raise a new stock. I have found that is far wiser to plant out new plants in the spring for this ensures they get a quick start, although they are unlikely to flower in most instances until the following year. Seed is best sown in the spring under glass and the seedlings pricked out into individual pots as soon as they have produced their first true leaf.

P. spicatum is available from a number of different nurseries and seed is occasionally listed in catalogues, being generally found under the name *P. heldreichii*.

Papaver triniifolium Boiss   [Pl. 101]

Another rarely cultivated species but an intriguing one in that it is one of the few biennial species in the genus. In this respect and in the character of its handsome first year leaf-rosettes it is perhaps more reminiscent of several of the species of *Meconopsis*. However, once seen, the typical *Papaver* fruit-capsules leave one in no doubt as to which genus it truly belongs. Reginald Farrer wrote of it being in 'the group of monocarpic or biennial poppies . . . the most beautiful we have, however (in foliage at least), is *P. triniifolium*, which comes, like all the others, from the hills of Asia Minor. Here the silver-glaucous leaves are cut and cut again into the finest silver fringe work . . . The resulting pyramid of bloom seems hardly a worthy conclusion to so much beauty, for the flowers are small, pale coloured . . . in utmost haste to shed their petals'.

P. triniifolium forms a rather dense spreading, grey-green leaf-rosette in the first season; this up to 30 cm (12 in) across in vigorous specimens. The narrow, stalked, somewhat bristly leaves are lanceolate in outline but pinnately-lobed to 20 cm(8 in) long, the segments rather distant and further lobed or toothed into narrow oval or elliptical divisions, each terminating in a bristle-tip. In the second season a central, leafy stem rises to 40 cm (16 in) with spreading glabrous branches bearing a succession of flowers. The flowers are small, 2.5–4 cm (1–1⅗ in) across and pale red or scarlet. The fruit-capsule, 8–12 mm (⅓–½ in) long, is smooth and greyish-green, the stigmatic disk with four to six rays.

This is a pretty little species, not spectacular like some, but worth growing if only for its handsome first year leaf-rosettes. Indeed, some gardeners think it is more interesting in its rosette form than when it is in flower, although I would not support this view. *P. triniifolium* is hardly, the leaf-rosette persisting through the winter months. Because it is biennial, seed needs to be collected regularly to ensure a supply of new young plants – I have not known it self-sow in my own garden but, in any event, it is readily raised from seed sown in pots in a cold frame early in the year. Pricked out as soon as they are large enough to handle, the seedlings grow away rapidly and can be planted out by mid-summer. This is an ideal plant for the rock or scree garden, planted close to a path where its subtle beauty can be best appreciated.

Plants prefer a moist, though well-drained, light soil but do not seem to be affected by winter wet providing these conditions are met. This is probably a reflection of its native home in Turkey where most rain falls during the winter months. Strangely enough, unlike some of the rosette-forming species of *Meconopsis*, slugs do not appear to like *P. triniifolium* and the rosettes survive the winter unchewed. In the garden it usually comes into flower during May.

P. triniifolium is native to eastern Turkey, being found from southern Cappadocia to the Pontic Ranges. It was first described by Boissier from material collected by Balansa in the so-called subalpine region of Mesmeneu Dağ, part of the Ala Dağ Range in Cappadocia.

Plants are occasionally offered in the horticultural trade, though it is probably easier to obtain seed from specialist seed merchants or society seedlists. Plants are self-fertile and a single plant can be expected to produce copious good seed.

The closely related *P. armeniacum* (L.) DC. (syn. *Argemone armeniaca* L.; *Papaver roopianum* (Bordz.) Sosn.) can be easily distinguished by its numerous stems, which arise from the basal leaf-rosette and by the racemose rather than paniculate inflorescence. In addition, the flowers are smaller and orange-red, the petals not more than 15 mm (⅗ in) long. *P. triniifolium* inhabits limestone rocks and screes at 2,600–3,400 m (8,500–11,150 ft) in eastern Turkey and neighbouring north-western Iran.

INTERESTING SPECIES NO LONGER IN CULTIVATION
[not in key]

Papaver belangeri Boiss.

See *P. minus* (p. 149).

Papaver bornmuelleri Fedde

This species is endemic to the Kermanshah region of Iran and the neighbouring area of Iraqi Kurdistan. It probably finds its closest ally in *P. macrostomum*, but can be distinguished by having sparsely bristly fruit-capsules. A generally smaller plant with purple flowers.

Papaver chelidonifolium Boiss. & Buhse

This is a delicate species restricted to the Caucasus and northern Iran, where it is to be found in cultivated and bare fields and in scrub or on stony slopes. It is an annual with slender, rather membranous, pinnate leaves, one to three pairs of small lateral lobes and a large terminal lobe often three-lobed; the upper leaves are generally smaller and more dissected. the flowers are pale red, 2–3 cm (⅘–1⅕ in) across; the oval petals have a dark, almost black, basal blotch. The fruit-capsules are smooth and small, only 6–7 mm (¼ in) long and more or less club-shaped, with five to seven stigmatic rays.

Papaver cylindricum Cullen

A close relation of *P. fugax* (p. 142) being distinguished primarily in fruit. The fruit-capsule is smaller and narrower, 8–15 × 3–5 mm (not 14–16 × 4–8 mm) (⅓–⅗ × ⅛–⅕, not ⅗–⅔ × ⅙–⅓ in) and with a decidedly more conical stigmatic disk.

   P. cylindricum is restricted to Iraqi and Iranian Kurdistan between 1,400–1,800 m (4,600–5,900 ft) altitude.

Papaver gorgoneum Coutinho

This is the only species of *Papaver* endemic to the Cape Verde Islands. It comes closest to *P. pinnatifidum* Moris. Both species have red flowers with pale yellow anthers. The main difference is to be seen in the fruit-capsule, which in the former is more or less cylindric, but clearly contracted at the base, whereas in the latter the capsule is more club-shaped.

Papaver hookeri Bak. ex Hook. f.

A plant from the western Himalaya scarcely distinguishable from *P. rhoeas*. The flowers are pale pink to bright crimson-red, the petals with a basal black blotch.

Papaver laevigatum Bieb.

Very similar to *P. dubium* but the plant scarcely hairy and the flowers rather smaller, the petals not more than 15 mm (⅗ in) long. A plant of Europe and Turkey, as well as part of south-eastern central Asia.

Papaver monanthum Trautb.

See *P. bracteatum* (p. 138).

Papaver nordhagenianum Lōve

A Scandinavian variant of *P. radicatum* to 35 cm (14 in) tall and bearing numerous yellow flowers.

Papaver paucifoliatum (Trautb.) Fedde.

See *P. bracteatum* (p. 138).

Papaver persicum Lindl.

See *P. fugax* (p. 142).

Papaver pseudocanescens Popov

Like *P. radicatum* but with broader leaf-lobes and flowers with more numerous stamens. A native of Siberia and Mongolia.

Papaver pygmaeum

A tiny poppy of the *P. radicatum* persuasion endemic to the American Rockies where it is only found on the high moraines and screes of the Glacier National Park region. Not in cultivation.

The Long-fruited Poppies
Roemeria

The genus *Roemeria* contains three to four species native to the eastern Mediterranean, western and central Asia, with one species, *R. hybrida*, extending west into the western Mediterranean and southern Europe.

Although the species look superficially very similar to the true poppies, *Papaver*, the genus is more closely allied to *Chelidonium* and *Glaucium* in its long, parallel-sided fruit-capsules which, when ripe, split from apex to base into two, occasionally four similar valves.

The genus is named in honour of Johann Jakob Roemer (1763–1819) who was Professor of Botany at Zurich.

All the species are rather slender annuals with yellow sap and finely-divided, pinnately-lobed leaves.

Roemeria hybrida (L.) DC.

(Syn. *Chelidonium hybridum* L.; *C. violaceum* Lam.; *Glaucium violaceum* (Lam.) Juss.; *Roemeria violacea* Medicus)

VIOLET HORNED POPPY, WIND ROSE

A rather distinctive poppy with violet-coloured flowers. Although confined primarily to the Mediterranean region and the drier parts of Asia, this plant was at one time well-naturalised in East Anglia in the UK where it was a weed of arable land, particularly wheat fields. However, in recent times it has become very scarce there due to modern farming practises.

Roemeria hybrida

The plant was well known to Gerard. In his *Herbal* of 1633 he lists it as 'Papaver cornutum flore-violaceo (Violet coloured horned Poppie)' and commented: 'There is another sort of horned Poppie altogether less than the last described [*Glaucium flavum*], having tender leaves, cut into fine little parcels: the flower is likewise lesser, of a blue-purple colour like the double violets.'

R. *hybrida* is a hairy annual 10–50 cm (4–20 in) tall, generally with branched stems. The alternate leaves, up to 20 cm (8 in) long, are two- or three-pinnately divided, glabrous or somewhat bristly, the segments narrow and bristle-tipped; the upper leaves are smaller and sessile, the lower clearly stalked. The solitary flowers, 5–7 cm (2–3 in) across, are borne on long slender stalks and are lilac, violet or purplish-red with a dark basal blotch to each petal; sepals two, hairy, soon falling; petals four, roundish with a broad wedge-shaped base; stamens numerous, with violet-filiform filaments. The fruit-capsule is narrowly cylindrical, 4–8 cm (2–3 in) long, straight or curved and bristly in the upper part; when ripe it opens by three or four valves.

R. *hybrida* has a wide distribution from the Iberian Peninsula and northwest Africa eastwards to Turkey, Iran and the neighbouring regions of central Asia. It is primarily a plant of cultivated, waste and fallow land from sea level to 1,500 m (4,900 ft), sometimes higher; flowers March to May.

This is an attractive poppy for a light well-drained soil in full sun. Seed should be sown in the early spring where the plants are to flower. It is well worth selecting out the better violet-coloured forms from the wishy-washy lilac flowers or the muddier purplish-reds. In gardens plants will generally flower from late June to August or early September; they normally set abundant seed and sometimes self-sow, especially on lighter soils. Although very striking in its best coloured forms, the flowers are fleeting beauties, opening at dawn with their petals generally falling by midday. For this reason it is often overlooked on arable land.

Roemeria orientalis Boiss.

This plant has been much confused with *P. hybrida* but differs in its squatter habit, short and broader leaf-segments, smaller flowers and shorter, thicker fruit-capsules, covered with bristles. This species, which is not in cultivation,
grows in the drier desert regions of Egypt and Sinai, north-eastwards through southern Iran to the regions of the Aral Sea. The relationship between these two species requires further investigation.

Roemeria refracta (Stev.) DC.   [Pl. 102]
(syn. *Glaucium refractum* Stev. ex DC.; *Roemeria bicolor* Regel; *R. rhoeadiflora* Boiss.)
ASIAN CORN POPPY

If the true poppies (*Papaver*) did not exist then this splendid species would surely rate very highly in our gardens. As it is, its effect in flower is so similar to that of *Papaver rhoeas* or *P. pavoninum* that it is sadly much neglected.

The plains around Samarkand and Taskent in Soviet Central Asia, where

I have seen it, are stained with the deep scarlet of *R. refracta* during April and May – a sight as unforgettable as the poppy fields of western Europe.

Plants grow 40–50 cm (16–20 in) tall and are branched from close to the base; stems hairy or rather bristly. The leaves are two- or three-pinnately-lobed, with elliptical or oblong, slightly bristly segments, the lower leaves stalked but the upper sessile usually. The solitary, long-stalked flowers, 4–7 cm (1⅗–3 in) across, are pendent in bud but become erect as they open; sepals two, bristly, petals four, bright red to scarlet with a large black basal blotch, which is often outlined with white, half-spreading to form a deep cup-shape; stamens numerous, with black filaments, which are somewhat dilated at the top, and yellowish-brown anthers. The fruit-capsule is linear-cylindrical, to 10 cm (4 in) long, smooth or bristly.

R. refracta is native to an area stretching from Armenia to Iran, Afghanistan and western Pakistan to Kazakstan and Kirghizia where it is a plant of cultivated, fallow and waste ground and the foothills and lower mountain slopes, flowering there during April and May.

Seed of this species is sometimes offered and should certainly be tried. Cultivation is the same as for *R. hybrida* or indeed any annual *Papaver*.

The colour of the flowers ranges from an orange-red to scarlet, those of the deepest scarlet hues being the most splendid of all. I would dearly love to see plants with 'violet or near blue flowers' reported in *The Plantsman* (Sept. 1991) but suspect this is a wholly erroneous report; petals of a number of red poppies often dry purplish and violet and this may have been the basis of such a record.

In the wild, populations are quite variable. Var. *albomarginata* is a name given to flowers in which the black basal blotch is outlined in white, whereas var. *setosa* applies to those plants with bristly fruits. However, I have observed large populations of these plants in the Samarkand area, in northern Afghanistan, as well as in western and eastern Iran and can only record that all these manifestations can be found quite readily within the same population. Of course in cultivation the white ring is a most attractive feature of the flower; a similar ring is found in forms of *P. rhoeas* and *P. pavoninum*.

The Californian Tree Poppies
Romneya

The genus *Romneya* was named in honour of the Reverend T. Romney Robinson, astronomer of Armagh, Ireland (1792–1882). The type species was discovered by Dr Thomas Coulter, an Irish botanist and friend of the Rev. Robinson, in California in 1833; the type species commemorates both friends in *Romneya coulteri*. Seed was not introduced into cultivation until 1875, the first plant flowering at the Glasnevin Botanic Garden in Dublin the following year.

Romneya is without doubt one of the most spectacular members of the poppy family with its striking grey leaves and flamboyant white flowers set off by a huge boss of yellow stamens. It has become deservedly popular in gardens. Many gardeners think that this splendid plant is too tender for their own gardens, coming as it does from the sun-drenched regions of California, but this is not so. Romneyas are suckering subsbrubs with the stems becoming woody towards the base; even when they survive unscathed these stems are never long-lived. Instead shoots spring from the base of the stems or from underground suckers; these will often flower during the same season. A vigorous mature plant will produce countless flowers over a long season from July to September.

Both the known species require similar conditions in cultivation. A warm sunny site is ideal, especially if backed by a south- or west-facing wall, but sheltered corners in the open garden will often prove satisfactory, although in more exposed cooler positions plants cannot be expected to grow so tall. The soil should be light and well-drained, preferably deep and well prepared with well-rotted compost or manure added; plants are equally happy on neutral or calcareous soils.

Young vigorous pot-grown plants should be purchased and planted out in the spring once the worst danger of frost has passed by. Romneyas hate disturbance once established and no attempt should be made to move them. Their suckering habit can prove annoying, although excess suckers can be removed with a sharp spade – suckers can in fact arise at a considerable distance from the parent plant.

Pruning consists of tipping back shoots in the spring or removing old or dead growth to ground level. Some gardeners regularly prune the entire plant to ground level without adverse effect.

Propagation is often rather tricky. Cuttings of firm young stem sections can be attempted, though the success rate is often very poor. Suckers removed and replanted rarely succeed, although young suckers carefully removed with some roots attached, potted up and placed in a propagating frame can produce good results, but the resultant plants should preferably not be planted out until the following year. The best means of propagation, however, is by root cuttings. Thick, healthy pieces of roots should be unearthed, taking care not to damage the parent plant unnecessarily. These can then be sliced up into 5 cm (2 in) portions and laid flat in trays of sharp sand and peat (60:40 per cent) and covered to a depth of 2.5–5 cm (1-2 in). Placed in a propagating frame or over a heated bench in the glasshouse, these will, with luck, sprout in due course.

Against a sheltered wall plants can be most spectacular and certainly more floriferous than those in the open garden, the stems reaching as much as 3 m (10 ft) in height in a good hot summer. In Britain these highly desirable plants can be grown in all but the very coldest regions, providing some shelter is possible. In my own garden in East Anglia *R. coulteri* has survived in an open position for several years despite severe winter frosts and biting east winds that have devastated other plants from less favourable parts of the world. *Romneya* would appear to come close to *Dendromecon*, another

Californian genus, which, however, is readily separated on account of its entire leaves and smaller, yellow flowers. However, the two genera are widely separated in the family (belonging to separate subfamilies) and have markedly different fruits.

Romneya coulteri Harvey
CALIFORNIAN TREE POPPY

A subshrubby, suckering plant with rather fleshy erect, sometimes branched stems to 3 m (10 ft) tall, though often only half that height. Leaves rather leathery, grey-green, variable in size according to vigour but generally 7–12 cm (3–5 in) long, ovate to lanceolate, the lower with five to seven narrowly triangular lobes, the upper with fewer lobes, or coarsely toothed or occasionally entire, glabrous save for a few bristles on the short stalk and midrib. The large white flowers are solitary or paired and mostly terminate short twigs near the top of the stems, each 10–13 cm (4–5 in) across and with a large central, rounded boss of numerous golden-yellow stamens; there are five or six overlapping satiny petals; the three leathery, smooth sepals quickly fall once the flowers begin to open. The fruit-capsule is egg-shaped, covered with stiff, golden, spreading bristles and is many seeded.

This glorious plant, with its showy, rather floppy flowers, which carry a sweet fragrance on a warm sunny day, comes from a limited area of southern California, but is especially abundant in the mountains to the south-east of Los Angeles where it inhabits sunbaked rocks and gullies.

R. coulteri is a larger plant than its close cousin R. trichocalyx but is less invasive with its suckers and for that reason it is perhaps the better one to choose for the smaller garden. It would make a spectacular plant for a mass planting in large gardens or parks in a sheltered site, though few have attempted such an effect.

Romneya trichocalyx Eastw.   [Pl. 103–104]

This species is superficially very similar to R. coulteri, indeed for many years they were considered to be one and the same species. However, in 1898 Alice Eastwood separated it, having studied plants closely in the Golden Gate Park in San Francisco.

R. trichocalyx differs primarily in its slender stems, more finely cut and less leathery foliage and more clustered flowers. In addition, the flowerbuds are adorned with appressed bristles close to the apex (they are not beaked as in R. coulteri) and the fruit capsules also bear appressed, rather than spreading, bristles. Because of early confusion with R. coulteri the date of introduction of R. trichocalyx into cultivation is uncertain, though it was probably around the turn of the present century.

This species hails from California (primarily to the south of R. coulteri in San Diego and Ventura Counties) and extending southwards into the Mexican state of Baja California.

Romneya trichocalyx

Hybrids with *R. coulteri* have been called *R. × hybrida* Hort. (syn. *R. × vandedenii* Correvon *nom. nud.*). This interesting hybrid is almost intermediate in its principal characteristics between its parent species; this is especially noticeable in the beaked flowerbuds, which bear a few bristles close to the top. The plant generally seen in cultivation of this cross has a bushier habit than *R. trichocalyx* but the flowers bear the fragrance of *R. coulteri*.

'White Cloud' is an especially fine cultivar of the hybrid raised in the USA. It has exceptionally large and fragrant flowers contrasting with attractive blue-grey foliage.

The Wind Poppy
Stylomecon

The genus *Stylomecon* contains a single species, *S. heterophylla*, from western North America. Originally described as a species of *Meconopsis* (*M. heterophylla*) by George Bentham it was subsequently transferred to its own genus by George Taylor in 1930, although the plant has been cultivated since 1826. As in *Meconopsis* the fruit-capsule has a distinct, though short style, however, its annual habit and dimorphic leaves serve to distinguish it clearly from *Meconopsis*.

Stylomecon heterophylla (Benth.) G. Taylor   [Pl. 105–106]
(Syn. *Meconopsis heterophylla* Benth.)
WIND POPPY

A slender-stemmed, somewhat bristly, annual to 60 cm (24 in) tall, though often less; stem unbranched or few-branched, with a yellow sap when cut. Leaves rather few, grey-green, the lower pinnately-lobed, with oval to elliptical, often toothed segments, long-stalked; upper leaves linear, generally unlobed, toothed or not, more or less sessile. The solitary bright orange-red or coppery-orange flowers, 3–3.5 cm (1–2 in) across, have a distinctive dark purple centre and are pendent in bud but become erect; sepals two, bristly at the apex, soon shed as the flowers open; petals usually four, broad and somewhat overlapping one another, with a slightly frilled margin; stamens numerous, with purplish filaments and golden anthers; style short, capped by a rather flaired, whitish stigma. The small, erect fruit-capsule is club-shaped with an undulate, turban-like, disk at the apex crowned by the short style, many-seeded.

This delightful and colourful annual is a plant of grassy and bushy habitats in California, especially on the north coast ranges, the foothills of the Sierra Nevada and the offshore Channel Islands; it also extends southwards into Baja California, flowering in these places during April and May.

The flowers, although rather delicate looking, are surprisingly long-lived and have a pleasing fragrance reminiscent of that of Lily-of-the-Valley (*Convallaria majalis*). One interesting feature of the flowers is the way in which most of the stamens are crowded above the ovary – the flowers generally face sideways.

S. heterophylla is surprisingly rare in our gardens. This is a great shame for it is a very cheerful little annual and quite hardy. Seed can be sown in the spring where the plants are required to flower. A light, well-drained soil is preferable and a sunny sheltered site. They will generally come into flower in late June or early July and bloom through until September.

Alternatively, seed can be sown earlier in pots under glass, pricking the young seedlings out into deep pans for flowering indoors in the later spring and early summer; 5–7.5 cm (2–3 in) between plants should be sufficient, keeping them in a light airy position to avoid the plants becoming too drawn.

Although the usual colour is a rich deep orange, pale orange or reddish orange forms also occur in the wild. A splendid pure white cultivar, which is grown in California in particular, has the cultivar name 'White Satin' [**Pl. 107**].

The Wind Poppy is unlikely to be mistaken for any other member of the poppy family except perhaps for one or two *Papaver* species. The short style and leaf characters are sufficiently distinct to enable accurate identification.

Stylomecon heterophylla

IV
Subfamily
Platystemonoideae

Meconellas
Meconella

This is another small, western North American genus, little known in cultivation but certainly worthy of attention. The name *Meconella* perhaps conjures up a dainty *Meconopsis* – the name from the Greek literally means tiny or diminutive poppy (*mekon*, poppy, and *ella*, tiny). However, the genus finds its closest ally not in Old World genera but in the Cream Cups, *Platystemon*. It differs in two major characteristics: firstly, the flowers have few stamens, generally only 6–12; secondly, the fruit consist of three fused carpels, which eventually dehisces to form a three-valved capsule. As in *Platystemon*, the plants are slender annuals with long flower-stalks (pedicels) and bear six-petalled flowers with two or three sepals.

The species look superficially very similar to *Platystemon*, but can be clearly differentiated by their smaller flowers and distinctive slender, twisted, fruit-capsules. They differ from *Platystigma* in their leafy, branched stems and twisted fruit-capsules; in *Platystigma* the leaves are apparently all basal, their scapes unbranched and the fruit-capsule is untwisted, although a similarly three-valved capsule.

Meconella californica Torr.   [Pl. 108]

A slender glabrous annual to 15 cm (6 in) tall with most of the leaves basal, elliptical to almost spathulate, entire, to 4 cm (2 in) long, though usually less, generally narrowing into a short petiole at the base; stems slender and erect, branched, bearing several pairs of opposite leaves, rarely in threes. Flowers solitary, white, or cream or yellow with a white centre, 17–20 mm (¾–⅘ in) across, borne on slender stalks, erect or half-nodding in bud; sepals often reddish, soon falling; petals six (rarely eight), ovate to elliptical; stamens 8–12. Fruit-capsule linear, twisted, to 3 cm (1⅕ in) long, borne on erect or deflexed stalks.

M. californica is native to California from San Francisco Bay Region southwards along the Sierra Nevada foothills, where it grows on rocky slopes, flowering there during March and April. This delightful little species, like some of the other Californian annual 'poppies', is sometimes found in large numbers, particularly after a wet winter.

Not in cultivation but it would make a dainty little annual for the front of the flower border.

Meconella oregana Nutt. ex Torr. & Gray
(syn. *M. denticulata* (Jepson) Greene; *M. californica* var. *denticulata* Jepson; *M. oregana* var. *denticulata* Jepson)

Rather similar to *M. californica* but often taller, to 30 cm (12 in), and glabrous. The leaves vary from oval to spathulate or linear, the basal ones being the broadest, entire and stalked, the upper sessile and sometimes finely toothed. The small white flowers are only 10–18 mm (⅖–¾ in) across; sepals soon falling; petals six, rarely four, oval; stamens six. The fruit-capsule is linear and twisted, to 3 cm (1⅕ in) long at maturity.

M. oregana is found in California from the foothills of the Sierra Nevada and the coastal regions, southwards into Baja California as well as on Santa Cruz Island. It is a plant of rocky and sandy places, often on grassy hillslopes or openings in chaparral or sagebrush, as well as in shaded canyons, generally below 1,000 m (3,300 ft); flowering from March to May. Plants are often frequent but are rather inconspicuous.

Not in cultivation.

Cream Cups
Platystemon

This charming little genus comes from California and adjacent regions. Most modern authorities recognise a single species, *Platystemon californicus*, but it is extremely variable from one population to another. It is not therefore surprising that various other species and subordinate categories have been proposed in the past. In fact almost 60 different names exist; fortunately most of these have been sunk into synonymy. However, some of the variants are worth recognising at varietal level.

The genus gets its name from its relatively broad stamens (from the Greek *platus*, broad and *stemon*, stamen); the stamens have expanded, almost petal or staminode-like, filaments. *Platystemon* is very distinctive in fruit; there are between six and 20 carpels, which are united in a ring at first but at maturity they become monilliform (bead-like) and separate, breaking off transversely into single-seeded units. No other genus has this type of fruit in the Papaveraceae. Despite this, *Platystemon* finds its closest ally in another primarily Californian genus, *Meconella*. In this latter genus the fruit consists of a three-valved capsule which splits to release the seeds. Both genera usually have six-petalled flowers, rather than the more usual four.

Platystemon californicus Benth.   [Pl. 109–111]
CREAM CUPS

A small, rather slender, softly-hairy annual to 30 cm (12 in) tall, occasionally more, with stems branched below, spreading to erect; juice colourless. The leaves vary from alternate at the base to opposite or whorled above, but are generally crowded into the basal half of the plant; they are linear-lanceolate to almost linear, to 8 cm (3 in) long, though often not more than 5 cm (2 in), with an untoothed margin. The cream to yellow flowers, which are nodding in bud, are borne on long, slender, hairy stems, which may be as much as 15–20 cm (6–8 in) in length, each flower 18–25 mm (¾–1 in) across; sepals three, softly-hairy; petals six, in two series, elliptical to oval; stamens numerous cream or yellowish, with distinctly dilated filaments. The cylindrical fruit consists of three or more carpels fused around a hollow core, 10–16 mm (⅖–⅗ in) long, each carpel topped by a persistent filiform style and becoming beaded on maturity.

The species has a distribution from southern Oregon to western Colorado, Utah, Arizona, California and Baja California at altitudes rarely exceeding 1,500 m (4,900 ft). It inhabits open grassy, sandy or clayey soils, scrub or desert fringes, sometimes sowing profusely in areas that have been burnt over; flowering in the wild from February to early June, depending on locality.

Of the various variations in this polymorphic species, the following can be recognised here:

Var. *californicus* (including *P. leiocarpus* Fisch. & Mey.) has cream, cup-shaped flowers; plants moderately hairy. Oregon, Utah, Arizona, California and Baja California, generally on grassy slopes and coastal hills.

Var. *crinitus* Greene is similar but the whole plant more shaggily hairy and flowers yellow. Western Colorado to California and Baja California, growing on the desert and mountain slopes primarily.

Var. *horridus* (Greene) Jepson is similar to var. *californicus*, but with the petals spreading widely to form a flat flower and the fruit-carpels covered in stiff white hairs at first; in var. *californicus* they are glabrous or softly-hairy. Western foothills of the Sierra Nevada, especially in the south.

Var. *nutans* Bdg. This variety has distinctive nodding fruits, otherwise it is rather like var. *californicus*. California from Western San Diego County to Santa Cruz and Santa Rosa.

Platystemon californicus var. *californicus* (left) and var. *crinitus* (left)

Var. *ornithopus* (Greene) Munz is very like var. *californicus* but it is a small hairless plant not more than 10 cm (4 in) tall and with the fruits scarcely beaded. California from San Miguel and San Nicolas to Santa Rosa.

Var. *ciliatus* Dunkle is very like the previous variety, but the plants adorned with short hairs. California in Santa Barbara County.

Of these varieties only the widespread var. *californicus* is seen in cultivation. Of the others the most attractive is the deep yellow-flowered var. *crinitus*.

P. californicus is a cheerful and hardy little annual for the front of a flower border. It will also succeed in the cracks in paving, terraces or on the scree garden. Seed can be sown in the autumn in mild warm areas; however, a safer bet is to sow it along with other annuals in the early spring. It prefers a warm sandy or loamy, well-drained and sunny position, although plants will wither in the very hot weather of mid-summer. The pale airy flowers, produced in quantity, are a charming foil to other small summer annuals such as *Linum grandiflorum*, *Nemophila menziesii*, *Omphalodes linifolia* or *Phacelia tanacetifolia*. In favoured gardens it may self-sow, although it cannot be relied upon to do so, therefore it is wise to collect some seed each year.

Platystigmas
Platystigma

Another western North American genus consisting of eight to nine annual herbs related to *Platystemon* but differing in having a three-valved capsule, rather than a fruit consisting of six or more carpels, which are free at maturity. The genus is also closely related to *Meconella* but can be quickly separated by having basal leaf tufts and scapose flowers. Two species are cultivated but are rarely seen in our gardens today.

Platystigma lineare Benth.
(syn. *Meconella linearis* (Benth.) Jepson; *Hesperomecon lineare* Benth.)

A slender annual to about 20 cm (8 in) tall, occasionally more. The leaves are crowded into a dense basal tuft and are linear to linear-elliptical, entire to 6.5 cm (2⅗ in) long. The small pale yellow flowers, 16–22 mm (⅔–⅞ in) across, are borne on slender, unbranched, bristly scapes; sepals three, brownish, soon falling; petals six, oval to elliptical or obovate, stamens 12–15, sometimes more, with linear filaments. The fruit-capsule is elliptical to narrow pear-shaped in outline, to 18 mm (¾ in) long, not twisted.

This is a little Californian poppy, found along the coast ranges but extending northwards into Oregon and southwards to the foothills of the Sierra Nevada and the Tahachapi Mountains. It grows primarily in sandy and gravelly soils and flowers during March and April.

Platystigma lineare

This little annual can be treated as a hardy annual, sowing the seed in the early spring where the plants are required to flower. It has been cultivated since 1833 (originally as *Hesperomecon lineare*) although seed is rarely available today.

Platystigma pulchellum Greene
(syn. *Meconella linearis* var. *pulchellum* Jepson)

Rather similar to *P. lineare*, but a somewhat hairier plant with flowers 22–28 mm (⅞–1⅛ in) across with the outer petals yellow, the inner narrower and white; stamens numerous with filaments winged in the lower half.

A rather rare plant in the wild, being a Calfornian endemic found along the coast from San Francisco to Sonoma County, where it inhabits sandy and stony ground.

This pretty little poppy first came into cultivation round about 1836 but is rarely seen in gardens today. It is sometimes recorded in cultivation as *P. lineare*, but is very distinctive with diverse petals and winged stamens. Treat as for *P. lineare*.

Allied Genera
(formerly subfamily Hypecooideae)

(Two genera sometimes included in the Papaveraceae, p. 23).

The Little Poppies
Hypecoum

A small genus of charming little annuals wholly neglected in gardens but pretty and effective *en masse*. There are about 15 species scattered primarily in the Mediterranean region and western Asia, but with one or two species found as far east as northern China and Mongolia.

Plants are rather delicate, often glabrous and glaucous, herbs with watery latex and finely cut foliage, reminiscent of some of the smaller species of Californian Poppies, *Eschscholzia*. The small yellow flowers are borne in a cymose inflorescence; sepals two, minute, quickly falling as the flowers begin to open; petals four, in two rows, the outer two unlobed to three-lobed, the inner, deeply three-lobed, with the outer lobes narrow and the middle one often fringed with hairs; stamens four only, with winged filaments. Fruit-capsule long and narrow, jointed and splitting transversely into numerous one-seeded portions, or splitting longitudinally into two valves, usually many-seeded.

In *Hypecoum* an interesting pollination device can be observed. The middle lobes of the inner two petals are somewhat stalked and with an expanded, sometimes somewhat hooded, apex. These apices wrap around the stamens before the stigma is receptive and form a chamber that collects the pollen shed from the anthers. When visited by an insect (nectar is secreted at the base of the filaments) these lobes spring apart dusting the insect with pollen, which it then transports to the next flowers it visits. The stigma of the first flower then becomes receptive and can then receive pollen from another insect.

Hypecoums are hardy annuals and prefer an open sunny position in the garden and a well-drained soil. As they are low growing they require the front of the flower border, though to my mind they look best in a gravel area, seeded along the edge of a path or driveway where they are not likely to be trampled on. If you can acquire seed, these friendly and cheerful little plants are worth encouraging. Direct sowing where the plants are to flower is recommended as they dislike being moved and will sulk or die as a result. From a spring sowing they will provide a display of little blooms from June until late summer.

Key to Species

1. Flowers yellow and violet or pale whitish-violet 2
   Flowers yellow or orange, not bicoloured, but inner petals
   sometimes violet-spotted 3

2. Flowers pale whitish-violet; fruit-capsules scarcely lined or
   thickened at the margins: **H. leptocarpum**
   Flowers yellow and violet; fruit-capsules lined and thickened
   at the margins: **H. aegyptiacum**

3. Stems smooth; outer petals almost twice as long as wide, unlobed 4
   Stems lined; outer petals almost as wide as long, three-lobed 5

4. Fruit-capsule pendent on recurved stalks, not jointed; middle
   lobe of inner petals rounded and stalked: **H. pendulum**
   Fruit-capsule erect, weakly jointed; middle lobe of inner
   petals linear: **H. ponticum**

5. Bracts leaf-like with many divisions; petals pale yellow usually,
   the outer with a large middle lobe: **H. procumbens**
   Bracts linear, not leaf-like, entire or with few divisions; petals orange
   usually, the outer with more or less equal lobes or the middle one
   somewhat smaller 6

6. Fruit-capsules erect to ascending, jointed and readily breaking into
   segments: **H. imberbe**
   Fruit-capsules pendulous and with thick walls, breaking with
   difficulty: **H. trilobum**

Hypecoum aegyptiacum (Forsk.) Aschers. et Schweinf.
EGYPTIAN HYPECOUM

A rather distinctive little species with bicoloured flowers. It is a spreading to ascending annual, not more than 25 cm (10 in) tall, though often less, with finely cut leaves, the segments acutely pointed. The flowers are about the same size and shape as *H. imberbe*, with large bright yellow, three-lobed outer petals; however, the smaller inner petals are yellow with a contrasting purple-brown or violet base or blotch. The erect fruit-capsules are lined and somewhat thickened at the margins.

   H. aegyptiacum can be found in cultivated and wastelands, stony and sandy habitats, in the extreme eastern Mediterranean region – Palestine, Egypt and the surrounding regions in particular. Unfortunately this is yet another charming little poppy rarely seen in cultivation.

Hypecoum imberbe Sibth. & Smith   [Pl. 112]
(Syn. *H. grandiflorum* Benth.)
ORANGE HYPECOUM

Very similar to *H. procumbens*, but it can be readily distinguished by its more finely cut foliage, small linear bracts (not leaf-like) and more pronouncedly branched inflorescence. In addition, the flowers are generally orange-yellow, 10–20 mm (½–1 in) across, with the outer petals evenly lobed or with the

Hypecoum imberbe

central lobe somewhat smaller than the lateral lobes; the inner petals are often spotted with violet. The fruit-capsule is scarcely jointed.

H. imberbe has a similar distribution to *H. procumbens*, although its range extends eastwards to Iraq and Iran. However, it is not a coastal species, being generally found inland on cultivated, fallow and waste ground, both lowland and in the hills and low mountains and flowering from January to June.

Formerly cultivated in gardens but now seldom seen, which is a pity for it is a true little delight and very floriferous.

Hypecoum leptocarpum Hook. f. & Th.

A biennial species that forms a small rosette of greyish leaves in the first season but, in the second, spreading stems produce a series of small pale whitish-lilac flowers. The outer petals are oblong and unlobed and only 5–6 mm (½ in) long. The linear fruit-capsules, up to 3 cm (1⅕ in) long, are borne on erect stalks and are jointed, readily breaking into segments.

This species, which is not in cultivation, is a plant of dry rocky ground, riverbeds and stony slopes from the Pamir Mountains to the western Himalaya, Xizang (Tibet) and Mongolia.

Hypecoum pendulum L.
PENDENT HYPECOUM

A small annual with erect or ascending, smooth stems to 20 cm (8 in) tall, often less. The fennel-like leaves are two- or three-pinnately lobed, with greyish green linear lobes; bracts thread-like. The pale yellow flowers are borne in small cymes, 8–15 mm (⅓–⅗ in) across; outer petals unlobed, oval to diamond-shaped, but the inner deeply lobed, with the lateral lobes lanceolate whilst the middle lobe is stalked, rounded and with a hairy margin. The fruit-capsule is clearly pendent, 4–6 cm (1⅗–2⅖ in) long, with four distinct angles but not jointed, tapered at both ends.

Like the previous species *H. pendulum* is a plant of cultivated fallow and waste land, sometimes being found along roadsides, often in large colonies and sometimes mixed with *H. imberbe*. It has a wide distribution including the Mediterranean Basin, North Africa, east to the Caucasus.

H. pendulum is a dainty and floriferous annual and I look forward to the day when seed is more freely available.

Hypecoum ponticum Velen.
PONTIC HYPECOUM

A lesser-known species allied to *H. pendulum*, but with the middle lobe of the inner two petals linear, rather than rounded, and fruit erect. The sepals are also sharply pointed rather than blunt, but soon fall off, so that they are often difficult to observe.

H. ponticum inhabits coastal sands of the Black Sea region, primarily in Bulgaria and Turkey. It is not in cultivation.

Hypecoum procumbens L.
PROCUMBENT HYPECOUM

A small procumbent to spreading annual not more than 25 cm (10 in) tall, often as little as 5 cm (2 in); stems lined, often more or less erect at first, but becoming gradually procumbent as the fruits mature. The leaves are in a basal tuft, two-pinnately lobed, with grey- or bluish-green, slender, linear divi- sions, generally pointed. The flowers are borne in one- to five-flowered cymes and are pale to bright yellow, 8–16 mm (⅓–⅗ in) across; outer petals broadly rhombic and three-lobed, the middle lobe somewhat longer than the others; inner petals are deeply three-lobed, the outer (lateral) lobes oblong and hairless, the middle lobe spatular-shaped and with a hairy margin. The fruit-capsule is erect to ascending, straight or curved, 4–8 cm (1⅗–3⅕ in) long, with prominent transverse joints.

   H. procumbens is a plant of sandy habitats, especially close to the sea, although it can occasionally be found growing inland. It occurs throughout the Mediterranean basin as well as coastal Portugal and the region of the Black Sea, where it can be found in flower from February to early June.

   This delightful little species has been cultivated in gardens since 1596, however, it is seldom seen in cultivation today, indeed seed is not easy to obtain, except from the wild.

Hypecoum trilobum Trautv.   [Pl. 113]

This Asian species is similar in flower to *H. imberbe*, being seldom more than 15 cm (6 in) tall and differing primarily in having pendulous rather than erect fruit-capsules. In addition, the fruits of *H. trilobum* have thickened walls and do not break readily at the joints. The flowers are somewhat larger, bright yellow with the inner petals spotted with violet.

   H. trilobum is a plant of fields, arable land and roadsides in the semi-desert steppes of Central Asia from Iran to the Pamir Mountains and the Tienshan. I have seen it along the roadsides south of Samarkand towards the frontier of Afghanistan where it grows in abundance, often in association with *Roemeria refracta*, and forming a haze of yellow. Although apparently not in cultivation outside the CIS, this is a cheerful and floriferous little annual well worth seeking out.

The Fern Poppy
Pteridophyllum

Japan has many exciting little woodlanders to offer our gardens. Few are as unusual and charming as *Pteridophyllum racemosum* Sieb. & Zucc. Out of flower this tufted perennial could be all to easily mistaken for a fern in the neat divisions of its frond-like leaves; hence the generic names which clearly alludes to this deception. Even in flower, the airy little 'racemes' scarcely betray their family affinities. However, look at one of the tiny flowers closely and they do clearly resemble a scaled-down poppy flower, especially in their two sepals and four petals, although there are rather few stamens.

The genus *Pteridophyllum* contains just one species, native to the mountains of central Japan where it was discovered in the province of Sinano by Siebold in the middle of the nineteenth century (it was described in 1843).

It is difficult to ascertain the affinities of this little gem and it appears to hold a rather isolated position within the family. The fruit, a two-valved siliqua, clearly puts it close to subfamily Chelidonioideae together with *Chelidonium*, *Dicranostigma*, *Stylophorum* and several other genera (p. 23). Some authors have suggested that it makes an obvious link with *Hypecoum* and hence the Fumariaceae, which contains the fumitories and corydalis, but this is by no means certain and, besides, this aspect needs further careful research. The Fumariaceae was of course once part of the poppy family but is now generally regarded as being distinct.

Pteridophyllum racemosum Sieb & Zucc. [Pl. 114]
FERN POPPY

This is a small tufted perennial, not more than 25 cm (10 in) tall in flower, often less; the shoots arise from a short branched rhizome, all the leaves being basal. The short-stalked leaves, up to 15 cm (6 in) long, are oblanceolate to elliptical in outline, but divided into many small, oval to almost linear, leaflets; these leaflets are largest in the middle of the leaf, decreasing in size at both ends and touching or slightly overlapping one another, being held at right angles to the midrib (rachis); the leaflets are sometimes slightly notched at the apex and are glabrous except for a few bristles beneath. The scapes inflorescence is erect and appears to be racemose but is actually a narrow cymose panicle. The flowers are white with pale yellow stamens, being borne on slender stalks; sepals two, rounded, quickly falling once the buds start to open; petals four, half-spreading, oval, 5–6 mm (¼ in) long, soon falling; stamens few. The fruit-capsule is a two-valved siliqua.

The species is native to Japan's Honshu Island where it inhabits montane coniferous woodland.

This plant was introduced into cultivation in 1914 and there is a fine picture of it in *Curtis's Botanical Magazine* (tab. 8743). It has never found great favour in gardens and today it is only listed by one or two nurseries. In *The English*

Rock Garden Reginald Farrer says of it that 'In the midst (of the tuft of leaves) rises in July a stem six inches or a foot (or more), unfolding a spike, most airy and graceful, of tiny white flowers, which, though poppies, look much more like the loose spire of some small-flowered white crucifer'. However, for those who, like me, are excited by these cool little woodlanders then this is certainly a gem not to be overlooked.

P. racemosum is quite hardy in the open garden though it needs a cool, shady place; in the woodland or a peat bank, where there is moist leafy or peaty soil. Its pleasing ferny appearance also make it suitable for a nook in the rock garden; it greatly dislikes summer drought. In favoured mild gardens plants remain more or less evergreen, however, elsewhere the leaves tend to die away during the winter. Grown like a choice petiolarid primula, it will also make a first rate pan plant for the shaded frame or alpine house; a compost of fibrous loam, leaf-mould and grit will suit it admirably.

In my experience the young leaves are very prone to attack from marauding slugs and snails and these little horrors must be kept at bay, otherwise the plant will quickly succumb.

Propagation is by seed, when available, or by division of the parent plant in the early spring before growth commences, although this is not always easy. Plants flower from May to July. Despite the fact that the flowers are all to fleeting in appearance, the attractive leaf tufts add interest at other times of the year.

Major References

Cobb, J.L.S. (1989). *Meconopsis*, Christopher Helm/Batsford, London/Timber Press, Portland, Oregon.

Cullen, J. (1965). Papaveraceae in Davis, P.H., *Flora of Turkey*, volume I.

—— (1966). Papaveraceae in Rechinger, K.H., *Flora Iranica* 34/16.

Debnath, H.S. and Nayar, M.P. (1986). *The Poppies of the Indian Region*. Botanical Survey of India.

Ernst, W.R. (1962). *Comparative Morphology of the Papaveraceae*.

Farrer, R. (1928). *The English Rock-Garden*.

Fletcher, H.R. (1975). *A Quest for Flowers*.

Gerard, J. (1597). *The Herball or Generall Historie of Plantes*, London.

Hussain, A. and Sharma, J.R. (1983). *The Opium Poppy*. Central Institute of Medicinal and Aromatic Plants, Luchnow, India.

Huxley, A. (Ed.) (1992). *The New Royal Horticultural Dictionary of Gardening* – in 4 volumes.

Lloyd, C. and Rice, G. (1991). *Garden Flowers from Seed*.

Meikle, R.D. (1977). *Flora of Cyprus*. Bentham-Moxon Trust, Royal Botanic Gardens, Kew.

Miller, P. (1768). *The Gardener's Dictionary*, 8th ed, London.

Munz, (1974). *A Flora of Southern California*.

Ownbey, G.R. (1958). Monograph of the Genus *Argemone* for North America and the West Indies in *Memoirs of the Torrey Botanical Club* 21(1).

—— (1961). The Genus *Argemone* in South America and Hawaii in *Brittonia* 13.

Popov, (1937). Papaveraceae in Flora *USSR*, volume 7.

Taylor, G. (1934). *An Account of the Genus Meconopsis*. Reprinted in 1985 by Waterstone, London.

Tutin, T.G. *et al* (1964). *Flora Europaea*, volume 1. Cambridge University Press.

Glossary

Amplexicaule – clasping; generally refers to leaves that have heart-shaped bases that clasp the stem.

Anther – the male organ of the flower that contains the pollen.

Anthesis – flowering time, when the flower bud opens (more accurately when the pollen is shed).

Appressed – lying flat against another organ – as hairs on a stem.

Capsule – a dry, many-seeded, fruit that dehisces (splits) in various ways (according to the species) when ripe to expel the seeds.

Carpel – the basic female unit of the flower which contains the ovules and makes up the ovary; an ovary may consist of one or several separate or united carpels.

Cultivar – a plant, species or form (often with a name, e.g. 'Goliath'), maintained by cultivation.

Decumbent – spreading to prostrate stems that bend upwards in the upper part.

Dimorphic – in two forms.

Elliptic – a flat shape broadest in the middle and pointed at each end.

Entire – not toothed or lobed – leaf-margin usually.

Ephemeral – an annual that completes its life-cycle in just a few weeks.

Filament – the stalk that joins the anther to the receptacle or corolla.

Filiform – thread-like.

Glabrous – hairless.

Glaucous – bluish-green or bluish-grey in general colour – generally applies to leaves.

Globose – shaped like a globe – spherical.

Inflorescence – flowers aggregated into formal arrangements (branched or not) together with their accompanying bracts and pedicels (i.e. the whole structure).

Lanceolate – an ellipse that is broadest just below the middle; same as narrow-ovate.

Latex – milky juice; can be white or yellow or orange in poppies.

Leaf-axil – the angle between the leaf and the stem.

Monilliform – bead-like.

Obcordate – reversed heart-shape.

Oval – a flat shape broadest in the middle and with rounded ends.

Ovary – the female organ of the flower that contains the ovules which, upon fertilisation, develop into seeds.

Ovate – egg-shaped.

Petiole – leaf-stalk.

Pinnate – a compound leaf in which the leaflets are placed in pairs along a common axis (rachis); 2–pinnate where the prime divisions of the leaf are themselves pinnate.

Procumbent – trailing along the ground.

Prostrate – growing flat on the ground.

Rachis – the axis of a compound leaf or an inflorescence to which the leaflets or flowers are attached – not the stalk.

Scape – a leafless flowering stem on plants which have entirely basal leaves.

Scapose – with scapes.

Sessile – stalkless; leaves, without a petiole.

Siliqua – a two-valved pod-like fruit which is at least three times longer than broad.

Stamen – the male organ of the flower; consists of the filament and the anther that bears the pollen.

Stigma – the receptive tip of the style that receives the pollen.

Style – the stalk-like appendage on top of the ovary that bears the stigma(s).

Torus – a semicircular disk-like ridge.

Trifoliate – a leaf composed of three leaflets.

Zygomorphic – asymmetrical flowers, which have bilateral (one plane of) symmetry.

Index

Synonyms in *italics*; ★ indicates a line drawing; Pl. refers to a colour plate